DRP:
Distribution
Resource
Planning

DRP:
Distribution
Resource
Planning

The Gateway to True Quick Response and Continuous Replenishment

REVISED EDITION

by **Andre J. Martin**

Foreword by Walter E. Goddard

John Wiley & Sons, Inc.

New York • Chichester • Brisbane • Toronto • Singapore

To:
Régine
Geneviève
Philippe

Contents

Foreword

A Better Solution

Andre Martin and I go back many years. We first met in 1975 at a Five-Day Class taught by Oliver Wight and myself. At the time, Andre was working for Abbott Laboratories in Montreal.

His accomplishments have contributed enormously to the field of resource planning. As director of materials management at Abbott, Andre led the successful implementation of a closed-loop MRP system. He then extended the planning and scheduling capabilities to include Abbott's distribution operations. This became the first installation of what is now known as Distribution Resource Planning, DRP. Additionally, he integrated the financial planning functions, leading Oliver to create the term Manufacturing Resource Planning, MRP II, to describe this broader application of what started as simply an inventory management system.

Because of the many successful companies using it, DRP has become the accepted planning process for manufacturing companies with make-to-stock products. This new edition reflects an equally important milestone.

Andre's dedication to helping business people operate their companies more effectively has led him to new ground. Andre recognized that the same concepts could apply to wholesalers, retailers, and distributors. Looking further ahead, he could see the dramatic advantage that would occur by linking each step in the industrial pipeline—raw material suppliers to manufacturers to wholesalers to distributors and finally to consumers. Andre's vision is for a two-way flow of valid information, strengthening each link in the chain, to enable products to flow through the pipeline faster, more reliably, and less expensively.

In 1982, this was simply an idea. In 1983, two companies were willing to try it—American Hardware Supply (now called Servistar) and Mass Merchandisers Inc. were the first wholesalers to apply Andre's advice. Both were highly successful. These trailblazers deserve special recognition.

Other companies have followed. This book contains their names and their experiences. The prerequisites and the pitfalls have been sorted out. A body of knowledge has emerged. Applied properly, predictable results occur: inventory levels drop, operating costs are reduced, and customer service is increased.

Their experiences can help you gain similar benefits for your company. Although what must be done is known, it will not be easy. Four issues distinguish the successful users described in this book. Each of these issues is a contributor when installed separately; however, operated together they become a powerful competitive edge:

- *The Right Planning Process*—A steady stream of changes comes from your customers; frequent surprises occur daily within your company; suppliers cannot always do what they promise or provide what you need. Analyzing these changes, ignoring the trivial and correctly responding to the significant, requires effective operating systems. Andre explains how Manufacturing Resource Planning, MRP II, provides this capability for manufacturing companies and how DRP offers a proven process for wholesalers, retailers, and distributors.

- *People Skills*—Operating DRP and MRP II to their potential requires knowledgeable users. Unfortunately, many managers have been raised using the alternative approach, called the informal system. Order launching and expediting are its characteristics. A formal system demands accurate data and must represent what you "can do," not simply what you would "like to do." For managers used to fire fighting, this is a difficult transition to make.

- *Communication Techniques*—Electronic Data Interchange, EDI, and bar coding are becoming commonplace. Swift and economical transfers of information are what they are good at. Old, correct information is no better than timely, poor information. An effective decision maker needs data that is accurate, up to date, and correct.

• *New Attitudes*—Two words frequently appear throughout this book: Teamwork and Partnership. Although they are used interchangeably, let me temporarily separate them to describe two changes in behavior.

Internal to your company, each person must be striving to do his or her job to the best of his ability, and at the same time, be willing to help his or her teammates. Whenever there is a conflict, the company's benefit must outweigh that of the individual. This is the essence of teamwork. Too often this is not the case. Instead, time and energy are spent blaming other people for problems rather than fixing them. When fingerpointing replaces cooperation, the team is not pulling together, but rather, pulling apart.

External to your company are your customers and suppliers. Are you a good partner to them? This includes providing your suppliers with believable information to help them improve their performance. This means being genuinely concerned for their success. The same spirit of cooperativeness should exist with your customers. If they provide you with reliable information, you must be prepared to convert it into improved service, better quality, and lower costs.

Building teamwork inside of the company and nurturing partnerships outside of the company are what the successful users are doing. They realize that this is in their own interest, and that by doing so, they will achieve the goals of their company.

Those companies capable of accomplishing these changes will achieve a competitive breakthrough. It is an approach whose time has come. It makes sense; it has been tried; and it works.

Andre Martin is a pioneer with an excellent track record. He has two unique abilities; to see better solutions and to help companies obtain them. Both of these are important to the readers of this book. He predicts a major improvement for the 1990s, and this book will contribute to you making it happen for your company: "This will be the decade when industries finally reap the benefits of total integration. Executives will learn to accelerate the flow of their products, not only through the supply and manufacturing pipeline, but also through the entire industrial pipeline."

Walter E. Goddard
Sunapee, New Hampshire

Preface

In the two years since the second edition of this book was published, the concept of Quick Response/Continuous Replenishment (QR/CR) has become a well-accepted way of doing business and a major competitive tool. Those companies that adopt QR/CR techniques will create their own futures, while those that don't will have their futures handed to them on a plate.

While Quick Response/Continuous Replenishment offers significant opportunities to lower costs, improve efficiency, and boost customer service, it is also fraught with perils. That's why it is essential to understand the potential pitfalls of QR/CR and what you can do about them. In chapter 1, I report on what I've learned about QR/CR through my research on companies such as Wal-Mart, Kmart, Procter & Gamble, Nabisco Foods, Kellogg, Quaker Oats, Kroger, Nestlé Carnation, Campbell Soup, Hunt-Wesson, Dominick's, Von's, H. E. Butt, Giant Food, Frito-Lay, Super Value, Kraft General Foods, Lever Brothers, Dial, Ocean Spray, and others. In the chapter, common problems are noted in companies using QR/CR and solutions are shared, so you won't have to reinvent the wheel.

Whether your company is in the talking or the refining stage, my observations, conclusions, and analyses can help you make QR/CR an important means of gaining a competing edge. I invite you to take a unique glimpse at the promising new world that Quick Response/Continuous Replenishment offers today's retail, wholesale, and manufacturing companies.

Acknowledgments

Since the first edition of this book was published in 1983, a significant number of advances have occurred, and DRP is now recognized as a proven concept. As a result, this has prompted me to update the book and share these experiences. With this revised edition, I have fulfilled the goal of explaining how nonmanufacturing companies can benefit from DRP. As a consequence, many thanks are in order.

First of all, thanks to Brant Slade and Michel Leroux for their help in critiquing the draft. Second, my special thanks to Walter Goddard and Darryl Landvater for their excellent suggestions on presentation and organization. Third, I owe a debt of gratitude to Bill Perry for his contribution to the forecasting chapter, and his many recommendations that helped improve the manuscript.

I would also like to thank those folks who worked behind the scenes, putting this book together. Thanks to Patricia Carriere for help with the figures. In addition, a special thank you to Steve Bennett, who helped me organize my thoughts into a more readable style and format.

Last, but not least, I want to thank my wife, Régine, and my two children, Geneviève and Philippe. It's hard enough for a family to put up with Dad being away much of the time, but to give up cherished weekends on top of it is beyond what a husband and father could expect. I owe this book to them; they made it possible, and I was merely the instrument.

Andre Martin
Rosemere, Quebec
October 1992

DRP:
Distribution
Resource
Planning

Introduction

Total Marketing Channel Integration:
The Last Frontier

I believe history will prove that the 1990s was the decade when industry finally reaped the benefits of total marketing channel integration. In the 1990s, we will finally understand how to compete profitably in domestic and international markets. We will see how manufacturers can accelerate the flow of their products not only through their internal supply and manufacturing pipeline but through the entire industrial pipeline. Quick response to change will become a way of life. This will require organizations to undergo significant internal restructuring to break down internal functional barriers.

Companies that succeed in the twenty-first century will understand natural linkages[1], which will result in multiple customer/supplier partnerships and completely different ways of doing business. Of course, the traditional roles of marketing, sales, logistics[2], manufacturing, and purchasing will change dramatically.

How will we get there? How will we do it? Where do we start? In fact,

---

[1] Natural linkages are fully explained in chapter 1.

[2] The term "logistics" has been adopted in recent years as a substitute for "distribution," because it is more encompassing and reflects the true dynamics of distribution. The term will therefore be used in lieu of distribution throughout the book. Since the term "Distribution Resource Planning (DRP)" has become deeply entrenched in the vocabulary of management of today's managers, however, it will be used throughout the book to avoid confusion.

everything we need to totally integrate a marketing channel is here today; a number of leading-edge companies are doing it and enjoying the competitive advantage that results. To achieve accelerated velocity of the flow of information and products across the industrial pipeline, we need three ingredients:

1. Systems that generate quick information flow.

2. Systems that generate quick material flow.

3. Systems that facilitate both quick information and material flow.

Planning and scheduling systems like Distribution Resource Planning (DRP) and Manufacturing Resource Planning (MRP II) generate and maintain valid plans across the entire industrial pipeline; plans that not only correctly reflect the needs of the company, but do so as things constantly change, and are attainable as well. Just-in-Time/Total Quality Control (JIT/TQC) generate quick material flow, and attack all forms of waste (i.e., inventory that sits too long, long manufacturing setups, large manufacturing lot sizes and safety stocks), thus reducing costs and improving quality. Finally, electronic data interchange (EDI) and bar coding facilitate information flow and material flow. These ingredients, available now, are tried and proven—it's a question of combining them in a logical and sensible sequence.

GENERATORS OF QUICK INFORMATION FLOW

Competitive levels of customer responsiveness require planning and scheduling systems that will continually and rapidly communicate changes in market demands from point of sale to the beginning of manufacturing, and even to the beginning of a supplier's manufacturing. DRP is designed to efficiently communicate changes in the marketplace. MRP II is designed to effectively communicate change in manufacturing. Chapters 1 through 5 cover these issues in significant detail.

GENERATORS OF QUICK MATERIAL FLOW

Competitive levels of customer responsiveness also require manufacturing to quickly and economically respond to changes in the marketplace. JIT/TQC are designed to continuously drive economic improvements in quality, delivery responsiveness, and cost throughout the entire supply, manufacturing, and distribution pipeline. DRP and MRP II provide responsive planning information. JIT/TQC drive responsive execution throughout the supply pipeline.[3]

FACILITATORS OF QUICK INFORMATION AND MATERIAL FLOW

Today people are beginning to use EDI effectively as a facilitator of quick information flow. Using EDI to transmit information like purchase orders, acknowledgments, invoices and payments of invoices reaps little benefit for most people. The real payback of EDI is not to use it as a facilitator of information flow from which business decisions have already been made, but to marry it to DRP and MRP II. As planning and scheduling tools for retailers, wholesalers, distributors, and manufacturers, DRP and MRP II quickly and accurately generate time-phased future requirements of material flow across the industrial pipeline. By combining EDI with DRP and MRP II, you use EDI as a means of communicating information that will be used as the basis for future business decisions. Chapter 1 provides actual practical examples of how this is accomplished.

Bar coding facilitates communications regarding material flow. Multiple bar-coding applications are in use today in the retail/wholesale, manufacturing, and transportation of products and materials. Bar coding not only eliminates errors and saves time; it is very efficient in identifying and tracking the movement of material from supplier to customer. When properly used as a facilitator of quick material flow, bar coding joins EDI as an ideal partner for facilitating the flow of information and material across the total marketing channel.

CHANGING WINDS

Many industrial leaders now are beginning to see the advantages of total marketing channel integration, and are looking at the benefits of high-velocity customer response. Roger Milliken, chairman and CEO of

---

[3] The principles of JIT/TQC are beyond the scope of this book. For a thorough discussion of the topic, refer to William A. Sandras, Jr., *Just-in-Time: Making It Happen: Unleashing the Power of Continuous Improvement* (Essex Junction, VT: Oliver Wight Limited Publications, 1989).

textile manufacturer Milliken & Co., commented: "Quick Response is a strategy that looks at the entire supply pipeline . . . quick response is a revolution not an evolution. You either move ahead by using it or lag behind your competitors."[4]

Other visionary business leaders also see the value of Quick Response. "Do something now," advises Patrick Galvin, vice president, Federal Express. "Remember, if you sit on the tracks you get run over . . . Offering the best product or the best service at the right price is not good enough. Meeting your customers' needs sooner or better than your competitor is the new critical success factor. A simple axiom of time and competition prevails: 'The firstest with the mostest' wins."[5]

And consider John Smale's, CEO, Procter & Gamble, statement: "I have the growing conviction that the product-supply concept is perhaps the single most important thing that can influence our profit performance over the next several years."[6] Smale estimates that the creation of product-supply managers will slash costs by $1 billion over the next two years.

A common thread transcends each leader's thinking. In their own words, these executives have proclaimed that it's no longer good enough to look inward; if you want to win (not just survive), you must look outward to your customer—you must look at the entire marketing channel. You must develop the ability to offer not only the best product or the best service at the right price; but you must be able to do it better and faster than your competition.

THE STEPS TOWARD QUICK RESPONSE TO CHANGE

Clearly each channel member can benefit significantly by implementing DRP and/or MRP II. Implementation will give them the capabilities to anticipate change, and to manage and control inventories and resources in a superior manner. Next, manufacturers, after implementing MRP II, will certainly benefit from applying the JIT/TQC philosophy. Wholesaler/distributors and retailers will also gain.

For example, let's take wholesaler/distributors. As manufacturers

[4] Speech at the Quick Response '89 seminar and show, Dallas, TX.
[5] Speech at 1989 EDI international seminar, Vancouver, BC.
[6] *Fortune*, November, 1989: p. 46.

reduce their lead times, lot sizes, safety stocks, forecasting, material handling, transportation, etc. through JIT/TQC, wholesaler/distributors can begin to reduce their lead times, lot sizes, and safety stocks, too. Ultimately, as lead times, lot sizes, and safety stocks are reduced, the flow of products will smooth out and velocity of products across the marketing channel will increase. This may take a few months to several years, and will depend on how well channel members do their homework in implementing DRP, MRP II, and JIT/TQC, how well they understand the changes they are making, and how well they communicate information about the proposed changes.

Manufacturers' Role in Channel Integration

Very often, manufacturers are the constraints in given marketing channels. Manufacturing's strategy is clearly one of implementing MRP II and JIT/TQC at the same time. Manufacturers need to improve both information flow and material flow capabilities. They must then explore using EDI and bar coding to facilitate the flow of both information and material. In addition, EDI and bar coding will give manufacturers the opportunity to move quickly when the opportunity for customer connectivity marketing (CCM) arrives.

Wholesaler/Distributors' Role in Channel Integration

Wholesaler/distributors will gain on two fronts. First, implementing DRP will give them all the benefits described in this book, as well as help them to improve information flow to manufacturers. Second, wholesaler/distributors will reap additional benefits as manufacturers' lead times begin to drop. Ultimately wholesaler/distributors will be in a position to respond better and more quickly to demand from retailers.

Retailers' Role in Channel Integration

Retailers will gain by implementing DRP. Clearly some retailers will gain more than others in terms of balancing and reducing inventory investment. But there is no reason why retailers cannot do business with far less inventory and associated cost reductions once DRP is implemented and fine-tuned.

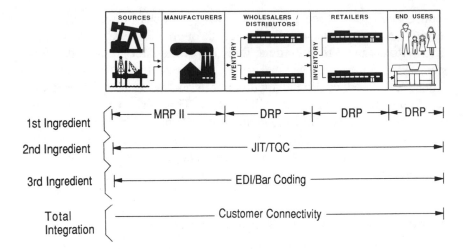

Figure I-1

LINKING THE CHANNEL THROUGH CUSTOMER CONNECTIVITY MARKETING

This is the final step toward total channel integration. Its rewards are so great that I cover it in one entire chapter—chapter 1. Chapters 3 through 5 cover the building blocks to customer connectivity marketing. Every member of the channel is now poised and ready for customer connectivity marketing. Although, in principle, customer connectivity marketing is easy to understand, it is the most demanding step because it deals with people inside and outside the company who have different cultures, different methods of organization, and different viewpoints. And there are the usual problems with functional barriers and tunnel vision.

On the customer side, people in inventory control, purchasing, receiving, and accounts payable are involved. On the supplier side, marketing and sales, customer service, order entry, billing, accounts receivable, manufacturing, and production and inventory control are involved.

Many a promising idea has died a quick death when confronted with multifunctional sign-offs. Why? Turf, territory, and the "not-invented-here" syndrome are some reasons. Whatever the specific cause, the effort requires top management people with a vision who have a profound desire to win. Executives must rise above their functional barriers and examine strategic roles in their respective marketing channels. They must arrive at the inevitable truth that everyone in the channel is linked naturally.

Once the three ingredients of total channel integration (see figure I-1) are institutionalized by each member of the marketing channel, customer connectivity marketing becomes the glue that binds everything together. And, in the process, it generates not only survivors but winners.

Chapter 1

Quick Response/
Continuous Replenishment

New Thinking

Some might say that the old saw, "Information is power," has become hackneyed or clichéd. In the world of retail, wholesale, and manufacturing, however, it accurately describes what can happen with "Quick Response/Continuous Replenishment" (QR/CR)[1] systems. Quick Response/Continuous Replenishment refers to an approach for increasing product velocity across a distribution pipeline. This is accomplished by speeding up the flow of information, which in turn speeds up the flow of product from the factory to the point of end use. As product flows faster through the distribution pipeline, all companies involved enjoy higher customer satisfaction, lower inventory investment, and lower operating costs.

Many well-known companies have established Quick Response/Continuous Replenishment links between themselves and their customers and suppliers, and are enjoying improvements in customer service and efficiency, and reductions in costs. In most cases (for example, Wal-Mart, Kmart, and H. E. Butt), the retail chain is the initiator, while in others, such as that of Procter & Gamble, the manufacturer initiates the relationship. Regardless of who initiates the arrangement, a well-functioning QR/CR system has the potential to increase the flow of product from plant to point of sale.

---

[1] "Partnerships in merchandise flow," "Just-in-Time Distribution," and "Stockless Materials Management" are sometimes used to describe QR/CR. To avoid confusion, I refer to the technique as "Quick Response/Continuous Replenishment" or QR/CR.

11

Success with QR/CR is predicated on getting the *right* information into the *right* hands at the *right* time. Only then can information become a substitute for inventory and lower real costs across the distribution pipeline. In this chapter, we'll look at how QR/CR functions ideally and where the information flow can become derailed or misdirected. We'll also examine carefully the constraints with which a supplier must operate, since these ultimately determine whether or not a QR/CR system functions with optimal efficiency.

THE PIPELINE CONCEPT

To understand the power of a Quick Response/Continuous Replenishment program, think of a relationship between suppliers and ultimate customers as a giant conduit. This analogy is depicted in figure 1-1.

Grocery "Pipeline"

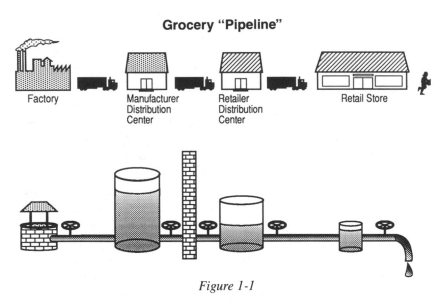

| Factory | Manufacturer Distribution Center | Retailer Distribution Center | Retail Store |

Figure 1-1

The top portion of figure 1-1 shows a set of linkages that begins with a factory and ends with a store. The bottom portion interprets the flow of goods through the pipeline as a series of holding tanks and control valves along the way. Now think of your distribution system as a similar pipeline, and imagine product flowing from beginning to end point. If you want to reduce inventory while at the same time improve availability (service), you must increase velocity. To do this, consider the entire pipeline, not just single or isolated segments of it (which is unfortunately the case with most QR/CR programs today). In addition, it is important to identify all possible constraints and "lumpy demand factors" that can distort or impede the flow (see figure 2-2, chapter 2, for a detailed listing of such factors). Finally, make sure that your inventory planning systems consider the constraints and amplifiers as early as possible so that the closer you plan to the point of end use (in figure 1-1, the retail store), the better off you'll be.

Finally, the pipeline model is just that—a theoretical construct. As explained in the second part of this chapter, in the real world there are real constraints and tradeoffs across the entire channel. These will diminish performance and payback potential if they are dealt with too late. The sooner you plan for the constraints, the greater your chances of eliminating or at least dampening their impact on the total performance of the pipeline.

NEW THINKING AND NEW TOOLS FOR NEW TIMES

For a Quick Response/Continuous Replenishment program to work, companies must use a different approach to planning customer requirements and synchronizing them with supplier capabilities. Traditionally, the interactions have been limited to those between buyers and sales reps. With the new thinking in QR/CR, the interactions must be expanded throughout the entire pipeline. This means involving people from all "pipeline constituents" on intercompany cross-functional product flow teams. These teams should meet regularly and address the topics shown in table 1-1 on page 14.

In working through the topics shown in table 1-1, the teams will use DRP and related planning models, such as transportation and warehouse capacity planning, which are not conventionally used in retail settings to generate the best solutions to specific problems.

As a result of the above-stated planning, the information about customer inventory requirements has "built-in intelligence" vis-á-vis capacity issues, in transportation, and in warehouse receiving. This also enables the buying and traffic distribution sides of the business (on behalf of the retailer) to synchronize the ordering process with the transport and receive products before requirements are passed to suppliers. This level of integration is greatly needed but is not usually done in most retail inventory management practices.

In the ideal setting, inventory requirements planning is first initiated on the customer (retailer or wholesaler) side, with the close participation

Topics for Intercompany Cross-Functional Flow Team Review
Merchandising/Marketing • Sales forecast reviews • Promotions, deals, specials • End-of-season sales • New products • Others
Buying/Logistics/Manufacturing • Modes of transport to be used • Types of pallets to be used • Lead-time reviews • Receiving capacity planning • Transportation capacity planning • Manufacturing capacity issues • Others
MIS • EDI standard reviews • System changes/enhancements • Others
Finance/Accounting • Billing issues • Payment issues • Receiving issues • Shorts (credits/debits)
Performance Measures • Service levels achieved • Inventory turns achieved • Safety stock reviews

Table 1-1

and coordination of suppliers. The customer and supplier also conduct additional planning that takes into account warehouse receiving and transportation capacity. Ultimately, this information feeds into the supplier's inventory management system, and an execution plan is developed. (Note: Prior to "opening up the pipeline," the customer establishes customer service and inventory turn objectives with the suppliers in its distribution pipeline. It's not uncommon to hear of customer service goals of 98 percent, and 20 to 30 inventory turns per year.) The flow of information is summarized in figure 1-2.

The Ideal QR/CR Model

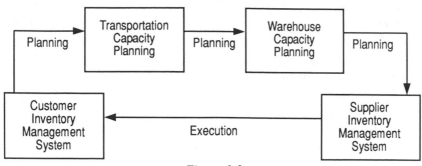

Figure 1-2

THE BUILDING BLOCKS TO THE NEW THINKING

There are three building blocks necessary to build a successful QR/CR partnership: systems (hardware and software), information, and people. The relative importance of each is shown in figure 1-3. But, in fact, most companies juxtapose the importance of the people and the systems factors. This is understandable, given the traditional view in which people are considered "fixed costs," and new hardware and software are the largest cost items on any new system proposal. While choosing the right hardware and software is important, the quality and level of education you give the people who use the system is far more important. This holds whether you're implementing an MRP II system, DRP, or QR/CR program—people make or break the effort.

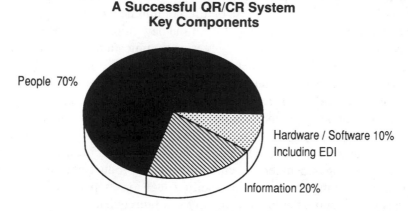

Figure 1-3

Consider the mechanics of the ideal QR/CR model. As mentioned earlier, they involve making sure that the right information flows to the right people at the right time. In part, this has been made easier by the establishment of various communication standards such as ANSIX12, VICS, USC, and so forth, and the emergence of data communications networks such as Tymnet, IBM Information Network, and OrderNet. All of these have made it significantly easier to share data with customers and suppliers.

But just because you can transmit a piece of information doesn't mean that anything worthwhile will happen to it. Too much attention has been placed on the technology and the act of getting information from A to B than on how to streamline the information so it can be used more efficiently. For example, rather than trying to automate manual systems, why not try to eliminate them and use EDI more effectively?

Take purchase orders, for example: Why work on automating them when you can eliminate them altogether, along with PO acknowledgments or invoices? There are many other opportunities to cut unnecessary paper and labor, too—if you shift your attention from the hardware to "brainware." With that in mind, let's take a closer look at the people component of a QR/CR system, then move on to the information and hardware/software factors.

People

For QR/CR to work optimally, people must adopt new patterns and modes of communication. Figure 1-3A shows a typical QR/CR communications flow between a customer (the retailer) and a supplier (the manufacturer). Note that most of the communication takes place between the buyers and sales reps. With the new thinking in QR/CR, this changes dramatically since it involves communication across intercompany cross-functional product flow teams. See figure 1-3B.

This approach to communications between customers and suppliers is dramatically different and calls for a complete re-engineering of customer/supplier communications. It's no longer good enough to be a professional salesperson or buyer. For QR/CR to work well, we must expand our understanding of business beyond our specific area of expertise. Becoming a member of a cross-functional product flow team is the answer. Learning how buying and selling decisions impact all functional areas within and outside the company is a prerequisite.

Typical QR/CR Communications Flow

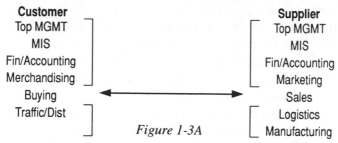

Figure 1-3A

The New Thinking in Communications Flow

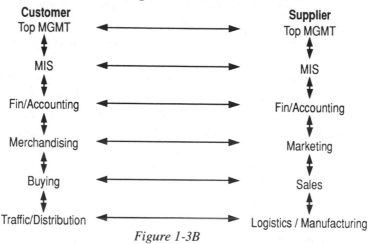

Figure 1-3B

The days of functional experts must be counted if we are to succeed in this new game of pipeline management. It's no longer acceptable to live within the four walls of manufacturing, wholesale, or retail businesses. We must remove these walls to ensure smooth communication and understanding of what it really takes to synchronize a total distribution pipeline.

Information

To be of value, information must enable people to take action that leads to performance improvements and profits. The root of information is data, and for data to be of value, it must be factual, accurate, and current. Unfortunately, more work and effort has gone into facilitating the passage of data between customers and suppliers in the typical

QR/CR arena than in ensuring the quality of the data. In a sense, the need to ensure data quality has been obscured by progress in the data communications field; we have now established communication standards that enable us to transmit just about any set of data we want. But in the fields of procurement, manufacturing, logistics, and inventory management, transmitting data from point A to point B is merely academic and does not necessarily accomplish anything.

What you *do* with data is what matters. For as Richard Wurman describes in his groundbreaking book *Information Anxiety*, a "black hole" often exists between data and knowledge. Data alone simply does not help us make important decisions or take action. The typical QR/CR, in my opinion, is riddled with such information "black holes" that lead to wasted communications. And the wasted communications in turn create unnecessary inventory and unproductive costs throughout the distribution pipeline.

The rest of this book describes how quality data can be translated into information. It will teach you how to gather data at the source, make sure that someone is accountable for the data's accuracy and timeliness, and convert data into a usable form—in other words, bridge the gap between data and knowledge. Finally, you'll learn how to enhance the information with "built-in" intelligence before transmitting and sharing it with suppliers. Ultimately, valid information will contribute as much as 20 percent to your chances of succeeding with a QR/CR program.

Hardware and Software

Hardware and software are to business decision makers what hammers and saws are to cabinet makers—tools to help get the job done. The danger is that sometimes too much importance is placed on them at the expense of training for those who use the tools. True, properly designed hardware/software systems are essential for helping business professionals convert the data to useful information. Because of their capacity to quickly process massive amounts of data, they can help turn people's goals and visions into day-to-day reality. But again, even the "smartest" system can only juggle ones and zeros; people alone can translate the data into meaningful information.

While hardware/software should not be the centerpiece of any QR/CR arrangement, it is essential that systems provide the right kind of data. Current systems, unfortunately, are incapable of meeting two essential requirements for effective QR/CR: time-phasing a distribution network and scheduling. Users of QR/CR must be able to work proactively and by exception. Their systems should do the "grunt work," leaving them time to evaluate alternative plans and make better decisions.

Finally, hardware and software for QR/CR must be capable of recognizing the difference between dependent and independent demand. In other words, they must be able to distinguish between demand that can be calculated and transmitted from one level of the distribution pipeline to the next as opposed to forecasting demand at each level in the network. The ability to distinguish between the two types of demand is essential for effectively integrating planning and scheduling throughout a distribution pipeline.

TYPICAL QR/CR IN THE REAL WORLD: CASE STUDY

As mentioned above, the perfect flow of information and goods represents an ideal. In the field, though, there is quite a difference between QR/CR in its ideal form and QR/CR as commonly practiced; in some cases, the ideal and as-practiced forms are 180 degrees apart.

Whereas in the ideal system intelligence about transportation, warehouse receiving capacity planning and other functions is integral to the flow of information (refer to figure 1-2), in practice customers typically "dump" a significant amount of raw data into the supplier's system (see figure 1-4), including store demand on DCs by product, store sales, store cuts (back orders), balance on hand, and the product on order. The result is another example of the information "black hole" between data and meaningful information, as described earlier. Indeed, typical QR/CR pipelines are often hampered by a disconnect between data and knowledge so that suppliers are left to their own devices to manage a

Typical Quick Response Model

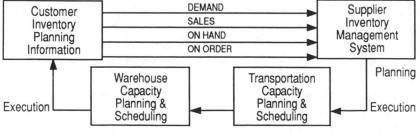

Figure 1-4

customer's inventory and to manage difficult transportation and receiving issues "after the fact."

The supplier, for example, must construct a customer-specific inventory model that makes recommendations for replenishment orders. At this point, the supplier in essence takes responsibility for managing the customer's inventory. Some might say, "That sounds like a beneficial thing for the customer." But in fact, when the time comes to ship the order, the supplier is often faced with a number of constraints in terms of how and when the order should be shipped and received. As a result of working out the constraints, the supplier must make numerous changes to his manufacturing and shipping plans. Again, the problem is that suppliers operate in something of a vacuum when they should be working out details with customers before the information reaches Wurman's so-called black hole.

Constraints on Suppliers

Many suppliers in typical QR/CR systems must navigate through a veritable mine field of constraints, any of which can slow down or even crimp the flow of product through the pipeline. The constraints are itemized in table 1-2 on page 21.

It might sound as though the cards are stacked against the supplier, but if the customer has a good inventory management system, strives for the QR/CR approach described earlier, communicates frequently, and works closely with suppliers, the results can be a high degree of efficiency for all parties involved.

QR/CR in Action

ICI Explosives, a division of Imperial Chemicals, embarked on a DRP QR/CR program in 1987. The company decided to use DRP with its customers because it was having problems forecasting demand, which in turn affected its customer service. The marketing department made forecasts based on experience and historical data, but it had difficulty identifying product demand in the short-term cycle. I recommended using DRP on a pilot basis with two customers to determine if the situation would improve.

The DRP pilot was impressive and resulted in shorter order cycles and better inventory management by the customers; they were able to hold inventories down even when there was a 20 percent increase in business. ICI Explosives also became convinced during the initial pilot

Constraints on a QR/CR System

- *No back orders (cuts).* Suppliers must ship full orders; the systems are not designed to handle partial shipments. In the event that a supplier can't make a full shipment, he must inventory the product at his own expense until he can make the full shipment at the next approved ship date.

- *Preference for full truck loads or palletized freight.* The system might recommend orders that add up to two-thirds of a truck. Unfortunately, customers prefer full truckloads because they are more economical. This means suppliers must often scurry about to find ways of filling the truck. Suppliers might also be required to use certain types of pallets that are different from those used internally by the supplier's own handling system.

- *Extra charges for LTL.* Customers in QR/CR arrangements discourage LTL shipments because their receiving systems are geared mostly for unloading full trucks. Since LTL trucks are sometimes not loaded in the ideal manner, they may actually take longer to unload.

- *Collect freight terms are preferred.* QR/CR customers want the flexibility of being able to specify the mode of transport. In some cases, they will send their own trucks, which does not help the supplier that has its own fleet. By letting the customer specify the shipping vendor, the supplier loses planning and execution flexibility.

- *One trailer to a PO for multi-trailer deliveries.* The supplier may have three truckloads of the same product, all of which should ideally fall under the same PO. But some QR/CR customers generally want one PO per truck, which in turn creates unnecessary paperwork.

- *Shipping appointments must be called in up to 14 days prior to a delivery date.* If a supplier has a good inventory planning system, this 14-day requirement can be built into the lead time. But many suppliers do not have a sophisticated inventory management system, so they might have to inventory product for two weeks before shipping it.

- *Up to a 5-day delivery window.* Once the supplier has called in for a shipping appointment, the customer will provide up to a 5-day window for the product's arrival date. Add this to the 14-day appointment constraint, and a supplier might have to wait 19 days before shipping product that is actually ready to roll.

Table 1-2

that DRP would smooth the company's inventory and production schedules, reduce operating and sales costs, and provide a better decision-making tool. And it did.

Figures 1-5 and 1-6 show actual copies of electronic transmissions for product demand from a customer for two consecutive weeks (9/30 and 10/7). These transmissions are updated and transmitted every week by each customer in the program. Every product at every customer location is modeled weekly. The following terminology is used in both figures:

FCST: sales forecast

INTRANSIT: in-transit shipments due from the supplier

PR ONHD: projected available inventory

PL ORD: suggested order quantity.

When you compare figure 1-5 with figure 1-6, some interesting observations can be made:

1. On September 30, the inventory position is 255. Compared to a sales forecast of 271 for the first week, the system is projecting a shortage of 16 (a potential back order) at the customer's inventory location by the end of the first week.

2. An in-transit of 1,200 items is scheduled to arrive the week of 10/7. The DRP dynamic inventory model has critiqued this in-transit and given an action message to expedite the shipment since it is needed now. The action message appears as the last line in figure 1-5.

3. One week later (week 10/7, figure 1-6), the on-hand balance is 1,155. Obviously, the 1,200 items were expedited and arrived in time to avoid a customer back order.

Figure 1-6 shows two time-phased displays. The top display is the original transmission as received by ICI Explosives every Monday morning. The bottom display is the confirming transmission sent back to the customer the same day. A close look at the top display of figure 1-6 reveals that suggested orders of 300 and 150 (Pln ord line), appear for the weeks of 10/7 and 10/14. On the bottom display, both orders have been replaced by an in-transit of 450 showing in the week of 10/21.

The confirming transmission reflects an action taken by ICI Explosives to ship the suggested orders for the first two weeks only. This action is part of the arrangement between the particular customer and ICI Explosives. In this instance, ICI Explosives is given the authority to ship anything that appears in the first two weeks of the horizon.

DRP for the Period Beginning 09-30

WEEK:	now	9-30	10-07	10-14	10-21	10-28	11-04	11-11	11-18
Fcst	0	271	262	262	262	262	262	262	262
In-Transit	0	0	1200	0	0	0	0	0	0
Pr onhd	255	-16	922	810	848	886	924	812	850
Pln ord	0	0	150	300	300	300	150	300	300

Reschedule in In-Transit for 1200 from 10-07 to 09-30

Figure 1-5

DRP for the Period Beginning 10-07

WEEK:	now	10-07	10-14	10-21	10-28	11-04	11-11	11-18	11-25
Fcst	0	271	262	262	262	262	262	262	262
In-Transit	0	0	0	0	0	0	0	0	0
Pr onhd	1155	884	922	810	848	886	924	812	850
Pln ord	0	300	150	300	300	300	150	300	300

Release planned order

WEEK:	now	10-07	10-14	10-21	10-28	11-04	11-11	11-18	11-25
Fcst	0	271	262	262	262	262	262	262	262
In-Transit	0	0	0	450	0	0	0	0	0
Pr onhd	1155	884	622	810	848	886	924	812	850
Pln ord	0	0	0	300	300	300	150	300	300

Figure 1-6

The DRP QR/CR model is used to release orders as if they were released against a purchase contract with scheduled deliveries agreed to ahead of time. The difference is that delivery dates and quantities are dynamically adjusted as sales come in above or below forecast. The first two weeks are considered firm. This induces up-front stability for both customer and supplier, and **allows for transportation and warehouse receiving capacity planning before orders are electronically transmitted by the customer.**

QR/CR and Supplier Scheduling

Other companies use a variation of the displays shown in figures 1-5 and 1-6 in their electronic communications with suppliers. In certain cases, customers are reluctant to share forecast and inventory information with their suppliers, and they merely "strip off" the suggested order quantities and maintain the time phasing to show when orders should be shipped. Figure 1-7 is an actual example of such a "stripped-down" report. In chapter 3, we will cover in detail how supplier schedules are developed and used.

The beauty of the system is that no purchase orders are issued, no confirmations are made, and no invoices are issued. Only a supplier schedule is issued to the supplier, who subsequently sends electronically a monthly statement to the customer. The statement indicates the total number of shipments made during the month.

In addition to the above benefits, the supplier gets an advance look at 28 weeks of requirements from his customer. Think about it: Companies can eliminate paperwork, unnecessary activities, and financial transactions. Most important, they can eliminate uncertainty about what the customer really needs. (This is also the elimination of waste in the purest sense of the Just-in-Time/Total Quality Control philosophy.)

ICI Explosives has extended QR/CR even further. The DRP transmissions received weekly from its customers are read directly in the master production schedule (MPS), as shown in figure 1-8. Every Monday morning after customers have transmitted their 28-week requirements, ICI Explosives performs a summary of transmissions. This is done by product for all customers 28 weeks out. The middle portion of figure 1-8 shows one transmission for Customer A for product 450-XXXX and the summary for all customers ordering the same product.

The total for week 10/7 is 3,500, and for week 10/14, 2,950. These summaries are then uploaded into ICI Explosives' master production

E.D. Smith Supplier Schedules for Perkins Inc.   Week of xx/xx/xx
Location: Portland DC   Firm Zone: first 4 Weeks

Buyer:

Unit Item Descr. Cost C/S	Current + Past due	Requirements			Next 4 Wks	U/M: Selling Units		
		Week 2/8	Week 2/15	Week 2/22		Next 4 Wks	Next 4 Wks	Next 12 Wks
2/42 16" Color TV Qty:	-	-	-	1100	2200	2200	2200	2200 / 3300
P.O. No.:				B1203				
175.00$				192,500	385,000	385,000	385,000	385,000 / 577,500
2/44 20" Color TV Qty:	-	-		-	1040	1040	1040	1040 / 2080
P.O. No.:								
200.00$					208,000	208,000	208,000	208,000 / 208,000
2/30 24" Color TV Qty:	70	70	70	70	280	280	280	280 / 840
P.O. No.:	B1120	B1146	B1180	B1203				
300.00$	21,000	21,000	21,000	21,000	84,000	84,000	84,000	84,000 / 252,000
2/00 28" Color TV Qty:	-	150			300	150	300	300 / 600
P.O.:		B1146						
470.00$		70,500			141,000	70,500	141,000	141,000 / 282,000
Weekly Total$	21,000	91,500	21,000	213,500	818,000	747,500	818,000	818,000 / 1,319,500
Cum Total$	21,000	112,500	133,500	347,000	1,165,000	1,912,500	2,730,500	4,050,000
Weekly Total WGT:	3,850	12,850	3,850	47,850	173,400	164,400	173,400	173,400 / 318,200
Cum Total WGT:	3,850	16,700	20,550	68,400	241,800	406,200	579,600	897,800
Weekly Total Std Hrs:	2	5	2	31	104	100	104	104 / 182
Weekly Capacity:	400							

Figure 1-7

schedule module for each product. ICI Explosives redesigned its MPS display to appear like the one shown in the bottom of figure 1-8. The DRP demands are displayed as the top line in the MPS. The displays also show actual customers' orders not yet shipped, along with the national forecast. The top three lines are added to show the total demand to be satisfied by the factory.

Before ICI Explosives implemented QR/CR, its MPS display showed only customer orders and the national forecast as demand, and the total demand line was the greater of the two. As DRP demands began to show on the MPS, they replaced the forecasts for the customers who were cutting over.

This approach changes the way customers and suppliers do business. It eliminates a significant number of activities. To appreciate the economies it offers, consider how customers and suppliers typically conduct business in a non-QR/CR environment. The top of figure 1-9 shows the normal information flow at the time of order placement. Initially, people working in the customer's inventory control department trigger a purchase requisition to the purchasing department. After negotiations with the supplier's sales rep, a purchase order is issued and then processed by the supplier's order entry system. The order is then picked, packed, shipped, and billed. Ultimately, inventory records are updated and a signal for additional production is triggered in the supplier's MRP system.

In contrast, once the new thinking in QR/CR becomes reality, customers and suppliers are able to directly connect their inventory control systems, as illustrated in figure 1-9. Because many steps are eliminated, the supplier can respond faster to changes in demand. This approach frees buyers from the need to issue POs, thus allowing more time for negotiations, value analysis, and so forth. It also frees supplier sales representatives from unnecessary paperwork and expediting, giving them more time to sell.

In addition, this approach is significantly different from typical QR/CR programs in use today. It's simpler, easier, and faster to implement and much more powerful. Typical QR/CR programs require suppliers to develop customer-specific inventory planning models and then incorporate them into their own system.

At ICI Explosives, the direct DRP input to the MPS enables the company to change production quickly. DRP takes the natural demand pull to manufacturing's doorsteps. Changes in the marketplace are totally visible to people responsible for scheduling logistics and pro-

Actual Customer Suggested
Order Report

DRP for the period beginning 10-07

Week:	now	10-07	10-14	10-21	10-28	11-04	11-11	11-18	11-25
Fcst	0	271	262	262	262	262	262	262	262
In-Tr	0	0	0	0	0	0	0	0	0
Pr onhd	1155	884	922	810	848	886	924	812	850
Plan ord	0	300	150	300	300	300	150	300	300

Release planned order

EDI 28-WK CUSTOMER DRP TRANSMISSIONS FOR PRODUCT 450-XXXX

Week	1	2	3	4	26	27	28
Customer	10/7	10/14	10/21	10/28	3/31	4/7	4/14
A	300	150	300	300			
B	150	-	300	-			
C	200	100	200	100			
D	-	200	-	200			
E	50	100	-	100			
F	100	-	100	50			
TOTAL	3500	2950	3200	3460			

ICI EXPLOSIVES MPS DISPLAY PRODUCT 450-XXXX

	Past Due	10/7	10/14	10/21	10/28	3/31	4/7	4/14
DRP Demands	-	3500	2950	3200	3460	3150	3400	2550
Customer Orders	-	550	490	320	120	-	-	-
National Fcst	-	12500	11000	11700	12220	12700	12400	11900
Total	-	16550	14440	15220	15780	15850	15800	14450
Sched Recpts	-							
Proj On Hand	47550	31000	16560	1340	20560			
MPS Start				35000				
MPS Rcpt					35000			

Figure 1-8

Customer/Supplier Information Flow

NORMAL FLOW

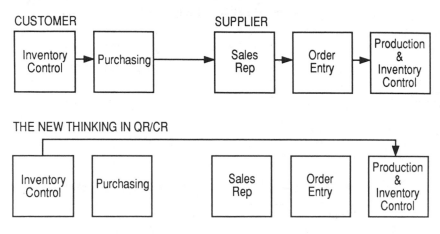

Figure 1-9

duction. Any significant change is picked up immediately, and demand uncertainty is significantly reduced.

ICI Explosives takes this even a step further. The company treats the first two weeks of DRP planned orders as the actual customer orders and calculates an available-to-promise (ATP), using both DRP planned orders and the actual customer orders. This is correct and makes perfect sense since ICI Explosives has been given authority by its QR/CR customers to ship the first two weeks of planned DRP orders.

Consequently, ICI Explosives is able to calculate an ATP and make this information available to its order-entry people for promising product to customers not on QR/CR. Ironically, this is being accomplished without actual customer orders ever going through the formal order-entry process. This approach may well cause a complete rethinking of how sales forecasting and order entry are practiced today in manufacturing companies.

This substitution of information for inventory unleashes the tremendous technological power of DRP. In addition, EDI is not reduced to a sophisticated electronic mailbox. Rather, it is used to transmit DRP-based customer requirements.

As ICI Explosives shows, DRP is a ticket to the new world of QR/CR. The customer-supplier relationships described in this chapter cut the information-cycle time significantly. Most important, they help reduce uncertainty. And the reduction of uncertainty has a domino effect: The newfound stability means predictable and realistic production schedules, which translate into predictable supplier deliveries. The predictable supplier deliveries mean fast responses, less inventory, and lower costs for customers.

To sum up, if gold is to be found in industry, you should stake your claim in the area of QR/CR. As stressed above, value-added benefits that accrue from the approach have an impact on many activities. Figure 1-10 depicts the benefits for customers and suppliers who enter into a new QR/CR arrangement.

CONCLUSION

For the new thinking in QR/CR to take hold, a paradigm shift is required. Retailers and wholesalers/distributors must take an active part in planning with their suppliers rather than abdicating responsibility to them.

All pipeline constituents have to see themselves as members of the same team if increased inventory velocity is to become a way of life across the channel. Implementing the principles described in this chapter and the rest of this book will elevate retailers, wholesalers/distributors, and manufacturers to a higher level of integrated management by:

- Setting the foundation for integrated forward planning. This results in integrated financial plans that include merchandising, buying, traffic, and warehousing plans.

- Creating a structure that significantly reduces demand uncertainty by pushing sales forecasting back to the point of end use (the retail store) as opposed to pushing it forward to suppliers.

- Making possible, in a seamless manner, fast reaction to change and synchronization from factory to store.

- Establishing one common language of pipeline management as opposed to forcing suppliers to create new systems to adapt to retailers' systems.

- Making proactive planning by exception possible, thus increasing productivity and the quality of life.

Value Added Benefits from the
New Thinking in QR/CR

Activity	Customer	Supplier
A/C Receivable	–	greatly simplified due to issuing monthly statements vs. invoices
A/C Payable	greatly simplified, no PO's, pay from statements	–
Purchasing	improved, simplified, no PO's, more time for professional buying	–
Order Entry	–	simplified, fewer orders working from supplier schedules
Receiving	less paperwork, visible inbound flow, improved manpower planning	–
Billing	–	almost eliminated, now issuing monthly statements
Forecasting	–	significantly reduced as more customers on system
Demand Uncertainty	–	same as forecasting
Inventory Investment	reduced	reduced
Operating Costs	reduced	reduced
Production Stability	–	improved
Customer Orders Deliver Stability	more dependable	higher customer service levels
Inventory Control	shared	shared
Shipping	–	smoother, more efficient

Figure 1-10

Chapter 2

Typical Problems in Logistics

Symptoms and Causes

LIFE IN THE FAST LANE

We've come a long way since the days when distribution was simply a matter of getting product from A to B. Today, logistics is a science in its own right, one that requires an ability to juggle conflicting needs in an effort to keep product flowing smoothly through the industrial pipeline. To understand the difficulties of maintaining a dynamic balance in the pipeline, consider the logistics perspective from the retail end of that pipeline.

Many retailers today have a network of distribution centers (DCs) that replenish the stock of the company's retail stores. Typically, the DCs have a high degree of freedom within the organization. Not only do they have their own buying plans and inventory budgets, but each has its own team of replenishment personnel, who report directly to the center's general manager. In many cases, the DC's general manager reports to a regional manager, who sets the inventory budgets.

The replenishment personnel at each DC independently forecasts its needs over a short future horizon to cover day-in and day-out regular sales. That group also forecasts the needs for future promotional events. Unfortunately, the forecast horizons for regular and promotional needs may not coincide, especially if the replenishers use a reorder point system to decide on the timing and quantity of orders to be placed. Future forecasts for regular and promotional sales over a limited horizon are compared to the total amount of product on hand and on order. If the amount is below the total needs, an order is triggered in multiples of the lot size for each item.

In addition to the organization that replenishes the DC, another organization often exists at a national level. In this case, the national buying organization is responsible for contracting with the various suppliers (supply sources) for merchandise that will be sold at the company's retail stores. The DCs stock only those items approved by the national buying organization.

A natural counterpart to a national buying organization is a national marketing organization. The marketing people are responsible for developing an advertising plan and an in-store presentation strategy for the merchandise. The marketing organization is also responsible for forecasting dollar sales on a monthly basis. This sales estimate is used for financial planning.

The national buying organization also estimates future sales. Done in units, sales are communicated to the suppliers on a monthly basis. Based on the marketing plan, the buying organization and the suppliers try to predict when the various independent replenishment organizations at the DCs will require shipments of merchandise.

One problem with this arrangement is that the DC replenishment organizations independently develop and execute purchasing plans, so there is very little, if any, communication about future needs with the buying organization or the supply source. On the other hand, the buying organization, along with the supply source, must predict when the replenishment organization will need merchandise. Since the plans of the DC and the plans of the buying organization rarely coincide, the company may find itself awash in expensive excess safety stock. Extra inventory typically exists at the supply source and at the DC—in case an item sells better than predicted, or there is a shortage at the supply source.

A final problem arises from each DC acting independently. As the supply of fast-selling merchandise dwindles, the replenishment organization at each DC orders as much of the source items as possible, which results in too much merchandise in the DCs that order first, and a short supply in the rest. The solution is often expensive reshipment of merchandise from one DC to another or lower future orders because of the overstock position. An additional consequence is that the buying organization or the supply source might interpret the situation as a change in demand. Either way, the results are potential stock outs or increased logistics costs.

Now that we've seen a sampling of the real difficulties that can arise from a typical distribution arrangement, let's look at some of the common assumptions about problems related to a company's logistics functions.

SURFACE PROBLEMS

If you ask people from a broad range of industries to identify their chief problems, you'll get answers such as high inventories, poor customer service, high logistics, and manufacturing costs, etc. Beginning in 1979, we did just that in our DRP classes. Figure 2-1 shows the results for 1986 through 1989. As you can see, 603 individuals from 101 different companies participated; the mix of companies responding to the questionnaire in class has been almost a fifty-fifty split—retailers and wholesaler/distributors on one side and manufacturers on the other. One response is particularly interesting; although high inventories account for 25 percent of the responses, that has not always been the case. During the past ten years, for example, shortage of product made it to the top spot twice. Nevertheless, in the same time period, high inventories, lack of visibility, shortage of product, and low customer service remained in the top four slots, and accounted for more than 70 percent of the responses.

Another important issue is the ability to handle change in business conditions. This issue has been rising steadily in importance for our respondents. Ten years ago, it was last on the list; in 1989, it became the fifth most important, and it continues to gain.

What do these numbers really mean? Are the issues cited the causes of the problems or the symptoms of deeper problems? In fact, they are merely symptoms. Companies that identified the root causes of the problems, such as lumpy demand, lack of integration, and reorder points and their derivatives, and then proceeded to correct them, achieved outstanding results. In the following pages and chapters, you'll read about some of these companies and how they tackled these underlying problems. For now, let's turn our attention to the first of the three major problems—lumpy demand.

1986–1989 DRP Class Surveys		
	No. of Respondents	% of Total
High inventories	150	24.9
Lack of visibility	108	17.9
Shortage of product	96	15.9
Low customer service	84	13.9
Change	63	10.4
High cost of distribution	40	5.6
Adversarial relationships	24	4.0
High cost of manufacturing	16	2.6
High cost of purchasing	11	1.9
Inter DC transfers	11	1.9
	603	100%

Figure 2-1

ROOT CAUSES

Lumpy Demand

Lumpy demand is a function of time and quantity impact across the industrial pipeline. Figure 2-2 shows the most common quantity and time factors creating lumpy demand. The list of factors can be broken down into two distinct categories—quantity and time-related. Some of the factors are externally induced, such as buying lot sizes, packaging lot sizes, and safety stock changes, while others, such as manufacturing lot sizes, inspection time, and move time are self-induced. A manufacturer's production process will dictate which factors will affect business and customers. The same holds true for people operating DCs, stores, etc.; they are responsible for the external factors that cause lumpy demand on their supply sources. These quantity and time factors cascade and amplify as they cross the various levels along the marketing channel.

Over time, the factors also change. For example, a manufacturer may start to produce in smaller lot sizes as it applies the JIT/TQC philosophy. A wholesaler may shorten order entry and processing times, as well as order picking, packing, and shipping time, and he may even receive smaller purchase quantities from the supplier who just reduced his

Factors of Lumpy Demand Across the Industrial Pipeline					
	Mfg.	**Mfg. DCs**	**W/D**	**Ret. DCs**	**Retail**
Quantity-Related					
Buying lot sizes	X	X	X	X	X
Mfg. lot sizes	X	X			
Packaging lot sizes	X	X			
Shipping lot sizes		X	X	X	X
Selling lot sizes			X	X	X
Stocking lot sizes		X	X	X	
Rejects	X				
Rework	X				
Batch order picking		X	X	X	
Safety stock changes		X	X	X	X
# stocking locations		X	X	X	X
Inv. stocking policies	X	X	X	X	X
Time-Related					
Inv. stocking policies	X	X	X	X	X
Seasonality		X	X	X	X
Promotions and deals		X	X	X	X
Price increases		X	X	X	X
End of season sales		X	X	X	X
Technology improvements		X	X	X	X
Packaging design changes		X	X	X	X
Product design changes		X	X	X	X
Order picking and packing time		X	X	X	X
Move time between customer and supplier		X	X	X	X
Mfg. queue time	X	X			
Inspection time	X	X			
Receiving time		X	X	X	X
Order processing time		X	X	X	X
Mfg. move time	X	X			
Mfg. equipment speed time	X	X			

Mfg. = Manufacturing
Mfg DCs = Manufacturing Distribution Centers
Ret. DCs = Retailers Distribution Centers
W/D = Wholesaler/Distributors
RETAIL = Retail Stores

Figure 2-2

manufacturing lot sizes. As a result, the wholesaler may also reduce minimum selling quantities to customers.

Likewise, a retailer may streamline an operation by closing DCs and stores in one location and opening new ones elsewhere. He may also switch to faster modes of customer deliveries by either going directly from DCs to customers, thereby bypassing the stores, or by switching modes of transport and methods of consolidation and break bulk. These are but a few examples of factors that ultimately cause and affect lumpy demand.

Depending on the industry, some factors have more influence than others in creating lumpy demand. For example, seasonality, promotions and deals, and price changes are more likely to cause lumpy demand than other factors.

Also, depending on location in the marketing channel, you may be forced to do business in a certain way, or you may add to or subtract from the factors listed in figure 2-2. For example, anyone in the marketing channel can and will change inventory stocking policies and decide to lower or increase inventories. This will affect every member of the channel.

Similarly, you may announce a big sale ahead of your competitor, who may than counter your maneuver with even lower prices. A manufacturer may experience technological improvements and introduce a superior product that will make your products obsolete, sending shock waves across the marketing channel. The factors are constantly changing for a variety of reasons.

To appreciate the consequences of the various factors, consider the example of a wholesaler operating three DC's located in Chicago, Montreal, and New York. If the manager of the Chicago distribution center visited every one of his customers, he would find that each customer has his own inventory management system. Some are manual; others are computerized. He would also find that customers have inventory investment targets. They know how much inventory they can afford, which affects their ordering patterns. Some customers order very frequently— as much as once or twice a week; others order less.

Also, certain customers sell more than others, and when you receive different order sizes at different intervals from different customers, you begin to see lumpy demand on your distribution center or factory from week to week.

The Chicago distribution center experiences different demand patterns compared to its counterparts in Montreal and New York. The three distribution centers also generate different demands on the manufacturers' distribution centers that support them—each has different ordering rules that are reflected in safety stock and order quantities. As sales in each distribution center materialize at different rates and are affected by order quantities, safety stock, and transportation lead times, lumpy demand will be very significant on the manufacturer's distribution center supplying the wholesaler's distribution centers.

Combating Lumpy Demand

The bad news is that lumpy demand is a fact of life. The good news is that with DRP, you can forecast it before it clobbers you. DRP will not only profile external lumpy demand, it will keep you up-to-date as conditions change. Figure 2-3 shows how this works, with actual DRP data from a company that operates a network of eight distribution centers. These eight locations are all serviced from the same regional distribution center (RDC).

Figure 2-3 shows on-hand, on-order, and weekly sales forecasts for each DC. Also planning data is indicated (ship order quantity, safety stock, and distribution lead time). DC #5, which hasn't opened for business yet, has no data, although 720 are in transit (on order). DC #8

	Basic Distribution Network Statistics					
DC	Inv on Hand	Inv on Order	Weekly Sales Fcst	Ship Order Qty	Safety Stock	Dist Lead Time
1	10540	-	1630	4800	3260	3 wks
2	5260	4680	1320	3960	2640	2 wks
3	13220	-	2760	8280	5520	2 wks
4	45240	-	12000	36000	12000	1 wk
5	0	720	240	-	-	-
6	23060	-	5115	15000	10230	1 wk
7	640	600	180	600	360	2 wks
8	960	-	-	120	0	2 wks
	98920*		23245*			
* = Total amounts						

Figure 2-3

has inventory on hand and no sales forecast. This DC is a public warehouse and is used to stock product for one large customer only. Since this is a relatively new setup, no demand history exists yet and a sales forecast has to be developed.

When you first look at the total weekly sales forecast for all eight DCs, it appears that the RDC could expect demand of about 23,000 units per week. In fact, people at the RDC use this weekly sales forecast and spread it across all DCs, taking into account historical sales. They also use this forecast in planning their inventory levels and purchases.

Is this a good method to use for managing and controlling inventory and purchasing? It's adequate if you don't have better numbers to work with. But will demand materialize close to the forecast of 23,000 per week? Absolutely not! Actual demand will likely show significant fluctuations—in other words, it will be very lumpy. Figure 2-4 shows the lumpy demand pattern.

The dynamics of this network have been calculated and simulated by DRP. Again, the lumpy-demand projection is very real, and it reveals how this company elects to conduct business. Will it or can it be changed? The answer is yes, if sales don't materialize as forecasted or if competitive conditions pressure the company into rethinking business as usual.

Until the advent of DRP, no system was capable of simulating the dynamics of external changes on logistics systems, and making lumpy demand visible. When you compare the lumpy demand to the national sales forecast, the two are far apart. For example, the national weekly sales forecast for all eight DCs in this network is 23,245, as shown in

Lumpy-Demand Profile	
Week	Demand on Supply Source
1	8280
2	56040
3	840
4	12480
5	56040
6	240

Figure 2-4

figure 2-3. Yet the demand for the first six weeks, as indicated in figure 2-4, has a low of 840 in week 3 and a high of 56,040 in weeks 2 and 5.

These are significant discrepancies. Nevertheless, most companies continue to forecast on a national basis. National sales forecasts are only valid when compared against actual total sales and financial goals. National sales forecasts are averages, and can be used safely for budgeting or for planning global manufacturing capacity. But for logistics planning and for manufacturing planning, they are far too inaccurate. Remember, customers don't buy nationally—they buy what they want when they want it and where they want it. Therefore, you need a system like DRP to simulate future demand if you wish to avoid excessive inventories and customer back orders at the same time.

In traditional inventory management systems, lumpy demand is tracked as "noise" that deviates from forecast and is used to recompute safety stock requirements that in turn increase inventory investment. This approach is misdirected. Moreover, because demand is so lumpy in the real world and invisible to supply sources, it causes severe back order situations, inventory overstocks, and major disruptions in operations at the same time.

In the example, there are eight DCs and one supply source. If sales materialize as forecasted, and if the planning rules don't change (safety stock, ship order quantity, and distribution lead time), the lumpy demand will materialize exactly as anticipated in figure 2-4. But when actual sales begin to vary from forecast or when someone changes the planning rules or conducts business differently, the lumpy demand will show different patterns. In chapter 3, examples illustrate these changes and their effects on supply sources.

Lack of Integration

If you look for books that address the need and importance of integrating inventory management/purchasing systems with other inventory management/purchasing/manufacturing systems, you will come up empty-handed. "Integration" is currently very fashionable. But you have to go beyond "surface connections," which entail integrating one system with another. Rather, people need to begin thinking about natural dependencies in inventory management, purchasing and manufacturing practices.

A wholesaler/distributor's inventories across his distribution centers are linked to the supplier's DCs which are linked to factories. The factories, in turn, are linked to outside suppliers, and so forth and so on.

These obvious connections have never been officially recognized. Just look at systems development—we develop stand-alone systems for retailers, stand-alone systems for wholesaler/distributors, and finally stand-alone systems for manufacturers. Even within a manufacturing company, you will find one system for logistics, another for manufacturing, and sometimes yet another for purchasing.

As explained earlier, natural linkages do exist and must be recognized when developing systems to manage and control inventories in purchasing, manufacturing and logistics. As early as 1958, Joe Orlicky, who coined the term Material Requirements Planning (MRP), recognized dependencies in materials needed to support production schedules— that's how MRP was born—yet true dependencies extend beyond the four walls of a factory.

Inventories are the common thread that link retailers, wholesalers, distributors, and manufacturers. We must stop developing stand-alone systems, and begin looking for linkages which provide visibility from one level to another. Planning and scheduling systems like DRP demand internal linkages; they can't work without them. They also set the stage for the external linkages, explained in detail in chapter 1. Remember, any change at any point will be felt elsewhere in the marketing channel—it's only a matter of time and quantity before the shock wave hits. If we aspire, as we should, to fully synchronized marketing channels, we must begin to install planning and scheduling systems, and then link them together.

Reorder Points and Derivatives

Reorder-point systems have been around since 1934. Initially, they were used by manufacturers to order material in support of production schedules, but eventually wound up being used throughout industry. Today, in fact, more than 99 percent of all retailers, wholesalers, and distributors use the classic reorder-point technique and its derivatives to manage and control inventories and conduct purchasing.

Although the reorder point is still widely used today in nonmanufacturing environments, manufacturing companies have moved on to more useful inventory management approaches. The shift in manufacturing began in the late fifties, when Orlicky, then at J. I. Case, began seeking alternatives to the reorder-point technique. What first started as requirements planning in the late fifties became, with the help of Ollie Wight, material requirements planning (MRP) in the late sixties. By the end of the seventies, Ollie, working with myself and others, ultimately transformed MRP into manufacturing resource planning (MRP II.) In the mid seventies, DRP appeared on the scene to help with distribution-related problems. Today, a significant number of manufacturers who service customers through distribution centers have set aside reorder points in favor of DRP.

Can we say the same thing about retailers and wholesaler/distributors? Unfortunately not. Is it because these kinds of organizations have not caught up with the times? Absolutely not; rather, they have not been exposed to DRP, or they have not seriously considered implementing DRP in their own operations. Of the three root causes of problems, reorder points are by far the most serious. To appreciate why, let's look at an example.

Figure 2-5 shows a generic situation. Three locations, Chicago, Montreal, and New York, are ordering product from a supply source. This is a generic situation because it can represent virtually any company, whether it is a retailer owning three stores supported by a distribution center, a wholesaler operating three distribution centers supported by a regional or central distribution center, or a manufacturer operating three distribution centers supported by a factory.

Generic Reorder-point Model			
	Chicago	**Montreal**	**New York**
Inventory on hand	225	164	350
Forecast	115/wk	47/wk	125/wk
Reorder point	345	141	375
POQ	500	200	500
Supplier lead time	2 wks	2 wks	2 wks
		Supply Source (DC)	
Inventory on hand		1170	
Reorder point		1150	
Order quantity		2200	
Supplier lead time (factory)		3 wks	

Figure 2-5

Let's assume the company in the example is a wholesaler that operates three distribution centers and orders product from a manufacturer (the supply source). This manufacturer operates a number of distribution centers. In our example, Chicago, Montreal, and New York are all supplied from the same distribution center owned and operated by the manufacturer. Both the wholesaler and manufacturer use the classic reorder-point formula—demand over lead time plus safety stock—to manage and control inventory and order material.

The wholesaler uses a computerized inventory control system that incorporates state-of-the-art techniques to dynamically compute and update reorder points and safety stocks, based on the most recent changes in actual sales versus forecasts. These reorder points and safety stocks are changed every week as necessary. In addition, reorder quantities are calculated on a period order quantity (POQ) rule of four-week supply for each distribution center. The POQ is then rounded to account for the minimum buy quantity of 100. For example, the four-week POQ for Chicago is 460 rounded to 500.

The wholesaler updates his data and makes buying decisions every Monday, taking into account sales for the previous week and inventory on hand as of the close of business Friday night. Before going further, it is important to mention that in this example, the wholesaler buys a product that is custom-packaged exclusively for him. Therefore, the only demand for this product at the supply source comes from Chicago, Montreal, and New York.

Consider what happens if you are responsible at the supply source for managing and controlling your inventory, as well as ordering from the factory. Are you okay? Are you in trouble? Do you need to do anything? You're all right, because you have 1,170 on hand and your reorder point is 1,150[2] (refer to figure 2-5). When your inventory reaches 1,149 or less, you will order from the factory and when you do, you will order 2,200—that's your minimum, and the factory lead time is three weeks.

Now, let's take a look at the wholesaler. Remember it's Monday morning and the computer just printed out the data. The system is

---

[2] The reorder points in the three DCs and the supply source have all been calculated the same way:

$$(\text{demand} \times \text{lead time}) + \text{one week of safety stock}$$

For example, the supply-source reorder point in this example would be:

$$(287 \times 3) + 287 = 1,148 \text{ (rounded to } 1,150)$$

recommending two orders for approval, the first for Chicago and the second for New York. Both locations have gone below their respective reorder points. Montreal is okay at this time, so no action is recommended.

The wholesaler reviews the recommendations and releases two orders for Chicago and New York for 500 units each. Monday afternoon both orders are transmitted electronically using EDI capabilities to your distribution center. Both orders are received, verified, picked, packed, and shipped within three working days. Now, it's Friday morning and your inventory has been updated and shows an on-hand balance of 170. The computer recommends that an order for 2,200 be placed at the factory. You review, approve, and release it.

That same afternoon you receive another order from the wholesaler for 200 to be shipped to the Montreal distribution center. Recall that on Monday, Montreal was okay. But now, sales have materialized close to forecast and the wholesaler reached his reorder point.

Do you have a problem? Obviously, you can't ship the whole order— you're short 30 units. And even though you have 2,200 on order, product won't be available for three weeks. So you must do two things. First, advise your customer you can only ship 170. Second, contact your factory to expedite the order you just placed that same morning. You are now out of stock and will be so for three weeks unless the factory can expedite the order.

So, one day things look great, and the next day you're out of stock. One day the factory receives an order with normal lead time; a few hours later the factory is told to expedite the order. Is this typical? Indeed—it happens all the time. What's the problem? The reorder point.

Reorder points don't tell the whole truth; they're reactive rather than anticipatory. In addition, reorder points assume that lead times are fixed and that demand during lead time is constant. That's why people carry safety stock. It's also why people who develop computer systems for inventory control pay a lot of attention to safety stock determinations. At the time of this writing, at least ten approaches were in vogue. But finding the right answer to safety-stock computations isn't the *real* solution to the problem; it's only an element. The main task is to find ways to stay in stock in the first place.

Another problem with reorder points is that they will often indicate something is needed when, in fact, it is not required for some time. This is illustrated by altering the numbers a bit from figure 2-5. As you can

Generic Reorder-point Model with Revised On-hand Balances			
	Chicago	Montreal	New York
Inventory on hand	225	330	880
Forecast	115/wk	47/wk	125/wk
Reorder point	345	141	375
POQ	500	200	500
Supplier lead time	2 wks	2 wks	2 wks
		Supply **Source (DC)**	
Inventory on hand		1600	
Reorder point		1150	
Order quantity		2200	
Supplier Lead Time (factory)		3 wks	

Figure 2-6

see in figure 2-6, the Montreal and New York distribution centers are well above their reorder points. They just received shipments and each has seven weeks of inventory on hand. This condition causes Chicago to order 500, which in turn causes the supply source to drop below it's reorder point (1,600 minus 500 equals 1,100) and signal the factory to produce 2,200.

This signal to produce is inappropriate because product is not needed at the manufacturer's distribution center for at least six weeks, which is about when New York will likely order. So not only do reorder points order late, as in the first instance, they also occasionally order too soon. Why is that? Because they were designed as ordering systems, not scheduling systems like DRP and MRP. Reorder points do not re-schedule when conditions change.

CONCLUSION

There's only one constant in industry and it's called change. We undersell or oversell the forecast, the shipment is late, equipment breaks down, products are rejected, damaged, need rework, and so on. These are normal day-to-day occurrences in most companies regardless of whether they are retailers, wholesalers, distributors, or manufacturers.

These conditions cause a lot of change in inventory management, and, as we just saw, purchasing systems that only tell you what to order and when to order it are greatly insufficient. In this day and age of Just-in-Time and Quick Response expectations, we need systems that recognize change and help us deal with it so we can gain control of the flow of raw material and finished goods.

Consider the effects of change on sales forecasting. As anyone in business will attest, there is only one sure thing about any sales forecast: *It's going to be wrong*. It is hoped you will be close and above forecast, but you'll still be off. Does that mean you should not try to improve sales forecasting? Quite the opposite. But there is a limit to forecast accuracy; no one can or ever will be able to forecast the future with 100 percent accuracy.

Everybody believes this, but seldom thinks about it. How did you react the last time you saw actual sales for a product that hit the forecast right-on? Probably it was similar to, "Hey, somebody must have fixed the numbers." Deep inside, we don't expect the forecast to be right, yet people relentlessly seek that perfect forecasting system. Let's hope they aren't holding their breath during the searching process.

Good forecasting is needed, but systems that can cope with changes are needed even more. Often people say, "We are not ready to change our system. We must first work on improving our forecasting capabilities." This is a waste of time because good scheduling systems like DRP go a long way in terms of compensating for erroneous forecasts. The worse the forecast the more you need DRP; the better the forecast the less you need it.

Finally, forecasting for a total business on a national basis is one thing. But taking that forecast and breaking it down by distribution location is another. If you service customers through a network of distribution locations (e.g. stores, distribution centers or warehouses) you cannot avoid the need to forecast by distribution location. This will inevitably lead to more, not fewer, forecast errors. In chapter 7 we cover forecasting in detail. We also show that eliminating the use of reorder points, obtaining visibility of lumpy demand, and integrating cross functionally within and outside the company is where most time, effort, and money should be spent in overcoming typical problems in logistics.

Chapter 3

The DRP Management Process

The ABCs of DRP

This chapter explains the DRP process and how it is used to solve the problems in logistics, manufacturing, and purchasing discussed in the previous chapters. The nuts-and-bolts details—the mechanics of DRP—will be covered in later chapters. Here, we focus on the DRP logic and how it compares to the traditional reorder-point concept.

THE LOGIC OF DRP: THE BIG PICTURE

DRP is a management process that determines the needs of inventory stocking locations (ISLs)[1] and ensures that supply sources will be able to meet the demand. This is accomplished in three distinct phases. First, DRP receives input from the following:

• sales forecasts by stock keeping unit (SKU) by ISL.

• customer orders for current and future delivery.

---

[1] For the purpose of this explanation, an inventory stocking location (ISL) can be any store, distribution center (DC), regional distribution center (RDC), central DC, manufacturing DC, or warehouse that maintains product for sale. The supply source can be a third-party supplier, a regional distribution point, or a factory. In this book, the term "supply source" is used generically.

- available inventory for sale by SKU by ISL.

- outstanding purchase orders and/or manufacturing orders by product purchased and/or manufactured.

- logistics, manufacturing, and purchasing lead times.

- modes of transport used as well as deployment frequencies.

- safety stock policies by SKU by ISL.

- normal minimum quantity of product to be purchased, manufactured, and distributed.

Second, once all inputs are received, DRP generates a time-phased model of resource requirements to support the logistics strategy. These include:

- which product is needed, how much, and where and when it is needed.

- transportation capacity needed by mode of transport by ISL.

- needed space, manpower, and equipment capacity by ISL.

- required inventory investment by ISL and in total.

- required level of production and/or purchases by product and by supply source.

Third, DRP compares the required resources to what is currently available at supply sources, and what will be available in the future. It then recommends what actions must be taken to expedite or delay purchases and/or production, thereby synchronizing supply and demand. This third phase forces integration and feedback into the system, thus closing the loop among manufacturing, purchasing, logistics, and the customers.

DRP Logic: The Math

At the core of this management process is a very simple, yet very powerful, logic. Its power is not found in math calculations, but in the overall system's ability to time-phase future activities, predict possible outcomes, critique ongoing activities, and recommend action.

Here's how the logic works. Let's assume that you are a retail store manager, and you are asked to predict when you will run out of product. The data given to you states that you will sell a given item at the rate of 200 per week. You have 500 on hand and 600 in transit, due to arrive at your store next week. If asked how long your inventory will last, your response will probably be, "Roughly five and a half weeks." In a nutshell, that's how the math of DRP works. *It attempts to predict future shortages, then recommends action to avoid them.* Figure 3-1 shows the entire DRP management process. All of the components are described in this chapter, as well as in chapters 4 and 5.

DRP IN ACTION

The math behind DRP is very simple. Let's look at an actual example of how DRP is used to plan and replan shipments to an ISL. The sample company manufactures, distributes, and sells pharmaceuticals and supports a network of six retail stores. Specifically, we'll track the planning for vitamin C tablets packaged in bottles of 100. The Los Angeles store has 500 of this product on hand, 200 as a safety stock, and a forecast that varies between 80 and 120 per week (see figure 3-2).

In figure 3-2, the projected on-hand balance is determined by means of the simple computations described earlier. This logic reduces the on-hand balance by the quantities forecast for each week. In the beginning of the first week, for example, 500 are on hand. Forecast sales for the week are 100; they are subtracted from the 500 on hand, leaving a projected balance of 400 at the beginning of the next week. The same mechanism ripples through the schedule. The projected on-hand balance dips below the safety stock of 200 in week 3 (projected on-hand balance of 190), at which point the store will probably run out of stock and go on back order in week 5.

In the example in figure 3-2, no product is in transit. If that were the case, the product in transit would be added to the projected on-hand balance in the week that it is due to arrive. (Some of the later examples will include a quantity in transit.)

The situation shown in figure 3-2 will occur if nothing is shipped from the supply source. The store manager needs more of the product delivered in week 3 to keep the balance from dropping below safety stock, which means that more product must arrive by week 5 to keep the product from going on back order.

The DRP Management Process
Distribution Resource Planning

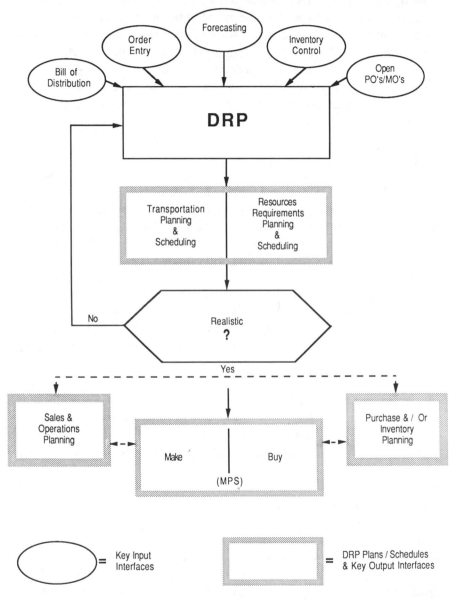

Figure 3-1

Los Angeles Store
Vitamin C Tablet 100/Bottle

On Hand Balance — 500
Safety Stock   — 200

	Past Due	Week							
		1	2	3	4	5	6	7	8
Forecast		100	120	90	110	120	100	80	120
In Transit									
Projected On Hand	500	400	280	190	80	-40			

Figure 3-2

The replenishment lead time for vitamin C at the Los Angeles store is two weeks, and normally 300 bottles, or four full cases, are shipped at a time. Therefore, a shipment of 300 units must arrive in week 3 to prevent the inventory from dropping below the desired safety-stock level. Since the replenishment lead time is two weeks, the shipment should be ordered from the supply source in week 1. Figure 3-3 includes this planned shipment (i.e., future order) from the supply source in the two lines labeled plnd shpmts. One shows the planned shipments on the date they are due to arrive at the store (plnd shpmts -rcpt date). The other

Los Angeles Store
Vitamin C Tablet 100/Bottle

On Hand Balance — 500
Safety Stock   — 200
Lead Time   — 2 wks
Order Quantity   — 300

	Past Due	Week							
		1	2	3	4	5	6	7	8
Forecast		100	120	90	110	120	100	80	120
In Transit									
Projected On Hand	500	400	280	490	380	260	160	80	-40
Plnd.Shpmts.-Rcpt.Date				300					
Plnd.Shpmts.-Ship Date		300							

Figure 3-3

Los Angeles Store
Vitamin C Tablet 100/Bottle

On Hand Balance— 500
Safety Stock   — 200
Lead Time   — 2 wks
Order Quantity   — 300

	Past Due	Week							
		1	2	3	4	5	6	7	8
Forecast		100	120	90	110	120	100	80	120
In Transit									
Projected On Hand	500	400	280	490	380	260	460	380	260
Plnd.Shpmts.-Rcpt.Date				300			300		
Plnd.Shpmts.-Ship Date		300			300				

Figure 3-4

shows the planned shipments on the date they are due to be shipped from the supply source (plnd shpmts -ship date).

The planned shipments provide enough stock to last until week 8, although the store will drop below safety stock in week 6. Therefore, another order must arrive in week 6. This order should be sent from the supply source in week 4. Figure 3-4 shows the complete picture for the vitamin C product at the Los Angeles store.

Now that we have seen how DRP functions in one store, let's expand it to all the stores for the vitamin C product.[2] The following examples (figures 3-5 through 3-10) show DRP displays for the other stores and are similar to the DRP display shown for the Los Angeles store.

In the case of the Montreal store in figure 3-5, an order of 150 is in transit. The order was shipped because the lead time is two weeks; and it is due to arrive in week 2. The in-transit quantity is added to the projected on-hand balance in the week the order is due to arrive. The store manager can now see what material is in route and when it should be expected.

[2] The example includes 6 stores. *There could be only 1 ISL* or as many as 82 if it were R. J. Reynolds, who uses DRP to manage and control cigarette inventories across the United States.

Montreal Store
Vitamin C Tablet 100/Bottle

On Hand Balance — 160
Safety Stock   — 75
Lead Time   — 2 wks
Order Quantity — 150

	Past Due	Week							
		1	2	3	4	5	6	7	8
Forecast		40	50	45	50	40	45	40	50
In Transit			150						
Projected On Hand	160	120	220	175	125	85	190	150	100
Plnd.Shpmts.-Rcpt.Date							150		
Plnd.Shpmts.-Ship Date					150				

Figure 3-5

In the case of the New York store (figure 3-6), a planned order is overdue for shipment. This is the planned shipment for 300, which appears in the past-due time period:

New York Store
Vitamin C Tablet 100/Bottle

On Hand Balance — 300
Safety Stock   — 100
Lead Time   — 2 wks
Order Quantity — 300

	Past Due	Week							
		1	2	3	4	5	6	7	8
Forecast		120	130	115	125	140	110	125	105
In Transit									
Projected On Hand	300	180	350	235	110	270	160	335	230
Plnd.Shpmts.-Rcpt.Date			300			300		300	
Plnd.Shpmts.-Ship Date	300			300		300			

Figure 3-6

There could be several reasons for the past-due order. Perhaps sales were greater than forecasted, so the product was needed in New York earlier than anticipated. Or, the shipment might not have been sent from the supply source on time. In that case, because of the visibility that DRP affords, the manager of the store could determine whether the supply source is shipping on time. Moreover, the manager could determine the problem well before a stock out occurs.

The situations at the Vancouver, Toronto, and Chicago stores, as shown in figures 3-7, 3-8, and 3-9, are similar to the Los Angeles store. Nothing is in transit, but there are several planned shipments from the supply source to the stores. The Chicago store is in the same city as the supply source, so its lead time for product is only one day.

The lead times, order quantities, and safety stocks are different for each store, so each store can be scheduled independently if desired. In addition, the lead times, order quantities, and safety stocks can be different for different products at the same store. (This is not apparent in the following figures because only one of many products is shown. Each product at each store, however, is scheduled independently.) As you can see, DRP gives the people operating the system complete flexibility in scheduling any item at any ISL.

Vancouver Store
Vitamin C Tablet 100/Bottle

On Hand Balance — 140
Safety Stock   — 50
Lead Time   — 3 wks
Order Quantity   — 150

	Past Due	Week							
		1	2	3	4	5	6	7	8
Forecast		20	25	15	20	30	25	15	30
In Transit									
Projected On Hand	140	120	95	80	60	180	155	140	110
Plnd.Shpmts.-Rcpt.Date						150			
Plnd.Shpmts.-Ship Date			150						

Figure 3-7

Toronto Store
Vitamin C Tablet 100/Bottle

On Hand Balance — 120
Safety Stock   — 50
Lead Time   — 1 wk
Order Quantity — 150

	Past Due	Week							
		1	2	3	4	5	6	7	8
Forecast		25	15	20	25	20	20	25	15
In Transit									
Projected On Hand	120	95	80	60	185	165	145	120	105
Plnd.Shpmts.-Rcpt.Date					150				
Plnd.Shpmts.-Ship Date				150					

Figure 3-8

Chicago Store
Vitamin C Tablet 100/Bottle

On Hand Balance — 400
Safety Stock   — 150
Lead Time   — 1 day
Order Quantity — 300

	Past Due	Week							
		1	2	3	4	5	6	7	8
Forecast		105	115	95	90	100	110	95	120
In Transit									
Projected On Hand	400	295	180	385	295	195	385	290	170
Plnd.Shpmts.-Rcpt.Date				300			300		
Plnd.Shpmts.-Ship Date				300			300		

Figure 3-9

In figures 3-8 and 3-9, forecasts for all the stores are nearly the same from week to week. Based on this, you might expect that the demand on the supply source would be smooth as well, with demand in any one week nearly the same as demands in other weeks. Yet, the opposite is true. The demand on the supply source is lumpy. Figure 3-10 illustrates this point very well. For example, in week 2 the demand is only 150, but in week 3 it jumps to 750.

Lumpy demand is one of the reasons why it is so important to have visibility in the logistics system. Because the demand on the supply source can vary so much from one week to another, a planner or buyer needs to be able to see what product is needed and when it must be shipped to meet the needs of the stores in the system. Without DRP, buyers must use averages—hence the inevitability of lumpy demand. With DRP, however, buyers see the true needs of the logistics system. This gives tremendous visibility into the distribution network, and enables buyers to realistically plan for the needs of the stores. The better buyers can see what the stores need in the future, the better they are able to meet those needs and resolve problems before they occur.

Flexibility through DRP

DRP can accommodate the unique constraints of any business environment. The ultimate goal of DRP is to simulate the real world in a way

Summary of Planned Shipments to the Stores

	Past Due	Week							
		1	2	3	4	5	6	7	8
Los Angeles		300			300				
Montreal					150				
New York	300			300		300			
Vancouver			150						
Toronto				150					
Chicago				300			300		
TOTALS	300	300	150	750	450	300	300	0	0

Figure 3-10

that truly mirrors what the company does and what it wants to do in the future.

The ability to represent your own environment is a function of feeding DRP information from a bill-of-distribution module, similar to the one in figure 3-11. Users of this module define their future distribution network by indicating how many inventory stocking locations they want to manage, who the supply sources are, which products will be stocked in the various locations, what modes of transport will be used, the shipping frequency, the size of shipment, etc.

In some companies, the distribution network consists of only one location (in which case it really isn't a network). In others, it contains three levels, as shown in figure 3-12. Regardless of the size or complexity of the network, DRP must have accurate and current information from the bill of distribution.

By including a bill of distribution in your DRP system, you actually induce a customer/supplier linkage. In other words, any change in any store will be passed on to its source of supply and become visible.

Managing Change

A key benefit of the visibility that DRP affords is the ability to react to change. As previously stated and stressed throughout this book, the nature of the industrial pipeline is constant change. The most apparent change in the pipeline occurs when sales differ from the forecast. Such events do not cause problems for DRP because the system not only plans each of the items in each of the stores and DCs, it also replans them continuously. In a DRP system, each item in each store or DC is

A Typical Bill-of-Distribution Module

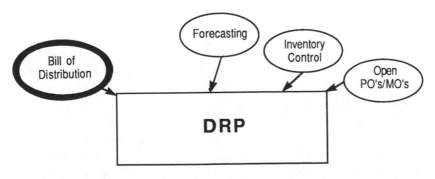

Figure 3-11

A Multitiered Distribution Network

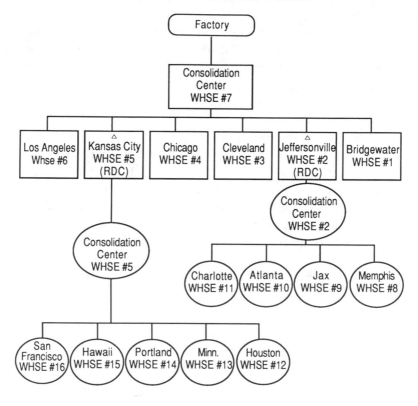

△=Factories playing dual roles-also RDC's.

Figure 3-12

replanned at least once a week. In some companies, replanning takes place on a daily basis so that people can respond quickly to change and handle large volumes of product to specific distribution points. (Companies such as Coca-Cola and R. J. Reynolds, which both use DRP, have no choice but to replan daily, given the enormous volume of product shipped from their factories to multiple distribution points every day. These are exceptions, though, and weekly replanning generally is sufficient in most situations.)

To illustrate the role of DRP in managing change, let's revisit the Los Angeles store, originally shown in figure 3-2. The first display in figure 3-13 shows a forecast of 100 in week 1. Let's assume that instead of selling the 100 that were forecast in week 1, 170 are actually sold. The following week the DRP display for this product at Los Angeles would change:

DRP Before and After Changes in Demand

Los Angeles Store
Vitamin C Tablet 100/Bottle

BEFORE CHANGE IN DEMAND
On Hand Balance –500
Safety Stock   –200
Lead Time   –2 wks
Order Quantity   –300

	Past Due	Week							
		1	2	3	4	5	6	7	8
Forecast		100	120	90	110	120	100	80	120
In Transit									
Projected On Hand	500	400	280	490	380	260	460	380	260
Plnd.Shpmts.-Rcpt.Date				300			300		
Plnd.Shpmts.-Ship Date		300			300				

AFTER CHANGE IN DEMAND
On Hand Balance –330
Safety Stock   –200
Lead Time   –2 wks
Order Quantity   –300

	Past Due	Week						
		2	3	4	5	6	7	8
Forecast		120	90	110	120	100	80	120
In Transit			300					
Projected On Hand	330	210	420	310	490	390	310	490
Plnd.Shpmts.-Rcpt.Date					300			300
Plnd.Shpmts.-Ship Date			300			300		

Figure 3-13

Because the sales are greater than the forecast, the planned shipments move up to earlier dates. The planned shipment of 300 due to arrive in week 6 is now needed in week 5, which is normal. In addition, a new planned shipment of 300 that did not exist in the previous week has been created for use in week 8.

In this case, the sales are so much greater than the forecast that the planned shipment dates are changed. This does not happen all the time—there must be a significant difference between what was sold and what was forecast, or the projected on-hand balance must be only slightly greater than the safety-stock level.

In figure 3-13, the Los Angeles store now has 300 units in transit (refer to figure 3-4 for original data). This 300 represents a planned shipment from the previous week. The order was shipped to Los Angeles, and now appears in transit under the week it is due to arrive.

As a result of the changes at the Los Angeles store, the total demands on the supply source have changed. Figure 3-14 shows the total demands from the previous week and the total demands for the current week:

**Summary of Planned Shipments
to the Stores**

BEFORE ABOVE-FORECAST SALES

	Past Due	Week							
		1	2	3	4	5	6	7	8
Los Angeles		300			300				
Montreal					150				
New York	300			300		300			
Vancouver			150						
Toronto				150					
Chicago				300			300		
TOTALS	300	300	150	750	450	300	300	0	0

Figure 3-14

AFTER ABOVE-FORECAST SALES

	Past Due	Week						
		2	3	4	5	6	7	8
Los Angeles			300			300		
Montreal				150				
New York			300		300			
Vancouver		150						
Toronto			150					
Chicago			300			300		
TOTALS	0	150	1050	150	300	600	0	0

Figure 3-14 (continued)

The change in the total demands on the supply source went from 750 in week 3 to 1,050; from 450 in week 4 to 150; and from 300 in week 6 up to 600. With this information, the inventory planner can determine the exact effect of the above-forecast sales in Los Angeles and other stores. The planner is also able to see the new demands on the supply source and can begin preparations to supply these needs. Conventional inventory management systems do not have this ability to look ahead accurately and revise the plan based on the changes that have occurred. The forward visibility offered by DRP allows buyers, master schedulers, and planners *to anticipate* what may change in the future rather than *reacting to* something that has already happened.

In the example above, the change to a planned shipment date occurred at one store (Los Angeles). In actual practice, it is likely that changes to planned shipments occurred during the week at several stores. It is even possible that a change to the planned shipments occurred at all the stores, although such a simultaneous set of changes is unlikely.

Sales that are greater or less than the forecast are not the only reasons that planned shipments change. Changes to the forecast quantities, safety stocks, lead times, and order quantities can cause the planned shipments to change. In other words, DRP picks up and reports any changes in the entire system. DRP can do this because it is a true simulation of a distribution network; it shows what is happening in the logistics system and what is predicted to occur.

To demonstrate the generic applicability of DRP to retailers, wholesaler/distributors, and manufacturers, in chapter 4 we use the data from the six stores to show how inventory planning, purchase planning, and purchase scheduling are carried out for retailers and wholesaler/distributors. In chapter 5, the same DRP data are used to show how a manufacturer can perform sales and operations planning, as well as master scheduling. Only the type of product changes.

DRP Versus the Reorder Point

In chapter 2, we referred to the use of reorder points and the problems they cause. Now we'll demonstrate the difference between DRP and a reorder-point system. To make the comparison, we'll use the same data from the example in figure 2-5 (reproduced below as figure 3-15).

Generic Reorder-point Model			
	Chicago	**Montreal**	**New York**
Inventory on hand	225	164	350
Forecast	115/wk	47/wk	125/wk
Reorder point	345	141	375
POQ	500	200	500
Supplier lead time	2 wks	2 wks	2 wks
		Supply Source (DC)	
Inventory on hand		1170	
Reorder point		1150	
Order quantity		2200	
Supplier lead time (factory)		3 wks	

Figure 3-15

The first reorder-point example, (figure 2-5) depicts a situation in which both Chicago and New York are below their reorder points; both order from the supply source. The two DCs are shown in figure 3-16.

With DRP, we have planned shipments to these two DCs that are

Chicago Distribution Center
Vitamin C Tablet 100/Bottle

On Hand Balance — 225
Safety Stock — 115
Lead Time — 2 wks
Order Quantity — 500

	Past Due	Week							
		1	2	3	4	5	6	7	8
Forecast		115	115	115	115	115	115	115	115
In Transit									
Projected On Hand	225	110	495	380	265	150	535	420	305
Plnd.Shpmts.-Rcpt.Date			500					500	
Plnd.Shpmts.-Ship Date	500				500				

New York Distribution Center
Vitamin C Tablet 100/Bottle

On Hand Balance — 350
Safety Stock — 125
Lead Time — 2 wks
Order Quantity — 500

	Past Due	Week							
		1	2	3	4	5	6	7	8
Forecast		125	125	125	125	125	125	125	125
In Transit									
Projected On Hand	350	225	600	475	350	225	600	475	350
Plnd.Shpmts.-Rcpt.Date			500					500	
Plnd.Shpmts.-Ship Date	500				500				

Figure 3-16

Montreal Distribution Center
Vitamin C Tablet 100/Bottle

On Hand Balance — 164
Safety Stock   — 47
Lead Time   — 2 wks
Order Quantity   — 200

	Past Due	Week							
		1	2	3	4	5	6	7	8
Forecast		47	47	47	47	47	47	47	47
In Transit									
Projected On Hand	164	117	70	223	176	129	82	235	188
Plnd.Shpmts.-Rcpt.Date				200					
Plnd.Shpmts.-Ship Date		200				200			

Figure 3-17

overdue. In other words, the reorder point never showed the problem. Also the safety stock in the DRP display is the forecast quantity for one week. This is the same as the quantity used in the reorder-point example.

Now, let's look at a DRP display for the Montreal DC, which shows that a planned order is due for release during the current week (see figure 3-17). We'll also look at the DRP display at the supply source (see figure 3-18). The inventory planner at the supply source is getting urgent messages from the DRP display to expedite an order from the factory to cover a shortage of 30 in week 1.

The reorder-point system does not indicate any trouble until the end of week 1 when the supply source received an order for 200 from the Montreal DC and only 170 were on hand. In contrast, DRP would have given us warnings many weeks before. DRP would have predicted the shortage at the supply source and warned the inventory planner and the factory of the problem. To illustrate this, let's go back in time by four weeks. Figure 3-19 shows the sales history by DC for the past four weeks. The actual sales were added back to the inventory to give a new on-hand balance, shown in figure 3-20. The sales forecasts are not changed, although we know better. This gives DRP a true test.

DRP Display
Vitamin C Tablet 100/Bottle
Supply Source

On Hand Balance — 1170
Safety Stock — 287
Factory Lead Time — 3 wks
Order Quantity — 2200

	Past Due	Week								
		1	2	3	4	5	6	7	8
Forecast	1000	200	0	0	1000	200	0	0	0
In Transit									
Projected On Hand	170	-30	-30	2170	1170	970	970	970	970
Plnd. Shpmts.-Rcpt.Date				2200					
Plnd. Shpmts.-Ship Date	2200								

Figure 3-18

Sales History

Weekly Forecast	Dist. Center	Week				Total	Current On Hand	New On Hand
		4	3	2	1			
115	Chicago	60	155	100	45	360	225	585
47	New York	50	33	40	45	168	164	332
125	Montreal	100	120	110	90	420	350	770

Figure 3-19

As you can see in figure 3-20, even four weeks earlier, DRP was planning for the distribution demands. In the example, DRP planned an order due for release to the factory in the current week, so that there will be enough to cover the distribution demands four weeks later. This order is visible at the factory as demand from the DC and is being ordered within the normal three-week factory lead time. Here, DRP is monitor-

New DRP Summary for Three DCs and Supply Source

Chicago Distribution Center
Vitamin C Tablet 100/Bottle

On Hand Balance −585
Safety Stock −115
Lead Time −2 wks
Order Quantity −500

	Past Due	1	2	3	4	5	6	7	8
Forecast		115	115	115	115	115	115	115	115
In Transit									
Projected On Hand	585	470	355	240	125	510	395	280	165
Plnd.Shpmts.-Rcpt.Date						500			
Plnd.Shpmts.-Ship Date				500					

New York Distribution Center
Vitamin C Tablet 100/Bottle

On Hand Balance −770
Safety Stock −125
Lead Time −2 wks
Order Quantity −500

	Past Due	1	2	3	4	5	6	7	8
Forecast		125	125	125	125	125	125	125	125
In Transit									
Projected On Hand	770	645	520	395	270	145	520	395	270
Plnd.Shpmts.-Rcpt.Date							500		
Plnd.Shpmts.-Ship Date					500				

Montreal Distribution Center
Vitamin C Tablet 100/Bottle

On Hand Balance −332
Safety Stock −47
Lead Time −2 wks
Order Quantity −200

	Past Due	1	2	3	4	5	6	7	8
Forecast		47	47	47	47	47	47	47	47
In Transit									
Projected On Hand	332	285	238	191	144	97	50	203	156
Plnd.Shpmts.-Rcpt.Date								200	
Plnd.Shpmts.-Ship Date						200			

Supply Source
Vitamin C Tablet 100/Bottle

On Hand Balance −1170
Safety Stock −287
Factory Lead Time −3 wks
Order Quantity −2200

	Past Due	1	2	3	4	5	6	7	8
Forecast		0	0	500	500	200	0	0	0
In Transit									
Projected On Hand	1170	1170	1170	670	2370	2170	2170	2170	2170
Plnd.Shpmts.-Rcpt.Date					2200				
Plnd.Shpmts.-Ship Date		2200							

Figure 3-20

Comparison of Reorder-point and DRP Systems		
Location	**Reorder Point**	**DRP**
Chicago	Below reorder point, order from supply source.	Planned order overdue for release from supply source.
New York	Below reorder point, order from central.	Planned order overdue for release from supply source.
Montreal	Beginning of week: above reorder point, no action needed. End of week: below reorder point, order from supply source.	Planned order overdue for release from supply source this week.
Supply source	Monday a.m.: above reorder point, no problem apparent. Monday p.m.: New York and Chicago order. Friday a.m.: New York and Chicago orders shipped. Supply source orders from factory. Friday p.m.: Montreal orders, not enough stock to cover at source. Expedite the factory. Montreal will be short for 3 weeks.	Four weeks earlier: predicts a shortage of 30 five weeks into the future and below safety stock four weeks out. Source places an order on the factory to cover need. Factory order due for release in normal lead time. Planned shipments are made, no back orders.

Figure 3-21A

ing and planning four weeks into the future. The reorder point did not anticipate the problem and when it did note it, there was no time to fix it.

Figure 3-21a summarizes and compares the information from the reorder-point system with the information from DRP for the previous example.

Though this example depicts the situation four weeks ago, the effects would have also been similar three weeks ago, two weeks ago, and one week ago. Figure 3-21b shows the math for each of the four weeks. It demonstrates that except for Chicago in week 1, the reorder-point approach decremented by the actual sales, as shown in figure 3-19, did not generate an order for any location at any time during the past four weeks.

Mathematical Explanation of Reorder-point Example
(Week by Week)

4 Weeks Ago

Chicago
OP – → 345
OH – → 585
(OH + 00) > OP   No order

Montreal
OP – → 141
OH – → 332
(OH + 00) > OP   No order

New York
OP – → 375
OH – → 770
(OH + 00) > OP   No order

3 Weeks Ago

Chicago
OP – → 345
OH – → 525
                 No order

Montreal
OP – → 141
OH – → 282
                 No order

New York
OP – → 375
OH – → 670
                 No order

2 Weeks Ago

Chicago
OP – → 345
OH – → 370
                 No order

Montreal
OP – → 141
OH – → 249
                 No order

New York
OP – → 375
OH – → 550
                 No order

1 Week Ago

Chicago
OP – → 345
OH – → 270
                 Order something, but still too late.

Montreal
OP – → 141
OH – → 209
                 No order

New York
OP – → 375
OH – → 440
                 No order

Figure 3-21B

If the factory is able to economically produce in quantities less than 2,200, the supply source might have requested a smaller quantity, since DRP shows that only 30 units are required in week 5 to cover all the orders. In other words, DRP is predicting a shortage of 30 five weeks out. The reorder point reacted to this same shortage by instructing the user to secure more product.

Now, let's look at the second reorder-point example from chapter 2 (reproduced below as figure 3-22a) using reorder points. In this situation, the reorder point at the supply source tripped because of an order from Chicago (1,600 minus 500 equals 1,100). The other two DCs had sufficient inventory, but the reorder-point system predicted that more product would be needed at the supply source immediately and an order for 2,200 was placed on the factory. This order was incorrect because it was placed much too soon.

Using DRP, the situation at the supply source would appear as shown in figure 3-22b.

Look at the difference between the two systems. DRP shows that for at least the next four weeks no additional product is needed. The current on-hand balance can satisfy the demand through the end of week 4 and most of week 5. In fact, many inventory planners and master schedulers, looking at the display shown in figure 3-22b, realize that the supply-

Generic Reorder-point Model with Revised On Hand			
	Chicago	**Montreal**	**New York**
Inventory on hand	225	330	880
Forecast	115/wk	47/wk	125/wk
Reorder point	345	141	375
POQ	500	200	500
Supplier lead time	2 wks	2 wks	2 wks
		Supply Source (DC)	
Inventory on hand		1600	
Reorder point		1150	
Order quantity		2200	
Supplier lead time (factory)		3 wks	

Figure 3-22A

Revised DRP Summary for Three DCs and Supply Source

Chicago Distribution Center
Vitamin C Tablet 100/Bottle

On Hand Balance -225
Safety Stock -115
Lead Time -2 wks
Order Quantity -500

	Past Due	Week 1	2	3	4	5	6	7	8
Forecast		115	115	115	115	115	115	115	115
In Transit									
Projected On Hand	225	110	495	380	265	150	535	420	305
Plnd.Shpmts.-Rcpt.Date			500				500		
Plnd.Shpmts.-Ship Date	500				500				

New York Distribution Center
Vitamin C Tablet 100/Bottle

On Hand Balance -880
Safety Stock -125
Lead Time -2 wks
Order Quantity -500

	Past Due	Week 1	2	3	4	5	6	7	8
Forecast		125	125	125	125	125	125	125	125
In Transit									
Projected On Hand	880	755	630	505	380	255	130	505	380
Plnd.Shpmts.-Rcpt.Date								500	
Plnd.Shpmts.-Ship Date						500			

Montreal Distribution Center
Vitamin C Tablet 100/Bottle

On Hand Balance -330
Safety Stock -47
Lead Time -2 wks
Order Quantity -200

	Past Due	Week 1	2	3	4	5	6	7	8
Forecast		47	47	47	47	47	47	47	47
In Transit									
Projected On Hand	330	283	236	189	142	95	48	201	154
Plnd.Shpmts.-Rcpt.Date								200	
Plnd.Shpmts.-Ship Date						200			

Supply Source
Vitamin C Tablet 100/Bottle

On Hand Balance -1600
Safety Stock -287
Lead Time -3 wks
Order Quantity -2200

	Past Due	Week 1	2	3	4	5	6	7	8
Forecast	500	0	0	0	500	700	0	0	0
In Transit									
Projected On Hand		1100	1100	1100	600	2100	2100	2100	2100
Plnd.Shpmts.-Rcpt.Date						2200			
Plnd.Shpmts.-Ship Date			2200						

Figure 3-22B

Supply Source
Vitamin C Tablet 100/Bottle

On Hand Balance — 1600
Safety Stock   — 287
Lead Time   — 3 wks
Order Quantity   — 2200

	Past	Week							
	Due	1	2	3	4	5	6	7	8
Forecast	500	0	0	0	500	600	0	0	0
In Transit									
Projected On Hand	1100	1100	1100	1100	600	0	0	0	0
Plnd.Shpmts.-Rcpt.Date									
Plnd.Shpmts.-Ship Date									

Figure 3-23

source order for 2,200 due in week 5 is just to satisfy a true need of 100, plus safety stock of 287. But with the visibility offered by DRP, does the inventory planner really need to release this order on the factory?

Since the master scheduler can see the real demands from the supply source, he does not typically schedule a lot of 2,200—most of it would be warehoused for several weeks. In such a case, the master scheduler evaluates the distribution demand in week 5 and, working with the inventory planner, decides to ship New York 400, rather than 500. The supply source display for this item, therefore, looks like the one shown in figure 3-23, so no order is placed on the factory at this time. To accomplish this, a firm planned order is created for release to the factory at a future week where demand would exist. (See chapter 6 for a detailed discussion of the use of the firmed planned order.) For example, if demands from any of the three DCs (Chicago, Montreal, or New York) exist in week 11, the inventory planner creates a firm planned order for release in week 8.

The forced linkage between logistics and manufacturing caused by DRP establishes the supply/demand integration between a customer and supplier. This, in turn, creates a win/win situation. DRP predicts future problems and gives people the information to solve them immediately. This often results in eliminating the problem before it occurs.

The reorder point, on the other hand, always orders material when-ever the on-hand balance is below the reorder point, regardless of whether more is actually needed. In this case, there is enough on hand to satisfy the demands. But the reorder-point system doesn't look at what is needed. Instead, it blindly attempts to keep a certain amount of inven-tory on hand at all times.

Let's compare the reorder point and DRP for the examples in figures 3-21 through 3-23. Figure 3-24 gives the results.

These examples serve to show that reorder points are an obsolete technique—an invalid inventory model—and should not be used in any situation where inventories are maintained. They simply do not provide the visibility to see when product is actually needed and when problems are likely to occur.

Operating in the Real World

Thus far, comparisons between the classic reorder-point approaches and DRP have assumed that supply sources are also using reorder-point systems. In reality, that is not always the case. During the past ten years, companies have used a variety of significantly different approaches when they plan at supply sources. The most frequently encountered approaches are represented in the following four scenarios.

Comparison of Reorder-point System and DRP		
Location	**Order Point**	**DRP**
Chicago	Below reorder point, order from supply source.	Planned order overdue for release from supply source.
New York	Above reorder point, no action needed.	Planned order due for release in week 5.
Montreal	Above reorder point, no action needed.	Planned order due for release in week 5.
Supply source	Beginning of week: above reorder point, no problem apparent. End of week: below reorder point, order 2,200 from the factory, due in week 3.	Enough inventory to last until week 5. Master scheduler may decide to release an order next week or may ship 400 to New York and not release an order to the factory.

Figure 3-24

Some companies plan monthly; others plan weekly. Some sources purchase product; others manufacture it. Some companies plan nationally and total all inventories at all locations; others do not. The impact of these different approaches will be evident as you read these scenarios. The first two involve nonmanufacturers; the last two examine companies with a manufacturing base. Although the data are the same across all scenarios, the companies use very different approaches to interpret them.

Scenario 1

This first scenario describes a company that purchases its products. In this example, the sum of all inventories in all locations, the supply source and all distribution centers, has been totaled to give a starting inventory of 1,909. (See figure 3-25.)[3] The sales forecast of 1,244 per month was calculated by taking the individual sales forecasts by week by DC, multiplying them by 52, and then totaling all the forecasts to arrive at a national forecast. This sum was then divided by 12 to arrive at a monthly forecast.

The objective is to have as a minimum at all times two weeks of inventory available nationally for the DCs:

Supply Source That Purchases Product

WHERE:
1. Source and DC's inventory is totaled
2. Plan monthly
3. Use Own sales forecast

O/H: 1909
O/Q: 2200
L/T: 3wks
S/S: 287 (1week)

Purchase Schedule Display

	Past Due	_Month_ 1	2	3	4	5	6	7	8
Sales Forecast		1244	1244	1244					
Planned Purchases			2200						
Proj. Avail. Bal.	1909	665	1621	377					

Figure 3-25

[3] The displays in figures 3-25 and 3-26 are a simplified version showing the sales forecast, future purchases (planned) and projected on hand (proj avail bal). This will be further explained in chapter 4.

A company using this approach has 2,200 as planned purchases during the second month. We can conclude from this example that companies using this approach are confronted with a major problem. Recall that the reorder-point example used in figure 3-15 indicated when Chicago and New York ordered against supply sources, 170 units were left to satisfy the next order of 200 coming from Montreal, thus creating a shortage of 30 by the end of the week. That created a severe problem. In this case, the supply source is only planning to purchase product during the second month, so the problem is amplified.

Scenario 2

Figure 3-26 displays another approach that several companies use. In this example, only inventory available at the source is used. Companies using this approach recommend the purchase of a quantity of 2,200 during their first month and again during the third month. This still does not solve the problem. This approach is frequently encountered when inventories in the DCs are the responsibility of people other than those at supply sources. For example, the store managers may be responsible for inventory in their stores while logistics or purchasing are responsible for inventories in the DCs.

Scenario 3

This case involves companies that use MRP II in manufacturing. The sales forecast is shown in weeks, and the starting inventory is the total

Supply Source That Purchases Product

WHERE:
1. Source inventory only is used
2. Plan monthly
3. Use own sales forecast

O/H: 1170
O/Q: 2200
L/T: 3wks
S/S: 287 (1week)

Purchase Schedule Display

	Past Due	_____ Month _____							
		1	2	3	4	5	6	7	8
Sales Forecast		1244	1244	1244					
Planned Purchases		2200		2200					
Proj. Avail. Bal.	1170	2126	882	1838					

Figure 3-26

Supply Source That Manufactures Product

WHERE:
1. Manufacturing and Logistics inventory is totaled
2. Plan weekly
3. Use own sales forecast
4. Use MRP II

O/H: 1909
O/Q: 2200
L/T: 3wks
S/S: 287 (1week)

MPS Display

	Past Due	Week							
		1	2	3	4	5	6	7	8
Sales Forecast		287	287	287	287	287	287	287	287
Sched. Receipts									
Proj. Avail. Bal.	1909	1622	1335	1048	761	474	2387	2100	1813
MPS-Receipt							2200		
MPS-Start				2200					

Figure 3-27

inventory available in the system, as in the first scenario. The Master Production Schedule (MPS) logic recommends that a manufacturing order be released in the third week to be available for shipping to the DCs in the sixth week, at which point the projected on-hand balance is to be below safety stock (see figure 3-27).[4]

Because these companies aren't using DRP, they still would not be in the position to accurately predict the timing of the release of the order in manufacturing to avoid a stock out.

Scenario 4

In this situation, companies are using MRP in manufacturing but only the plant inventory is being netted at the MPS level. Figure 3-28 indicates that the timing is improving. The material planning logic recommends that an order be released during the first week. Although this is closer to reality and the company is using MRP II in manufacturing, it is planning in weeks and is using only the plant inventory. The logic still recommends that a manufacturing order be released during the

---

[4] The displays in figures 3-27 and 3-28 are a simplified version showing sales forecasts, open manufacturing orders (sched recp), projected on hand (proj avail bal), MPS receipt, and start (MPS receipt and start). Chapter 5 expands on these examples.

Supply Source That Manufactures Product

WHERE:
1. Manufacturing inventory only is used
2. Plan weekly
3. Use own sales forecast
4. Use MRP II

O/H: 1170
O/Q: 2200
L/T: 3wks
S/S: 287 (1week)

MPS Display

	Past Due	Week							
		1	2	3	4	5	6	7	8
Sales Forecast		287	287	287	287	287	287	287	287
Sched. Receipts									
Proj. Avail. Bal.	1170	883	596	309	2222	1935	1648	1361	1074
MPS-Receipt					2200				
MPS-Start		2200							

Figure 3-28

first week, which means that inventory will not be available to ship for three weeks.

The preceding scenarios yield four different answers to the problem. In the first instance, the approach recommends that the company purchase products sometime during the second month. In the second instance, the approach recommends that purchases be made sometime during the first and third months. In the third example, manufacture is scheduled sometime during the third week. And, in the last scenario, the system indicates that the company should manufacture sometime during the first week.

In none of the cases are the companies in a position in which the planning approach can predict accurately when the company should begin to purchase or manufacture in order to provide sufficient inventory to handle the needs of the DCs.

You might ask why, even though companies are using MRP II in manufacturing, are planning by week, and are using the plant inventories, are they unable to predict when they truly need to create product. The point is very simple: If you refer back to the results of the DRP example, you will note that the basic difference is the forecast. DRP provides a simulation of requirements over the planning horizon that truly depicts the distribution demands as they will happen, as opposed to using a national sales forecast that may be in months or in weeks. That is the subtle difference between the two. In fact, the sum of the planned orders coming from the DCs and generated by DRP become the forecast that should be used in purchase planning and master scheduling. That is the key to the solution for this problem. Supply sources suddenly have visibility into distribution centers because the forecast is an accurate picture of what the DCs really need. If you are a retailer, wholesaler, or distributor, the DCs, the stores, etc. are integrated with the external sources of supply. If you are a manufacturer, logistics and manufacturing are totally integrated via the MPS.

It is important to recognize that even though companies may have an MRP II system operating in manufacturing, unless they integrate their MRP II system with DRP to plan and schedule inventories in the distribution network, they will not achieve the results anticipated with MRP II. They will have great difficulties in developing a proper MPS that truly represents what needs to be manufactured to support logistics operations, and will constantly be confronted with timing problems of this nature.

Companies that only have MRP II in manufacturing must invest in significant amounts of safety stock at the supply source to cut down on surprises of this nature and achieve some stability in master production scheduling. With DRP, there is no need to invest in more inventory. If you are a nonmanufacturer, the same situation regarding safety stock will prevail. You will be more able to synchronize demand from the field with supply at the source, using far less inventory.

DRP DISPLAY

For the remainder of this chapter and for the balance of the book, the format of the DRP display changes from the examples presented earlier. The display is standardized—it is exactly the same for items in a store or a distribution center, for manufactured items, or for purchased items. This is also the format used for purchased items.

There are a number of reasons for adopting a standardized format for retail/wholesale manufacturing and logistics. One is that the logic of the system works in exactly the same way. Therefore, there is no need to use different displays. Another reason is that it makes the system easier to understand; people in retail/wholesale manufacturing and logistics using the same display can communicate more effectively and reach a higher level of understanding.

Figure 3-29 shows an example of the DRP display using the previous format; figure 3-30 shows the same items using the standardized display.

Four aspects of the standardized display in figure 3-30 differ from the DRP display in figure 3-29:

1. The term Gross Requirements is used instead of Forecast. Gross requirements are the demands for an item. If the item is a product in a store or a distribution center, the gross requirements are the forecast. If the item is manufactured or purchased, the gross requirements are what is needed to be satisfied by manufacturing or outside suppliers.

2. The term Scheduled Receipts replaces In Transit. Scheduled receipts are quantities scheduled to come into stock. If these items are products in a store or a distribution center, the scheduled receipts are in transit from the supply source. Although they may not actually be on the road, the scheduled orders could be in the process of being picked or packed and still be a scheduled receipt. If these are manufactured or purchased items, the scheduled receipts are either manufacturing orders that have been released to the factory or purchase orders that have been released to suppliers.

3. The term Planned Orders is used instead of Plnd Shpmts-Ship Date. As the name suggests, planned orders are still in the planning stage and are unreleased, unlike scheduled receipts, which have either been shipped or are in process. If the item is a product in a store or a distribution center, the planned orders are the schedule for future shipments from the supply sources. If the item is a manufactured or purchased item, the planned orders are the schedule of what will be manufactured or purchased in the future. Planned orders are typically displayed by order start date. In the case of a distribution item, this is the date of shipment from the supply source. For manufactured and purchased items, this is the date the order is released to the shop floor or the date the order is placed with the supplier.

4. The Plnd Shpmts-Rcpt Date item is eliminated from the report. It is only necessary to see the planned orders at the start date. They are still added to the projected on-hand balance, just as they would be if the planned order receipt line were on the display.

DRP Display
Vancouver Distribution Center
Vitamin C Tablet 100/Bottle

On Hand Balance— 140
Safety Stock   — 50
Lead Time   — 3 wks
Order Quantity — 150

	Past Due	Week							
		1	2	3	4	5	6	7	8
Forecast		20	25	15	20	30	25	15	30
In Transit									
Projected On Hand	140	120	95	80	60	180	155	140	110
Plnd.Shpmts.-Rcpt.Date						150			
Plnd.Shpmts.-Ship Date			150						

Figure 3-29

Standardized Display
Vancouver Distribution Center
Vitamin C Tablet 100/Bottle

On Hand Balance— 140
Safety Stock   — 50
Lead Time   — 3 wks
Order Quantity — 150

	Past Due	Week							
		1	2	3	4	5	6	7	8
Gross Requirements		20	25	15	20	30	25	15	30
Scheduled Receipts									
Projected On Hand	140	120	95	80	60	180	155	140	110
Planned Orders			150						

Figure 3-30

CONCLUSION

In this chapter, we introduced and explained the ABCs of DRP in significant detail, and showed that whether you have one inventory stocking location or a very complex multitier network, DRP will plan and schedule equally well. We also showed you how DRP deals with changes in demand and how it helps you manage change.

We compared DRP to the reorder-point system and demonstrated the significant difference between the two and advantages of DRP. Then, we looked at four frequently used approaches to planning at supply sources in manufacturing, as well as nonmanufacturing, environments.

In the next chapter, we expand the use of DRP by showing application and actual use in nonmanufacturing environments. And, in chapter 5, we show you how DRP applies in a manufacturing company that supports its customers through its own distribution network.

Chapter 4

DRP in Nonmanufacturing Environments

Retailers, Wholesalers, and Distributors

Although the first users of DRP were logistics people in manufacturing companies, significant advances have been made since 1983, when wholesalers began using DRP. This chapter describes this evolution and explains how the DRP management process is used by retailers, wholesalers, and distributors.

Using DRP in Inventory/Purchase Planning in Retail/Wholesale

If you are a retailer or a wholesaler/distributor, you should plan at the least at two distinct levels of detail—the national level and the saleable stockkeeping unit (SKU) level. DRP plans at the SKU level, and then generates information for use in planning at the national level.

Companies generally plan inventories and purchases by product groupings. For example, a purchase plan[1] or purchase schedule might be stated as 10,000 color television sets per month. An inventory plan

---

[1] People use the term "purchase plan" to indicate what is to be purchased by product. Recently, some people using DRP have started to use the term "purchase schedule" instead of "purchase plan."

The same holds true for "inventory plan" and "open to buy plan"—both are used interchangeably.

might contain an investment target of $10 million for large categories of products such as furniture, home appliances, home electronics, house and garden supplies, etc. Normally, a purchase schedule is product specific, such as 16-inch color TVs; an inventory plan is broader, such as "home electronics," and typically will include several purchase schedules for specific items.

The buyer's responsibility is to manage the purchase schedules and ensure that the sum of the purchase schedules does not exceed the overall inventory plan. Often, people use the term "open to buy" as an indicator of a constraint within which a buyer must adhere to the overall inventory plan. For example, the inventory plan for home electronics products might be $10 million. The open-to-buy amount is the actual value of products on hand plus products on order, minus the products in the inventory plan. If the value of inventory on hand is $6 million and the value of products on order is $3 million, the open to buy becomes $1 million. Thus, open to buy is another version of the inventory plan, because it sets a definite ceiling on how much inventory is to be carried.

In our example, the buyer is authorized to buy up to $1 million worth of product. The buyer must spread this $1 million over every television set, black-and-white and color, size, brand, etc., every type of VCR, every type of cassette and disk player, stereo, etc. There could be dozens, or possibly hundreds, of different products in the home electronics category. In other words, the buyer must manage the mix to keep products in stock, and stay within the open-to-buy amount.

The management of mix represents one of the toughest challenges a buyer at the retail/wholesale level faces. Imagine a buyer for Wal-mart who must keep in stock a product line of 100 different products stocked in 13 DCs and sold in more than 2,300 stores. Clearly, the buyer in such a situation is dependent on the availability of good planning systems, as well as accurate and timely information.

DRP is the vehicle for generating the necessary information, and, as such, it is a vehicle for improving inventory planning and purchase planning. To demonstrate this, let's take an example for home electronics products and see how purchase schedules can be developed and tied to the inventory plan. For this example, we'll look at a 16-inch color TV sold through six stores that are supported by a distribution center (the internal supply source in this example.) Figure 4-1 shows a purchase schedule display for this item.

The distribution demands shown in figure 4-1 are the totals from the

**Internal Supply Source
16-inch Color TV Brand X
Purchase Schedule**

On Hand Balance — 1700
Safety Stock   — 0
Lead Time   — 3 wks
Order Quantity   — 1100

	Past Due	Week							
		1	2	3	4	5	6	7	8
Distribution Demands	300	300	150	750	450	300	300	0	0
Scheduled Receipts									
Projected On Hand	1400	1100	950	200	850	550	250	250	250
Purchase Schedule Receipt					1100				
Purchase Schedule Start		1100							

Figure 4-1

six-store network used in chapter 3 to explain the DRP logic. Figure 3.10 shows the sum of the requirements for this product from all the different stores.[2] This is the same set of numbers that appears in the distribution demands line because they are the demands that need to be satisfied to supply this product to the stores.

The scheduled receipts line shows any released purchase orders for this item at the date they are due into stock. The projected on hand line is the same type of calculation as shown in the DRP display. The on-hand balance is reduced by the distribution demands, and scheduled receipts and purchase schedule orders are added into the calculation. This calculation shows either a projected inventory buildup or a stock out (i.e., projected on-hand balance of less than zero).

The purchase schedule-start line in figure 4-1 shows the purchase schedule at the start date. The purchase schedule receipt line shows the

[2] In retail companies that have hundreds of stores and thousands of items, a subset of DRP logic is typically used to avoid numerous netting calculations. Normally, no forecasting is done at the store level, and a replenish-up to logic using safety stock is used instead.

date the order should be received from the supplier if released at the start date indicated. The DRP purchase schedule recommends when purchase orders should be released to suppliers. Buyers review these recommendations and then authorize their releases. When this is done, a purchase-schedule recommendation becomes a purchase order.

The Inventory/Open-to-Buy Plan

The inventory or open-to-buy plan acts as a constraint on the buyer. This means that purchase schedules, when totaled for a group of items, must equal the open-to-buy plan for that group. For example, let's assume that the sum of purchase schedules for the color-TV product group is as shown in figure 4-2.

With DRP, people can show an open-to-buy plan by month if they compare projected inventories from DRP to the monthly inventory plan. The difference is the amount in the open-to-buy plan. For example, let's say that the inventory plan for home electronics is $10 million for the end of January and $9.5 million for the end of February. Actual DRP projected inventory for all products in home electronics is $8.5 million for January and $9 million for February. The open to buy for January is thus $1.5 million and for February is $0.5 million; it becomes the constraint within which buyers must operate. DRP makes this time phasing of open to buy possible because it already knows how much inventory is on hand and on order. Moreover, DRP projects what and when product should be purchased and what the resulting inventory will be. In other words, all key information is available.

Summary of Purchase Schedules
Color TV Product Group

	Week				Monthly Totals	Week				Monthly Totals
	1	2	3	4		5	6	7	8	
16" Color TV				1100	1100					0
20" Color TV					0		1040			1040
24" Color TV	70	70	70	70	280		140		140	280
28" Color TV		150			150			300		300
Monthly Totals (TV's)					1530					1620
Open to buy plan: per month					1550					1600

Tolerance: 2%

Figure 4-2

In actual practice, clients usually calculate open-to-buy quantities one to two months out only. The reason is that supplier lead times rarely exceed two months in make-to-stock manufacturing environments. The open-to-buy plan for this product group is 1,550 color TVs for the first month (see figure 4-2). Based on the numbers given in the example, the purchase schedules for the first month (weeks 1 to 4) are 20 units below the open-to-buy plan. In the second month (weeks 5 to 8), the sum of the purchase schedules is 1,620, which is 20 units above the open-to-buy plan. The buyer, however, is given certain tolerances for making the sum of the purchase schedules agree with the open-to-buy plan. In this case, he is allowed a tolerance of plus or minus 2 percent. The 20 above the plan in the second month is thus well within this tolerance.

If the sum of the items in the purchase schedules exceeds the 2 percent tolerance, the buyer has to change some of the individual items. For example, if the sum of the purchase schedules is low, as in the case of weeks 1 to 4, the buyer can increase quantities or move future purchases from one month into another. If the sum of the purchase schedules is high, the buyer can decrease quantities or move future purchases further into the future.

To do this kind of time shifting, the buyer can use the purchase-schedule display and the DRP displays for each store or DC to determine how changing purchase schedules will affect the stores or DCs. The purchase-schedule display shows the distribution demands for the product, and the DRP display shows the situation for each product at each store or DC. This visibility gives the buyer a tremendous advantage in managing and evaluating the purchase schedules.

THE SUPPLIER-SCHEDULING CONCEPT

As mentioned above, part of the buyer's job is to balance the mix of purchase schedules to fit within the constraints of an open-to-buy plan. This, in practice, ultimately should lead to the determination of a firm-purchase time fence expressed in weeks. Such a time fence is negotiated with suppliers and, when used properly, becomes a very powerful tool for both the buyer and supplier. Firm-purchase time fences induce stability for the supplier and help buyers perform their purchasing jobs more professionally.

To illustrate the effectiveness of firm-purchase time fences, take a look at what is called the "typical supplier schedule," as shown in figure

4-3. It shows a listing of four purchase schedules for product (color TVs, in this case), all bought from the same supplier. As a matter of fact, this supplier schedule is identical to the sum of the purchase schedules listed in figure 4-2, as all the TVs listed are purchased from the same manufacturer of brand X. If a company carries multiple brands of the same sizes, several supplier schedules should exist. The sum of all supplier schedules for TV sets adds up to the purchase schedules that comprise a specific group of products within an inventory plan.

The supplier schedule represents the total planned purchases needed to support six different stores. (In fact, in the real world, such schedules often represent hundreds of stores.) Figure 4-3 shows 28 weeks of future purchases. The first 4 weeks are shown individually, the next 12 weeks are shown in increments of 4 weeks, and the last 12 weeks appear as a single total at the end of the display. Specific information such as product code, description, quantity, and cost are displayed for each TV set. Purchase order numbers are shown only for planned purchases displayed in the first 4 weeks.

Note the indication of a firm zone of four weeks. This is the firm-purchase time fence that has been negotiated with the supplier. It means that, although the buyer is showing the supplier 28 weeks of future purchases, he has only fully committed for the first 4 of the 28 weeks of future purchases. In other words, as conditions change in the stores because of selling above or under forecast, DRP will update the individual purchase schedules starting with week 5 and beyond.

For example, if sales for the 16-inch color TV occur well above forecast for 2 weeks, DRP will do two things. First, it gives the buyer action messages recommending that quantities inside the first 4 weeks be moved in. Second, it updates by increasing or decreasing future purchases starting in week 5 to reflect the latest changes that have occurred.

Such action messages and shuffling of orders are called "rescheduling." Rescheduling represents a very powerful aspect of DRP for retailers, wholesalers, and distributors. As conditions change, DRP reschedules, updates, plans, and communicates the changes rapidly.[3]

---

[3] The first company that embraced this buying approach using DRP was a major wholesaler in the health and beauty aids business. Today, roughly 75 percent of all its purchases are scheduled and shipped from the company's suppliers using supplier schedules. The result of fine-tuning the system is an almost paperless environment—no purchase orders to suppliers, and, in some cases, invoices are eliminated. Instead, suppliers send monthly statements referencing supplier schedule numbers and POs.

E.D. Smith supplier schedules for Perkins Inc. week of xx/xx/xx
Location: Portland DC   Firm zone: first 4 weeks

U/M: Selling Units

Buyer: / Unit / Item Descr. Cost C/S	Current + Past due	Requirements Week 2/8	Week 2/15	Week 2/22	Next 4 Wks	Next 4 Wks	Next 4 Wks	Next 12 Wks
2/42 16" Color TV Qty:	-	-	-	1100	2200	2200	2200	3300
P.O. No.:				B1203				
175.00$				192,500	385,000	385,000	385,000	577,500
2/44 20" Color TV Qty:	-	-	-	-	1040	1040	1040	2080
P.O. No.:								
200.00$					208,000	208,000	208,000	208,000
2/30 24" Color TV Qty:	70	70	70	70	280	280	280	840
P.O. No.:	B1120	B1146	B1180	B1203				
300.00$	21,000	21,000	21,000	21,000	84,000	84,000	84,000	252,000
2/00 28" Color TV Qty:	-	150	-	-	300	150	300	600
P.O.:		B1146						
470.00$		70,500			141,000	70,500	141,000	282,000
Weekly Total$	21,000	91,500	21,000	213,500	818,000	747,500	818,000	1,319,500
Cum Total$	21,000	112,500	133,500	347,000	1,165,000	1,912,500	2,730,500	4,050,000
Weekly Total WGT:	3,850	12,850	3,850	47,850	173,400	164,400	173,400	318,200
Cum Total WGT:	3,850	16,700	20,550	68,400	241,800	406,200	579,600	897,800
Weekly Total Std Hrs:	2	5	2	31	104	100	104	182
Weekly Capacity:	400							

Figure 4-3

In figure 4-3 PO numbers only appear for items listed for shipment in the first 4 weeks, the firm-purchase time fence. For any planned purchases in the same week, the PO number is the same, so the PO number is merely a reference point. No hard-copy POs are necessary. This approach eliminates the need to issue purchase requisitions and purchase orders, and therefore represents a significant reduction in paperwork.

Here is how the system works. Once a month, the wholesaler referenced in footnote 3 issues a prenumbered purchase schedule in four copies. The original is sent to the supplier. The second copy is retained by the buyer for file and follow-up. The third copy goes to accounts payable, and the fourth is sent to the receiving department. Every week, DRP updates the supplier schedules and changes are indicated with asterisks, one for each week between hard copies. For example, an item with three asterisks indicates a change that took place three weeks after the purchase schedule was issued.

The weekly schedules are communicated electronically to suppliers. When suppliers ship, they reference the purchase schedule number, the PO number, the product code, quantity, and cost. This information enables both the customer and the supplier to uniquely identify what is being shipped against the purchase schedule. As of this writing, several clients in retail/wholesale businesses have switched to this new way of conducting business with their suppliers. The benefits of this approach are numerous and have a profound impact on how their businesses are managed.

Applying the Supplier-Scheduling Concept[4]

With computers and formal systems like DRP, it becomes a practical matter to put the planning people in direct contact with the supplier. These planning people are called "supplier schedulers," and they typically communicate directly with scheduling people at the supplier's location.

With this arrangement, buyers now have the time to do the important parts of their jobs—sourcing, negotiation, contracting, value analysis,

---

[4] Most of the supplier-scheduling concepts discussed in the next few pages have been written by two Oliver Wight associates, John Schorr and Tom Wallace. See their book, *High Performance Purchasing* (Essex Junction, VT: Oliver Wight Limited Publications, Inc., 1986) for more details about using supplier scheduling in manufacturing.

etc. In this environment, there is normally a business arrangement called a "supplier agreement" between the customer and the supplier. The supplier scheduler enters the picture after the supplier agreement is finalized. His job is to operate DRP and provide the suppliers with purchase schedules that meet the terms and conditions stipulated in the supplier agreement. When the supplier has a problem meeting the schedule, he notifies the supplier scheduler, who helps him develop an alternative plan.

The Supplier Schedule—Content and Format

A purchase order is simply a contract with a schedule on it. The obvious question is: Why not separate the schedule from the contract? After all, schedules change frequently, every week or so. Contracts change infrequently, perhaps once a year, so there's little reason to reissue a new contract every time the schedule changes.

More and more companies are choosing to establish long-term supplier agreements and then issue schedules to them, typically one per week. In general, the buyer develops the supplier agreements, and the supplier scheduler supervises the schedules.

The Degree of Future Commitment

Questions sometimes arise regarding the degree of commitment to the suppliers involved in supplier scheduling. In other words, does a company find itself making firm commitments further into the future with supplier scheduling than with conventional purchase orders? Further than with blanket orders? Or further than with buying capacity?

In each of these cases, the answer is no. Supplier scheduling, done properly, results in a reduced, firm future commitment. Let's examine the alternatives:

- Conventional purchase orders require commitments to specific items, quantities, and time lines through the supplier's total lead time. Of course, this includes backlog time. Supplier scheduling keys on the supplier's true manufacturing time and firms up only those orders within that period. Since these times are shorter than the manufacturing time, the commitment period is correspondingly smaller.

- Blanket orders typically require a commitment to the supplier for a specific quantity, or perhaps quantity range, of a specific item over an extended period of time, often at a predetermined delivery schedule. With supplier scheduling, there is no long-term commitment to specific quantities and time.

• Buying capacity usually means committing to the supplier for a given level of volume per time period over an extended time into the future. With supplier scheduling, there is normally no such firm commitment. There are situations, however, when good supplier scheduling requires capacity buying.

Multiple Sourcing

Supplier scheduling does not require sole sourcing. Many companies do a great deal of sole sourcing, and there is a definite trend toward reducing the number of suppliers, but in fact, most of the companies using it today are multiple-sourced.

Good software for supplier scheduling makes multiple sourcing more practical because it enables the supplier scheduler to specify the share of an item's total requirements for Supplier A, Supplier B, etc. Moreover, the supplier schedules that the software generates will reflect this split. The supplier scheduler is typically not a decision maker with regards to apportioning volume to various suppliers. Rather, the scheduler executes decisions made by the buyer or the purchasing manager. Some companies show the supplier the total volume on the item as well as the supplier's share of it. This can serve as an incentive for each supplier to do a better job and gain a greater share of the business.

In any case, the best companies work very closely with their suppliers, maintaining frequent and open lines of communication. Since the schedules are valid, the dates are believable. The supplier knows the customer's environment, problems, and opportunities—and vice versa. Mutual trust, recognized as a critical element, is constantly nourished. The result of all these efforts? The suppliers are looked upon as "part of the team."

Why Help the Supplier?

Sometimes people question why they should help their supplier plan his capacity needs. One important reason is that without this forecast information, the supplier is forced to guess at the customer's future needs. The customer then has to rely on the quality of the supplier's guess rather than on the quality of the planned orders in the DRP system. In rising markets, customers often find themselves put on allocation when the supplier guesses wrong. The issue is not whether to forecast or not to forecast, but who forecasts.

Giving better information to suppliers enhances their ability to give customers what they need, when they need it. Many companies using supplier scheduling find high-quality information helps mediocre suppliers become good ones, and good ones become excellent. Their philosophy is: "Let's help them to help us. Their problems are our problems."

With supplier scheduling, companies can ask the same thing of their suppliers. Companies that do a good job of supplier scheduling using DRP or MRP II, find routine follow-ups of suppliers are unnecessary. Suppliers know that the due dates are valid, and that the company needs the items at those times. When a supplier has a problem and can't ship on time, he knows it's necessary to notify the company at once. Otherwise, he says nothing and ships on time. In these instances, silence is approval.

ORGANIZING FOR SUPPLIER SCHEDULING

Traditionally, most companies have a planner who determines the needs for purchased items. The planner enters the quantity and due date on a requisition and forwards it to purchasing. Upon receipt of the requisition, and barring any difficulties, the buyer creates the purchase order.

Unfortunately, in many companies, the planner and buyer do not work well together. Because the planner is usually held accountable for the dollars in inventory, he tends to requisition smaller quantities to keep the inventory low. On the other hand, the buyer is accountable for price. He'll tend to work toward getting the largest quantity price break possible. If he's unable to get the maximum price break, he may go back to the planner and ask him to increase the order quantity. In this way, the company can unwittingly set conflicting goals for these two functions.

A second problem prevents planners and buyers from working in concert. Without a valid planning and scheduling system, the initial due dates on requisitions may be incorrect, so they do not reflect when the material is really needed. In addition, constantly changing priorities make it very difficult for the due dates to be kept valid during the life of an order.

In this environment, the buyer doesn't really know when the orders are needed. If a company runs out before the shipment from the supplier arrives, the finger pointing begins. The planner blames the buyer for not respecting the dates on the requisitions, and, in return, the buyer accuses the planner of giving incorrect need dates.

In most companies, the planners are not allowed to talk to the suppliers, for two major reasons. The first concerns the due date. Since purchasing people believe that planners don't provide them with valid dates on requisitions, they don't want the unrealistic dates passed on to the suppliers. Purchasing people also fear that the planners may treat the suppliers unfairly by violating lead times or minimum order quantities. In other words, they're concerned that planners may break down the rapport the buyers have worked so hard to establish with their suppliers. Second, the planners in most companies are organized by product lines, not commodities. Therefore, two or more planners could possibly contact a supplier simultaneously and give him conflicting priorities.

THE COMBINED METHOD

As industry made the transition from manual to computerized inventory record keeping, certain opportunities opened up. For example, record keeping became less time-consuming, which in turn allowed one person—typically the buyer—to do both the buying and the planning. Accordingly, that person is often called a buyer/planner.

Under this combined form of organization, the buyer/planner receives computer-generated information on each of the purchased items. He reviews this output, reacting to the action messages on each item as needed. Once this planning is complete, he places the purchase orders with the supplier and performs all the normal purchasing functions.

This approach gives the buyer/planner much better information than he could obtain in the past. He can see the need dates on every item and can easily increase order quantities or combine items to get the desired price breaks. Freed of requisition paperwork, his overall paperwork burden is reduced. Further, with an effective DRP system in place, the dates can be kept valid, thus sharply reducing the buyer's expediting work load.

This is not to say that the buyer can sit back and relax; to the contrary, he now has planning, in addition to his buying responsibilities. Some, possibly most, of the time saved by the reduced paperwork and better dates now must be devoted to the planning function. Therefore, it's still possible for buyers to have insufficient time to do the really important parts of their jobs—sourcing, negotiation, value analysis, etc.

THE SUPPLIER-SCHEDULER METHOD

As a result, some very forward-thinking purchasing departments found a better way. Since DRP can generate and maintain valid need dates, much of the traditional conflict between the buyer and planner can be eliminated. Planners can be organized by commodity and work directly with the supplier on details of the schedule. Often, they're given a new title—supplier scheduler. The buyer's job changes to what it should have been all along—spending money well. Be aware that it's unnecessary to go through the combined method to achieve supplier scheduling. You can immediately implement supplier scheduling regardless of your current arrangement.

THE SUPPLIER-SCHEDULER'S JOB

What does the supplier scheduler do? First, he analyzes the DRP reports and reacts to the messages posed by the system. The types of messages he reviews include:

- Release an order.

- Reschedule an order in.

- Reschedule an order out.

- Cancel an order.

- Resolve data problems.

As explained in chapter 3, DRP forecasts the future and calculates when the company will need to receive more material from its suppliers on each purchased item. It then offsets by the supplier's lead time and recommends when to place an order. This is called a "planned order" because it is only a recommendation from the system. As time passes, that planned order release moves, for example, from week 4 to week 3, from week 3 to week 2, from week 2 to week 1. When it appears in week 1, the DRP system gives the supplier scheduler a message to firm up that order with the supplier. The supplier scheduler converts that planned order to a "scheduled receipt," which authorizes the selected supplier to produce the item. If there is a problem from the supplier's viewpoint, the buyer may need to get involved and resolve the problem prior to the placement of the order.

DRP is also constantly reviewing the need date against the due date, when the supplier has been asked to deliver the item. If the need date changes, either in or out, the system gives the supplier scheduler a message to move the due date accordingly, that is, to reschedule in or reschedule out. The supplier scheduler contacts the supplier and requests the change in due date. If the supplier agrees to the change, there's no problem. The scheduled receipt's due date on the computer is simply changed to reflect the new date. If the supplier cannot or will not change the date, the supplier scheduler may contact the buyer, who tries to resolve the differences.

On occasion, the system will also recommend canceling an order with a supplier. This can happen when a customer has canceled an order and no longer needs a scheduled purchased item. In these cases, the supplier scheduler contacts the supplier to try to cancel the order. If there are no problems, the order is canceled. If there are problems, such as cost implications, the buyer needs to get involved and negotiate the necessary settlement.

In short, the supplier scheduler does all the planning via DRP, handling the 90 to 95 percent of the items that are routine. The few exceptions are handled by the buyer.

The second area of responsibility of the supplier scheduler is to maintain the information in the system. If a price changes or the buyer negotiates a new lead time or selects a new supplier, the buyer passes the information on to the supplier scheduler, who inputs it into the system. After verifying that the master data is correct, he lets the buyer know that the change has been completed. Thus the buyer exercises management control over the DRP system, but is free of actually handling the time-consuming transactions.

The third area of responsibility of the supplier scheduler is to respond to changes to the schedule and to supplier delivery problems. "Can the supplier move the shipment from Thursday to Monday?" The supplier scheduler becomes the eyes and ears of both the supplier and the company.

The fourth and last area of responsibility of the supplier scheduler concerns the actual generation of supplier schedules. After all the necessary planned orders are converted into scheduled receipts in the DRP system, all the reschedule messages are complete, and all the changes are updated, the system is then authorized to generate the supplier schedule. The supplier scheduler is responsible for transmitting the weekly schedule to the supplier. He may also check with the supplier to ensure receipt of the schedule, and that the schedule is practical and attainable.

THE BUYER'S JOB

Because the supplier scheduler frees the buyer of paperwork and assumes the bulk of the day-to-day contact with the suppliers, the buyer can perform his job of value analysis, negotiation, supplier selection, alternate sourcing, etc. He has new opportunities to work with suppliers to find ways to satisfy the function of the item at a lower cost. He also has time to effectively negotiate on all the items, not just the high-ticket ones.

In 1985, Oliver Wight associates conducted a survey of more than 1,100 client manufacturing companies. Successful users of MRP II who also used supplier scheduling reported an average 11 percent annual purchase cost reduction. Why? Primarily because the buyers had the time to do their jobs, in addition, of course, to furnishing the suppliers with valid schedules generated by MRP II. Those companies having buyer/planners reported an average 7 percent annual cost reduction. Why the difference? Under the buyer/planner concept, the buyer has to spend time planning and following up. That subtracts time spent on the value analysis, negotiation, etc. Under supplier scheduling, the buyer's full-time job is getting the best return on the money he has available to spend.

Lead times can be negotiated more easily as well. By visiting the suppliers' plants, the buyer can determine the real elements of lead times. He can find answers to such questions as: When does the supplier need to order raw materials? When does the supplier set aside capacity to make the product? How long does it actually take to produce the item? By using the supplier's schedule to forecast raw material and capacity needs, the buyer can negotiate a shorter lead time based upon the supplier's actual manufacturing time. In short, the buyer is given the time to do all the functions of his job well. Since he's now an expert at buying, rather than paperwork and expediting, he can become a highly motivated, contributing professional in the purchasing department.

A POTENTIAL DILEMMA

To whom should the supplier schedulers report? The purchasing manager may feel that the supplier schedulers should report to him, since they're in direct contact with his suppliers. But the manager of inventory control might want the supplier schedulers to report to him since they're operating DRP. What's the solution to this potential dilemma?

The answer lies in the basic issue of accountability. The supplier-scheduling function should report to that manager who has accountability for the performance of the purchased material inventory. Inventory performance in this context means two things—service and turnover.

- *Service*—this means providing good customer service on finished goods.

- *Turnover*—this refers to keeping the inventory levels low.

The manager who can best be held accountable for purchased inventory performance is the logical choice to manage the supplier-scheduling operation. In some companies, this might be the purchasing manager, in others the inventory control manager, or the materials manager.

All things being equal, the supplier-scheduling group should be part of the purchasing department. In this arrangement, there's only one person to consult if there is a purchased-item problem—the purchasing manager. It makes no difference if the quantity is wrong, if the inventory level is incorrect on a purchased item, etc. The purchasing manager is ultimately responsible for all purchased-item problems. If the supplier scheduler reports to inventory control, there may be confusion about whom to call—the purchasing manager or the inventory control manager.

Also, if the supplier scheduler reports to inventory control, there may remain some conflict between order quantity and price breaks. If the supplier scheduler reports to purchasing, the purchasing manager is held accountable to manage pricing while staying below his total inventory dollar limit.

That's the theory. In actual practice, it really doesn't seem to matter very much. In the Oliver Wight survey, about half of the companies had the supplier schedulers as part of the purchasing department, and roughly half had them in inventory control.

In most companies, regardless of reporting structure, the supplier schedulers sit in proximity to the purchasing department. In this way, the supplier schedulers can easily update buyers on potential problems. In return, the buyers keep the supplier schedulers informed on key issues.

Quality problems can be handled jointly by the buyer and supplier scheduler. The supplier scheduler needs to get a replacement shipment, as the buyer needs to resolve the underlying reason for quality problem. The buyer also needs to keep the supplier scheduler up to date on pricing and buying quantity, so he can input the data and replan as necessary.

The buyer informs the supplier scheduler about pending changes in suppliers, new suppliers, and other related information. This can enable the supplier scheduler to help the new supplier with material planning, and to begin building new relationships.

In short, the buyer and supplier scheduler work together to resolve problems and handle changes. When a supplier calls to discuss quality or pricing, he sees the buyer. When he calls to discuss delivery, he sees the supplier scheduler. But because they work as a team, often both the buyer and supplier scheduler meet as a team with the supplier to be sure all bases are covered before the supplier leaves. Anything short of a team effort may cause a return to the unfortunate "your supplier, your schedule" finger-pointing routine, hot lists, and the associated decrease in performance.

How many supplier schedulers will a company need? Our survey showed an average of one supplier scheduler supporting two buyers. Since the buyers and supplier schedulers are set up on a commodity basis, it is fairly easy to arrange the commodities to enable a 2 to 1 ratio to work smoothly.

One question almost always arises: "Will we need to hire more people to staff the supplier-scheduling function?" The answer is usually no. The supplier schedulers can often be drawn from the existing planner group, as a result of reassigning planning responsibilities.

SUPPLIER EDUCATION

DRP education cannot be limited only to the people employed by the company. Because suppliers are key to the success of any scheduling system, they need to understand DRP. Education and training are vital for them.

Suppliers should be brought into the company for a one-day education program whenever practical.[5] It's important to have several representatives from a given supplier at the training. The representatives should include the supplier's customer service/order-entry manager, scheduling group manager, and perhaps the plant manager in addition to the local salesman. Even with a group this large, it's a very practical matter to educate a number of suppliers in one day.

The supplier education program should consist of basic education on the principles of DRP, plus more specific training on the supplier-scheduling process itself.

It is also necessary to develop a supplier education manual, a document created especially for the suppliers to take back to their companies for use in educating their own employees. It should cover the fundamentals of DRP, how the supplier schedule works, what's required of the supplier (for example, on-time delivery, quality, the principle of "silence is approval," etc.).

Here's an example of how an effective supplier education day might be structured. The first few hours of the morning are devoted to general DRP education, using videotapes plus training aids. This session covers the fundamentals and applications of DRP, mechanics of executing the purchase schedules, the open-to-buy plan, and how to operate DRP in purchasing.

For the balance of the morning, the emphasis shifts to the supplier schedule. The discussion covers what suppliers are authorized to produce, such as scheduled receipts, and how they can plan raw material and capacity, capacity units of measure, and so on. This is also a good time to verify lead times, lot sizes, minimum buy quantities, buy-quantity multiples above the minimum buy quantity, and supplier plans for vacation shutdowns, etc.

The agenda for the morning session also allows time to discuss what day of the week the supplier schedule should be sent to the supplier, the cutoff dates for the previous week's receipts, and the need for feedback on past-due orders. At this time, the principle of "silence is approval" is

---

[5] In some cases, because of geographical or other factors, it may be necessary to "take the show on the road"; that is, to conduct the education day at the supplier's plant. This approach can work well, although bringing the suppliers into one's own company seems to have more overall impact and generate better results.

stressed again. Suppliers must understand they will be held accountable for delivery on the dates shown on the supplier schedule, and that it's imperative they communicate in advance if they will miss a delivery date.

After lunch, the first couple of hours in the afternoon can be used to review the supplier manual. Since this is the document the suppliers will use to educate their people in their individual companies, they must thoroughly understand the manual.

The supplier education day ends with a commitment from the supplier to work to the supplier schedule, and the development of an action plan to bring performance on delivery and quality up to acceptable levels. Suppliers must realize because they will now be receiving valid need dates, they must ship high-quality products consistently on time. The action plan spells out the supplier's current performance levels on delivery and quality. A timetable shows when the supplier is at acceptable levels of performance in the areas of delivery and quality to support the supplier-scheduling program.

After designing the supplier education program, it's time to test the system with the suppliers selected for the pilot. This entails 20 percent of the suppliers who represent 80 percent of the dollars spent on purchased items. Later, it's time to educate the remaining 80 percent of the suppliers.

By then, all suppliers should be through the initial suppliers' education day. It's important to schedule follow-up education days with selected suppliers who do not understand either DRP or the supplier-schedule requirements. These follow-up education days reinforce how the DRP system works and what is required of a supplier receiving the supplier's schedule.

Pilot and Cutover

The best choice for a pilot supplier is a key supplier who is in close geographic proximity, well organized, well run, and willing to work with you to develop and perfect your supplier education program and supplier schedule.

The actual pilot with the key supplier lasts for three or four weeks, or longer if it's not working properly. If that is the case, go no further. Stop right there and fix what's wrong. Based on the feedback from the pilot supplier, fine-tuning of the supplier-scheduling system occurs during the pilot period. The measurement reports should also be piloted with the key supplier at the same time.

A word of caution: Don't assume that suppliers will automatically become perfect the minute they start to receive their supplier schedules. It won't happen. Initially, they will still have delivery problems. The last thing a company needs when cutting over onto supplier scheduling is to have serious stock outs.

Therefore, it's often a good idea during pilot and cutover to make prudent use of safety stock and/or safety time to protect against supplier problems. Then, as supplier performance improves, these cushions can be removed. Remember priority number one when implementing DRP—run the business.

The 20 percent of the suppliers that represent 80 percent of the dollars purchased should be cut over to supplier scheduling within two months. You will begin to see the improved results of having the pilot supplier and the larger suppliers on the system and experience better on-time delivery, lower inventory, reduced lead times, etc. If these results aren't occurring, something is wrong, either with the supplier schedule itself or the education program. Again, if there is a problem, go no further— fix what's wrong before proceeding.

With positive results, you can begin to cut over the 80 percent of the suppliers who represent the last 20 percent of the dollars purchased.

Once fully on the air, companies should measure results with all suppliers. They should determine which suppliers are not improving their performance on delivery and quality during the first three months. These suppliers need follow-up education. Goals and action plans for all of these suppliers should be established on delivery and quality and committed in writing.

CONCLUSION

In chapter 3, we explained the logic of DRP using one store—Los Angeles—and then an additional five stores. In this chapter, we continued with the same six-store example, changing only the product names. We summarized the total purchase requirements for all stores, and developed a purchase schedule. Next, we covered how purchase schedules should add up to an open-to-buy or inventory plan. A summary of these examples and how they integrate is shown in figure 4-4. The key point is that a planner/buyers or supplier schedulers or buyers evaluating

Example Summary

On Hand Bal.:   −500
Safety Stock: −200
Lead Time: −2 wks.
Order Quantity: −300

Los Angeles Store
16" Color TV

	Past Due	Week							
		1	2	3	4	5	6	7	8
Forecast		100	120	90	110	120	100	80	120
In Transit									
Projected On-Hand		400	280	490	380	260	460	380	260
Plnd. Shipments-Receipt				300			300		
Plnd. Shipments-Ship		300			300				

Summary of Planned Shipments to the Six Stores

	Past Due	Week							
		1	2	3	4	5	6	7	8
Los Angeles		300			300				
Montreal					150				
New York	300			300		300			
Vancouver			150						
Toronto				150					
Chicago					300		300		
Totals	300	300	150	750	450	300	300	0	0

Summary of Purchase Schedules

	Week				Monthly Totals	Week				Monthly Totals
	1	2	3	4		5	6	7	8	
16" Color TV				1100	1100					0
20" Color TV					0		1040			1040
24" Color TV	70	70	70	70	280		140		140	280
28" Color TV		150			150			300		300
Monthly Totals (TV's)					1530					1620
Open to Buy Plan: per month					1550					1600

Tolerance: +/− 2%

On Hand Bal.:   −1700
Safety Stock: −0
Lead Time: −3 wks.
Order Quantity: −1100

16" Color TV Purchase Schedule

	Past Due	Week							
		1	2	3	4	5	6	7	8
Distribution Demands	300	300	150	750	450	300	300	0	0
Scheduled Receipts									
Projected On-Hand	1400	1100	950	200	650	550	250	250	250
Purchase Schedule-Recpt					1100				
Purchase Schedule-Start		1100							

Figure 4-4

An Integrated Retail/Manufacturing System

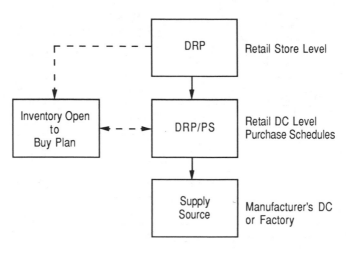

Figure 4-5

a change in business conditions have all the information they need to make good decisions.

If sales rise in certain stores, they can see it and know which store. If sales drop they see that, too. Buyers also see the aggregate impact of all the changes from every store and the significance those changes have on the purchase schedule. If changes are currently necessary because of suppliers' situations, buyers have sufficient visibility to take appropriate actions. If changes are very large, planner/buyers, supplier schedulers, or buyers will also see the impact on the open-to-buy plan, so they can recommend changes to management. Clearly, for professional buyers, this window on change is a very powerful tool.

The integration of activities as shown in figure 4-5 makes possible, for the first time, one set of logic from stores to DCs to suppliers in a continuous, seamless manner. It also provides the information that permits the development of open-to-buy budgets.

In the end, the process of integrating the various levels of inventory through DRP completely changes the traditional approaches to retail/wholesale inventory management used during the past 30 years.

Chapter 5

DRP in a Manufacturing Environment

Using DRP with Sales & Operations Planning and Master Production Scheduling

This chapter deals with the application of DRP in manufacturing companies who service customers through inventory stocking locations (ISLs). In such situations, the customer/supplier relationship described in chapter 4 should be perpetuated. In other words, the business conditions are still the same.

In a manufacturing company that sells products through a network of DCs, logistics becomes the customer of manufacturing. The problem is that few people think of logistics this way, and, as a result, the planning and scheduling systems in manufacturing companies are rarely developed with this relationship in mind.

For the most part, people view manufacturing and logistics as separate functions, which results in the development of different planning systems for the two. The pioneering effort that led to the development of DRP in 1975 was in large part a move toward a new mind-set that considered logistics and manufacturing as elements in a continuous pipeline. The effort proved that to fully satisfy customers, manufacturing companies must develop integrated planning systems able to answer two sets of questions:

The Universal Logistics Questions

What am I going to sell?

Where will I sell it?

What do I have?

What do I have on order?

What do I have to get?

The Universal Manufacturing Questions

What am I going to make?

What does it take to make it?

What do I have?

What do I need to get?

Today, people recognize that the answer to manufacturing's first question—"What am I going to make?"—is derived from the answer to the last logistics question—"What do I have to get?" That is because *what logistics must obtain is what manufacturing must create.* Look at the DRP management process chart in chapter 3 (figure 3-1). It answers the universal logistics questions and integrates the answers with manufacturing.

The inputs into the DRP process contain the information that answers the first four questions for logistics. Once this input is received by the DRP system, DRP answers the last logistics question and passes it on as input to manufacturing via the sales & operations planning (S&OP) process and master production scheduling. A summary follows:

LOGISTICS QUESTIONS	ANSWERS DERIVED FROM
What am I going to sell?	Today and near-term: order entry Medium and long-term: sales forecast
Where will I sell it?	Bill of distribution
What do I have?	Inventory control
What do I have on order?	Open purchase orders (POs) Open manufacturing orders (MOs)
What do I have to get?	DRP determines the answer and passes it to S&OP and MPS

The DRP Management Process
Distribution Resource Planning

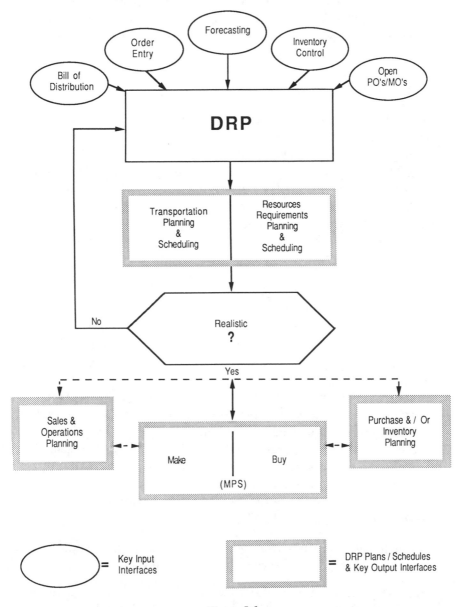

Figure 5-1

The totals from DRP represent the demands of the entire logistics system. The job of the manufacturing supply source is to plan production so that the demands from logistics can be satisfied. This process entails two activities: sales & operation planning, which refers to families of products, and master scheduling, which refers to specific end items.

Production Planning

The production plan[1] is a statement of production in gross terms. Typically, production plans are developed for products representing monthly totals. For example, the production plan for vitamin C might be 100,000 tablets per month. Other production plans might include the number of gallons per month of a certain color of paint, the number of gallons per month of orange juice or ice cream, the quantity of a particular style of chair per month, etc.

A production plan does not identify the specific package size in the case of orange juice, paint, etc., or the specific model in the case of chairs, etc. Rather, it is a statement of production in terms of families of products, not the individual products themselves.

A family of products for production planning purposes is a group that typically shares manufacturing facilities. For example, the pint, half-gallon, gallon, and five-gallon containers of a particular type of paint may use the same mixing tank and packaging line. These products are then grouped into the same family for production planning. The manufacturing families could be different from the marketing product groups.

The top management of a company is responsible for the accuracy and the validity of the production plan, although some top managers believe they aren't concerned with detailed planning. In actuality, though, the production plan is not a detailed plan; it is a broad summarized statement of production rates. And the production plan has tremendous influence over many of the things for which a top manager is held accountable. For example, the plan will determine:

1. Whether the demands from logistics will be satisfied and, consequently, what customer service problems will result.

[1] Production plans are the result of a sales & operations planning (S&OP) process that occurs in three stages. It starts with sales forecast and inventory targets and ends with rates of production, which are typically referred to as production plans. For more information on the S&OP process, read *Orchestrating Success* by Richard C. Ling and Walter E. Goddard (Essex Junction, VT Oliver Wight Limited Publications, Inc., 1988).

2. Whether the factory will be able to meet the production requirements and, if not, what other methods can be used to solve the problem.

3. What the staffing levels will be for the factory and how this fits with current labor contracts.

4. What the utilization of the factory and equipment will be and what the overhead cost of the product will be.

5. What the inventory investment level will be over the course of the year, as well as at the end of the year.

6. What the production cost will be, and whether the cash flow will support the plan.

All these outcomes are determined either directly or indirectly from the production plan. The production plan serves as the basic constraint on the master production schedule; the sum of the master production schedules, when totaled, must be within the constraints of the production plan. In this way, the production plan is management's single most powerful handle on the system. Because the production plan has such sweeping effects on the performance of the company, it must be reviewed and approved by the top manager. Typically, the production plan is developed and approved by the president or the general manager and his staff. It is not something delegated to lower-level management.

Developing a Production Plan

When developing a production plan for a family of products, three questions must be kept in mind:

1. What are the distribution demands that must be satisfied for the family of items?

2. What change in inventory is planned for the family of items?

3. What are the manufacturing or purchasing constraints that could limit production for the family of items?

To illustrate the basics of production planning, let's examine how a production plan could be developed for a family of paint products (see figure 5-2). In this case, the production plan is developed so that: (1) the ending inventory is nearly the same as the starting inventory; (2) the

Production Plan High-Gloss Enamel Paint						
All Numbers in Gallons						
Month	Distribution Demands	Change in Inventory		Inventory		Production Plan
		Monthly	Cumulative	Starting	Ending	
January	1655	+345	+345	1580	1925	2000
February	1770	+230	+575	1925	2155	2000
March	1750	+350	+925	2155	2505	2100
April	2300	−200	+725	2505	2305	2100
May	2470	−270	+455	2305	2035	2200
June	2650	−450	+5	2035	1585	2200

Figure 5-2

plan meets the demands from logistics, and (3) the production rate does not exceed 2,200 per month, which is the capacity for a three-shift operation.

The column labeled distribution demands in figure 5-2 is the total that comes from DRP. The total demands on the supply source (manufacturing, in this instance) for one product are added to the demands for the other products in a family of items. For example, the demands for the pint, half-gallon, gallon, and five-gallon sizes of the enamel paint are added together. In addition, the weekly demands for all the different sizes are combined to yield monthly totals. This total represents the demand that has to be satisfied to meet the requirements of the distribution centers.

The change in inventory column shows the planned increases and decreases in inventory. This is broken down into two rows—the monthly change in inventory and the cumulative change in inventory from the beginning of the year. The totals from the change in inventory column represent the sum of the inventories in all the DCs and the supply source.

In the example shown in figure 5-2, inventory is built in anticipation of a peak selling season. The months of January, February, and March are used to build up 925 gallons in inventory as indicated by the cumulative inventory in March, the starting inventory of 1,580 in January, and the ending inventory of 2,505 at the end of March. In April, May, and June, peak sales use up 920 of the 925 gallons in inventory. This is also shown by the cumulative inventory levels from March to June, where there is a starting inventory of 2,505 at the beginning of April and an ending inventory of 1,585 on the last day of June.

The production plan is more stable than the distribution demands or the planned inventory levels. The distribution demands vary from a high of 2,650 to a low of 1,655, while the inventory ranges from a low of 1,580 to a high of 2,505. The production rate is more stable because manufacturing is unable to sustain a rate of production for this family of products beyond 2,200 per month, and if production drops below 1,900, the company will have to lay off skilled people.

Reviewing the Plan

Typically, the production plan is reviewed once a month during the sales & operation planning meeting. This is advisable because situations will inevitably change over the course of a month. The distribution demands, for example, are likely to change because of sales that are greater or less than the forecast or because of changes in the forecast quantities, order quantities, methods of shipment, etc. In addition, other conditions may change, too. Situations might arise that dictate the building of more or less inventory. Manufacturing constraints may change and cause higher or lower rates of production than those used to develop the current production plan.

For reasons stated earlier, the president or the general manager and his staff review the production plan. This does not necessarily mean changing the plan; it should simply be reviewed in the context of current circumstances. For example, an increase in the sales forecast could lead to a change in the production plan, provided that manufacturing can handle the increased rate of production. The production plan would not be changed, however, if demand was close to the forecast. Every company should establish the ground rules concerning the necessity and desirability to change the production plan in advance. Discussions will then be focused on solving problems as they arise.

MASTER PRODUCTION SCHEDULING (MPS)

The MPS is the specific statement of what will be produced and when manufacturing will make it. In contrast to the production plan, which is stated in families of products, the MPS is stated in terms of specific items. For example, a company would have an individual MPS for the pint size of paint, the half-gallon size, the gallon size, and the five-gallon size.

An MPS is developed based on the following information for an item:

1. Distribution demands for the item.

2. Any other demands for the item.

3. The inventory balance, safety stock, lead time, and production lot size.

4. The production plan for the family of items.

Let's return to the vitamin C in bottles of 100, used in chapter 3 to illustrate how DRP operates in retail settings. As this chapter deals with DRP in a manufacturing environment, we will assume that the six stores are distribution centers supported by a factory (the supply source). Figure 5-3 shows an MPS display for this item.

The distribution demands are the totals from the distribution network. Figure 3-10 shows the sum of the distribution requirements for

Master Production Schedule
Supply Source (Manufacturing)
Vitamin C Tablet 100/Bottle

On Hand Balance — 1700
Safety Stock   — 0
Lead Time   — 3 wks
Order Quantity   — 1100

	Past Due	Week							
		1	2	3	4	5	6	7	8
Distribution Demands	300	300	150	750	450	300	300	0	0
Scheduled Receipts									
Projected On Hand	1400	1100	950	200	850	550	250	250	250
Master Schedule-Rcpt.					1100				
Master Schedule-Start		1100							

Figure 5-3

this product from all the different stores, DCs in this example. This is the same set of numbers shown in the distribution demands line of figure 5-3. In other words, these numbers represent the demands that need to be satisfied to supply the vitamin product to the DCs.

The scheduled receipts line shows any released orders for this item at the date they are due into stock. If the item is manufactured, the released orders are actually manufacturing orders that have been released to the shop. If the item is purchased, the orders are considered purchase orders that have been released to suppliers.

The projected on hand line is the same type of calculation as that shown in the DRP display. The on-hand balance is reduced by the distribution requirements, while scheduled receipts and MPS orders are added into the calculation. This calculation will show a projected inventory buildup or a stock out.

Two lines represent the MPS in figure 5-3: the master schedule-rcpt, which indicates the MPS at the receipt date, and the master schedule-start, which indicates the MPS at the start date. These are set and maintained manually by the master scheduler. The MPS lines in the display are not like the planned order release lines in the DRP display. Planned shipments at the DCs are generated by the computer; the MPS is not. Because the MPS can have a tremendous impact on the manufacturing facility since it is the source used to develop all supporting manufacturing schedules, it must be managed carefully by human beings who exercise sound judgment and decision making.

The management of a company is responsible for setting guidelines for master schedulers. The master schedulers are responsible for developing and maintaining schedules that are within established management guidelines. The computer can only provide the master scheduler with information regarding demands for the item, the inventory balance, ordering rules, lead time, etc. A master scheduler, using the display shown in figure 5-3, can interpret the information and evaluate the situation for the given product. He may decide that the MPS should be changed, that more information be added, or that the situation is correct and no changes are needed.

To reiterate, the production plan acts as a constraint on the MPS because the MPS, when totaled for a family of items, must equal the production plan for that family. To illustrate this concept, let's assume that the vitamin C family of products has the production plan shown in figure 5-4.

Summary of Master Production Schedules
Vitamin C Family

	Week				Monthly Totals (Tablets)	Week				Monthly Totals (Tablets)
	1	2	3	4		5	6	7	8	
100/Bottle				1100	110,000					0
250/Bottle					0		1040			260,000
500/Bottle		280			140,000					0
1000/Bottle				150	150,000			150		150,000
Monthly Totals (Tablets)					400,000					410,000

Production Plan: 400,000 per month
Tolerance: +/− 5%

Figure 5-4

The production plan for this family of products is 400,000 per month. Based on the numbers in figure 5-4, the sum of the MPS for the first month (weeks 1 to 4) agrees exactly with the production plan. In the second month (weeks 5 to 8), the sum of the MPS is 410,000. This is 10,000 above the production plan quantity. The master scheduler, however, is given some tolerances by management for making the sum of the MPS agree with the production plan. In this case, he is allowed a tolerance of plus or minus 5 percent. The 10,000 difference in the second month is only a 2.5 percent deviation.

If the sum of the items in the MPS exceeds the 5 percent tolerance, the master scheduler has to change some of the individual items. For example, if the sum of the MPS is low, the master scheduler could increase quantities or move work into one month from another month. If the sum of the MPS is high, the master scheduler could decrease quantities or schedule work into the future. To accomplish this, the master scheduler could use the individual MPS displays and the DRP displays to see how changing the MPS will affect distribution.

An MPS display shows the distribution demands for the product, and a DRP display shows the demand for each product at each DC. This gives the master scheduler a tremendous advantage in evaluating every item within every DC. As a result, he can do a more effective job of balancing supply and demand.

Using the MPS to Integrate Logistics with Manufacturing and Purchasing

In DRP, the distribution requirements end at the MPS. In manufacturing, everything begins with the MPS—all of the supporting manufacturing schedules are based on the MPS. The MPS is exploded, and demands for components and raw materials are created. This is done in the same way that the planned shipments to distribution centers are shown as demands on the MPS report.

For example, let's look at the MPS for vitamin C tablets to see how it is exploded and posted as requirements to the components. The MPS for this product appears in figure 5-5, as well as the MRP display for the K391 bottle, which is one of the component parts required to package the finished product, in this case the vitamin C tablet.

The MRP display is used to plan components and raw materials in the same way that the DRP display is used to plan an item in a DC. Notice that the gross requirements of 1,100 in week 1 are generated by the MPS for the vitamin C product packaged in 100 tablets per bottle. The gross requirements line shows the demands for the product. In this case, there

Master Production Schedule
Vitamin C Tablet 100/Bottle

	Past	Week							
	Due	1	2	3	4	5	6	7	8
Master Schedule-Rcpt.					1100				
Master Schedule-Start		1100							

MRP Display
K391 Bottle

On Hand Balance — 1500
Safety Stock   — 0
Lead Time   — 5 wks
Order Quantity   — 6000

	Past	Week							
	Due	1	2	3	4	5	6	7	8
Gross Requirements		1100	0	0	3300	0	0	2100	0
Scheduled Receipts					6000				
Projected On Hand	1500	400	400	400	3100	3100	3100	1000	1000
Planned Order Releases									

Figure 5-5

are other demands of 3,300 in week 4 and 2,100 in week 7, created by other products that use the same bottle.

The scheduled receipts line in the MRP display shows the released orders at the date they are due to arrive in stock. If the item is manufactured, the orders constitute released manufactured orders. If the item is purchased, it is considered a released purchase order. In our example, the bottle is purchased. In figure 5-5, the purchase order for 6,000 is due in week 4.

The projected on hand line is the same type of calculation shown in the DRP and MPS displays.

The planned order releases line contains any planned orders for the item. These are the same as the planned orders in the DRP display. They are created by the computer—figure 5-5 shows them at the release dates. The display does not show the planned orders at their receipt dates. This is just a convention; the planned orders can be shown at their receipt dates if so desired. The MRP display explained here is a key element within an MRP system.

The point is that the MPS is used to drive the schedules for all the components and raw materials. In addition, these schedules are used to calculate the capacity requirements by manufacturing work center. The MPS is the starting point for all scheduling in manufacturing. It is also the focal point between logistics and manufacturing. Problems between these two functional areas tend to surface at the MPS development when it is unable to meet distribution demands.

The solutions to such problems don't necessarily require changing the MPS. Rather, the MPS gives the problem visibility. Sometimes problems can be solved in logistics; other times they must be rectified in manufacturing or purchasing. Only as a final solution is the MPS changed. The important thing for a manager to realize is that there are opportunities in all four areas to solve problems.

Problems can be eliminated in logistics by manipulating the distribution plan as developed by DRP. If more product is needed than can be supplied, it is possible to reduce the demands. One way to do this is to reduce the quantity shipped to the DCs. Another is to drop below safety stock. In addition, there are a number of other methods that are available to logistics people.

Problems can be solved in manufacturing and purchasing by working overtime or extra shifts, using alternate equipment, splitting lot sizes, reducing move and queue times, etc. These methods will be explained in chapters 6 and 8.

And, problems can be resolved by changing the MPS itself. This is generally the last resort, however, the objective is to meet the MPS and change it only if there is no alternative.

The DRP display and the MRP display in figure 5-5 work in the same way. People in manufacturing and purchasing can see and understand how logistics operates, and, in turn, people in logistics can see and understand how manufacturing and purchasing operate. The same principles, the same methods, and even the same, or similar, reports are used for logistics, manufacturing, and purchasing. Whether someone is looking at an item in a DC or a manufactured or purchased item, the same logic is used. The system provides visibility from purchasing into manufacturing, and into logistics, and vice versa. This type of visibility, combined with the use of a common system using one common logic across the internal product supply pipeline, promotes communication, a better appreciation of the other person's problems, and teamwork. This common system crosses organizational boundaries, and allows people to work together.

In addition, when DRP is combined with production planning, master scheduling, and MRP, it tends to make some of the conventional ideas about inventory management across functional areas obsolete. Customer-service objectives are no longer a function of finding the correct inventory levels or target inventories. Customer service becomes a function of how well MPS, shop and supplier scheduling, and execution problems are identified and corrected.

Although this is a more difficult environment, it is a better simulation of the real world. DRP doesn't pretend that people can sit back and pick a number or use a formula to eliminate problems. Solutions result from identifying problems and then taking action. DRP—combined with production planning, master production scheduling, and MRP—makes it possible to identify these problems when there is still time to act.

CONCLUSION

The integration of DRP with the MPS and MRP gives a single, continuous seamless system that uses one set of logic across purchasing, manufacturing, and logistics. Figure 5-6 shows this linkage.

We saw how DRP applies in a manufacturing company, which operates from a factory and services customers through DCs. Used in this way, DRP integrates logistics, manufacturing, and purchasing. DRP contributes to the abilities of users to effectively control ongoing activ-

**A Seamless Logistics, Manufacturing
& Purchasing Planning System**

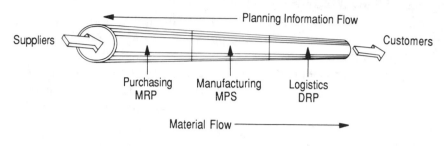

Figure 5-6

ities by comparing plans against operating budgets, as established in the sales & operations planning process.

Figure 5-7 shows this integration. The manufacturing integration makes possible this last step in integrating an entire marketing channel.

In chapter 1, I described the benefits of customer connectivity marketing. In chapter 4, I described how DRP applies to retailers and

An Integrated Logistics/Manufacturing System

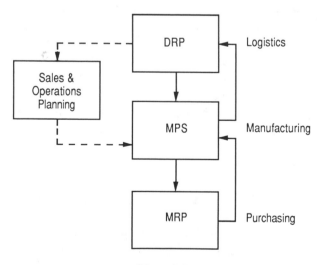

Figure 5-7

wholesaler/distributors. In this chapter you saw how it applies to manufacturing companies. Now total channel marketing integration is possible. In the Introduction, I gave you a vision of total channel integration. You should now be able to see how it all fits together. The rest of the book describes in significant detail how to use DRP to its maximum potential.

Chapter 6

Tools of the Trade

Getting the Most Out of a DRP System

Once the DRP management process is in place, many tools are at the disposal of its users for fine-tuning operating plans. This chapter describes how the tools are used. The following tools are available:

1. *The DRP display*: Either a printed report or a cathode ray tube (CRT) display, this is a tool that a supplier scheduler or distribution planner can use to plan an item. This same display also can be used to plan a manufactured or purchased item.

2. *The master schedule display*: Like the DRP display, this can be either a printed report or a CRT display. The master scheduler can use this to analyze the changes that have occurred for an item, and reevaluate the master production schedule. It can also be a supplier schedule if the item is purchased.

3. *Pegging*: This tool traces all the sources of the demands. Quite useful when all the demands for an item cannot be met, pegging is generally used only when a planner or master scheduler needs to find the source of the demands for an item.

4. *The firm planned order*: The firm planned order (FPO) allows a planner to override the order-planning logic and specify a date or a quantity for an order. It is used only when the planner wants to use a date or quantity that is different from what the order-planning logic would have calculated.

This chapter discusses each of these tools in depth in the context of a standard DRP display. The DRP display has two sections. One is the

Vancouver Distribution Center
Vitamin C Tablet 100/Bottle

On Hand Balance— 140
Safety Stock   — 50
Lead Time   — 3 wks
Order Quantity — 150

	Past Due	Week							
		1	2	3	4	5	6	7	8
Gross Requirements		20	25	15	20	30	25	15	30
Scheduled Receipts									
Projected On Hand	140	120	95	80	60	180	155	140	110
Planned Orders			150						

Figure 6-1

time-phased information—gross requirements, scheduled receipts, etc.—shown by date. This is covered in the explanation of how DRP works (chapter 3). The other section, see figure 6-1, is the descriptive information—the on-hand balance, the lead time, etc. It is described in detail in the following pages.

DRP Display

On-hand Balance

The on-hand balance is the quantity available for sale on the store shelves, in the stockroom, or in the distribution center. For a finished-goods stockroom or a DC, the on-hand balance is the quantity available to ship. For a component-parts or raw-material stockroom, the on-hand balance is the quantity available to issue to manufacturing. It does not include the quantity in transit or rejected material.

A high level of inventory accuracy is needed for DRP to work[1]; it will not work if inventory records are inaccurate. The on-hand balance is the beginning of the DRP calculation. If it is incorrect, everything that follows will be incorrect as well. Assume that the on-hand balance at the

---

[1] The only exception to this is the situation where replenish-up-to logic is used within DRP. Then, the accuracy of actual product movement becomes imperative.

Vancouver Distribution Center
Vitamin C Tablet 100/Bottle

On Hand Balance — 40
Safety Stock   — 50
Lead Time   — 3 wks
Order Quantity   — 150

	Past Due	Week							
		1	2	3	4	5	6	7	8
Gross Requirements		20	25	15	20	30	25	15	30
Scheduled Receipts									
Projected On Hand	40	20	-5	-20	-40				

Figure 6-2

Vancouver DC is 40 as shown in figure 6-2, and not 140, as shown in figure 6-1.

The distribution center is already below its planned safety stock, and next week, the product will be out of stock. Based on the old on-hand balance (figure 6-1), the next planned shipment to the DC is scheduled to arrive in week 5. In reality, this product is needed next week, as is a new planned order, which did not appear on the old report. A recalculated version of the DRP display appears in figure 6-3:

Vancouver Distribution Center
Vitamin C Tablet 100/Bottle

On Hand Balance — 40
Safety Stock   — 50
Lead Time   — 3 wks
Order Quantity   — 150

	Past Due	Week							
		1	2	3	4	5	6	7	8
Gross Requirements		20	25	15	20	30	25	15	30
Scheduled Receipts									
Projected On Hand	40	20	-5	-20	110	80	55	190	160
Planned Orders		150			150				

Figure 6-3

Several points are of particular interest. First, even if the scheduler realizes that Vancouver only has 40 on hand and makes a shipment, the product will not arrive until week 4, unless a faster, more expensive mode of transportation is used. That means Vancouver will be on back order for two weeks. This is no assurance, however, that the product is actually available in the supply source for immediate shipment. For instance, the planners at the supply source are planning to ship 150 to Vancouver in week 2, based on the old on-hand balance. It may be that there are 50 of this product available to ship, but it is also possible that Vancouver may be on back order beyond week 4.

Another ramification of this inventory error is the new planned order for 150 that appears in week 4. The people at the supply source have not planned for this demand, and will have to scramble to satisfy it. More than likely, DRP will help them respond, and they may be able to get the 150 that are needed. However, only so many of these surprises can be handled in a week. If this type of unexpected demand begins to occur at several inventory stocking locations (ISLs), planners and master schedulers may be unable to cope and the system may begin to collapse.

The opposite type of error, where more product is in inventory than the on-hand balance shows, also causes problems. Let's take the situation where 240 are really on hand instead of 140. In this case, the DRP display would look like this:

Vancouver Distribution Center
Vitamin C Tablet 100/Bottle

On Hand Balance — 240
Safety Stock — 50
Lead Time — 3 wks
Order Quantity — 150

	Past Due	Week							
		1	2	3	4	5	6	7	8
Gross Requirements		20	25	15	20	30	25	15	30
Scheduled Receipts									
Projected On Hand	240	220	195	180	160	130	105	90	60
Planned Orders									

Figure 6-4

In the situation shown in figure 6-4, Vancouver has enough in stock to satisfy the DC's needs to the end of week 8. No shipments are needed, but the DRP display calculated with the correct on-hand balance of 140 shows that a planned order should be shipped from the supply source in week 2.

Some people may say, "So what. It's better to have too much than not enough." But that's based on spurious logic. The obvious problem is that there is too much inventory in Vancouver. You have to pay for it, move it, and store it. The deeper problem, though, is the fact that the people at the supply source believe Vancouver needs a shipment in week 2. This may mean that other distribution centers or stores won't receive all the product they need if supplies are tight. In addition, in this example, if Vancouver is supplied from a factory, scarce manufacturing capacity or scarce materials may be used to produce the 150 units that are not really needed. As MRP pioneer Oliver Wight said repeatedly, "The real tragedy in business today is that we are using our scarce resources to make the wrong things."

Experience shows that a minimum inventory accuracy of 95 percent is needed to run DRP to yield the maximum benefits from the system. Because the accuracy of the on-hand balance is so critical to DRP, a number of things should be done to obtain and maintain that accuracy. See Appendix B.

Safety Stock

The second piece of descriptive information on the DRP display concerns safety stock, which is used to cover situations when the sales exceed the forecast.

Safety stock is handled differently in DRP than in traditional statistical inventory management systems. In the past, conventional wisdom said that the more safety stock, the better. The limitation was the amount of justifiable safety stock. Keeping all that safety stock was expensive, so studies were done to evaluate where it was needed most, what items had the most forecast variance, etc. But the idea was still the same—the more safety stock you could justify, the better customer service would be.

In reality, too much safety stock doesn't improve customer service; rather, it has a deteriorating effect. The application of the JIT/TQC philosophy proves this. Too much inventory hides problems; it's a liability and should be considered wasteful because the system no longer tells the truth about what and when product is needed. The strength of

Vancouver Distribution Center
Vitamin C Tablet 100/Bottle

BEFORE ADDING THE LARGE SAFETY STOCK QUANTITY
On Hand Balance — 140
Safety Stock   — 50
Lead Time   — 3 wks
Order Quantity   — 150

	Past Due	Week							
		1	2	3	4	5	6	7	8
Gross Requirements		20	25	15	20	30	25	15	30
Scheduled Receipts									
Projected On Hand	140	120	95	80	60	180	155	140	110
Planned Orders			150						

AFTER ADDING THE LARGE SAFETY STOCK QUANTITY
On Hand Balance— 140
Safety Stock   — 200
Lead Time   — 3 wks
Order Quantity   — 150

	Past Due	Week							
		1	2	3	4	5	6	7	8
Gross Requirements		20	25	15	20	30	25	15	30
Scheduled Receipts									
Projected On Hand	140	120	95	230	210	330	305	290	260
Planned Orders	150		150						

Figure 6-5

DRP is that it reliably shows the needs in terms of quantities and dates that items are needed. An excess of safety stock in the system weakens the integrity of the calculations.

Let's increase the safety stock from 50 to 200 at the Vancouver DC. A safety stock of 200 in Vancouver should result in excellent customer service, according to the old rules. The top of figure 6-5 shows the situation before safety stock is changed: the bottom shows the effect of the increased safety stock.

In comparing the two displays, the result of the increased stock is to create a new planned order for 150 due to be shipped from the supply source immediately. If this type of safety stock is added to all items, then the same situation will occur across the board with the result that the demand on the supply source jumps dramatically. Figure 6-6 shows the distribution demand on the supply source before and after the safety stocks have been added to several DCs:

Supply Source
Vitamin C Tablet 100/Bottle

BEFORE LARGE SAFETY STOCKS
On Hand Balance — 1700
Safety Stock　　— 0
Lead Time　　　— 3 wks
Order Quantity　— 1100

	Past Due	Week							
		1	2	3	4	5	6	7	8
Distribution Demands	300	300	150	750	450	300	300	0	0
Scheduled Receipts									
Projected On Hand	1400	1100	950	200	850	550	250	250	250
Master Schedule-Rcpt.					1100				
Master Schedule-Start		1100							

AFTER LARGE SAFETY STOCKS
On Hand Balance — 1700
Safety Stock　　— 0
Lead Time　　　— 3 wks
Order Quantity　— 1100

	Past Due	Week							
		1	2	3	4	5	6	7	8
Distribution Demands	450	300	1050	1050	450	300	300	450	0
Scheduled Receipts									
Projected On Hand	1250	950	-100	-1150	-500	-800	-1100	-1550	-1550
Master Schedule-Rcpt.					1100				
Master Schedule-Start		1100							

Figure 6-6

The MPS[2] is adequate to satisfy the demands from the distribution system before the large safety stocks are added. Once the safety stocks are increased, though, the MPS seems hopelessly insufficient. The reason is that the system is asking the master scheduler to satisfy the safety stocks right away. This creates a transient, or start-up, problem. To satisfy the new safety stocks, the MPS will have to be increased by adding two new MPS orders, as shown in figure 6-7.

Supply Source
Vitamin C Tablet 100/Bottle

On Hand Balance — 1700
Safety Stock   — 0
Lead Time   — 3 wks
Order Quantity   — 1100

	Past Due	Week							
		1	2	3	4	5	6	7	8
Distribution Demands	450	300	1050	1050	450	300	300	450	0
Scheduled Receipts									
Projected On Hand	1250	950	-100	-1150	600	300	0	650	650
Master Schedule-Rcpt.					2200			1100	
Master Schedule-Start		2200			1100				

Figure 6-7

Even if the new MPS orders are started immediately, and if the lead time is reduced from the normal three weeks, there will still be a week or two where the supply at the supply source will not be enough to satisfy the demands from the DCs. An additional problem is how to produce the two additional orders of 1,100 due in weeks 4 and 7. Where will manufacturing get the capacity and the materials to satisfy this demand?

Two aspects of this example need to be discussed. The first is to demonstrate the sudden demand that arises from significantly increasing

[2] If the supply source is a factory, changes in distribution demand will directly impact the MPS. If, however, the source is a DC supporting other DCs or stores, changes in distribution demands will impact the supplier schedules.

safety stocks. DRP tries to satisfy this additional demand, and, in doing so, the demands from the distribution system are likely to outstrip manufacturing's ability to produce.

The second point is that even after the initial surge of demand, the information from the system is questionable, and the demands are distorted. For example, the quantities are requested earlier than they would be without safety stock.

This becomes a significant problem when there is a limited amount of manufacturing capacity product at the source. In these situations, the distribution system must show real demands—accurate information that tells what is needed and when. Unfortunately, because of the large safety stocks, the system fails at a crucial point. As a result, we have to develop some other system so that scarce capacity or materials are used to the best advantage.

This is not to say that safety stocks should not be used. There are some legitimate uses for safety stock with DRP. However, the type of large safety stocks in the above example will prevent DRP from working well. Large safety stock is waste and should be avoided.

An argument can be made for keeping safety stock at supply sources. Safety stock can be used to ship to any ISL that needs it. On the other hand, supply sources do not have the same uncertainty of demand as stores or DCs. DRP is able to calculate distribution demands on supply sources, resulting in less uncertainty in demand and, consequently, less need for safety stock. The net result of these two conflicting factors is that there is still some uncertainty of demand at supply sources, and any safety stock stored there could be used to supply any stocking location. Therefore, most companies choose to keep some safety stock at supply sources. A golden rule to be adopted is to wait to commit inventory until the last possible moment.

The key issue with determining and using safety stocks with DRP is the credibility of the purchase/manufacturing schedules. If the schedules developed using safety-stock quantities are credible, those safety-stock quantities are realistic and reasonable. If, however, the schedules developed are not a credible description of the demand from the distribution system, the safety-stock quantities will be unrealistic.

Let's take some real situations as examples of the proper use of safety stock. In one situation, the lead time from supply sources to stocking locations is long, about five weeks, and the demand on the stocking location is a forecast. Sometimes the sales are greater than the forecast, sometimes less. In this example, the sales for the product are within plus or minus 20 percent of the forecast each month.

Such a situation is a legitimate use for safety stock. There may be a week or two where the sales are above forecast, and, at the same time, the on-hand balance is low (just before delivery of the next shipment). In case of a stock out, it is possible to send a special shipment by air freight or courier service to arrive before the normal shipment, which is in transit. This solution, though, can be prohibitively expensive.

The best way to handle the problem is by using safety stock. In this particular situation, the safety-stock quantity is not more than a week or two of forecasted demand. Remember that the amount of safety stock is not derived from a precise calculation. Rather, it is based on consideration of several factors that affect the need for safety stock. One is the lead time, which, in this case, is five weeks. This is fairly long for a stocking location, so there is a good possibility that there will be some weeks where the sales exceed the forecast.

Another factor is the variance between the actual sales and the forecast. In this case, the variance has been plus or minus 20 percent, measured over a four-week period. This could mean that each week might vary by 20 percent, but more than likely some weeks will vary as much as 50 to 100 percent. By having a week or two of safety stock, the stocking location can handle most variations, even if they occur when the on-hand balance is low.

Some people may argue with this simple approach because it is not based on complex algorithms and only yields an approximation. But with DRP, you don't need to perform difficult calculations to determine safety stock because DRP provides an early warning system that detects and reports changes to enable you to respond before you run out of product. In a statistical inventory management system, no action is taken until the reorder point is reached. The fact that things are happening at a faster or slower rate than anticipated is not apparent to the people operating the system. The reorder-point system is blind until the reorder point is hit.

With DRP, planners and master schedulers are alerted to the altered situation and can begin to take action. If, for example, sales are above forecast, planners can deliver the product to stocking locations earlier than originally scheduled.

Finally, approximations work well in practice because the safety-stock quantity can be monitored and adjusted as needed. DRP is a superb monitoring and tracking tool. If a safety-stock quantity you picked seems to be working well, stick with it. If, however, you find there are still situations when the stocking locations are out of product, look at factors such as lead time, forecast, and forecast error, and then make another try. The ability to refine these estimates for safety stocks in the real world is more valuable than all the sophisticated formulas and calculations combined.

Safety Stock Versus Safety Time

Two techniques can be used to provide safety stock with DRP. One is to set a safety-stock quantity. This is the method used in the above examples. The other method is to set a safety time. The safety-time method schedules the planned orders and scheduled receipts into stock for a specified period of time before they are actually needed. Figure 6-8 shows how safety time versus safety stock works. The first display in figure 6-8 shows a safety time of 2 weeks. The second display shows a safety stock of 50 items:

Vancouver Distribution Center
Vitamin C Tablet 100/Bottle

On Hand Balance — 140
Safety Time   — 2 wks
Lead Time   — 3 wks
Order Quantity — 150

	Past Due	Week							
		1	2	3	4	5	6	7	8
Gross Requirements		20	25	15	20	30	25	15	30
Scheduled Receipts									
Projected On Hand	140	120	95	80	60	180	155	140	110
Planned Orders			150						

Figure 6-8

On Hand Balance — 140
Safety Stock   — 50
Lead Time   — 3 wks
Order Quantity   — 150

	Past Due	Week							
		1	2	3	4	5	6	7	8
Gross Requirements		20	25	15	20	30	25	15	30
Scheduled Receipts									
Projected On Hand	140	120	95	80	60	180	155	140	110
Planned Orders			150						

Figure 6-8 (continued)

The timing approach to safety stock calculates the planned-order due date based on the date the projected on-hand balance will be less than zero. In figure 6-8, the projected on-hand balance will go negative in week 7, which is the planned-order due date. The planned order is then backed off by the lead time for the item.

In this situation, the planned orders are identical using either a safety time of two weeks or a safety stock of 50. Basically, safety stock and safety time are different ways of expressing the same thing. Safety time, though, is easier to maintain since you can decide on one week, two weeks, etc., rather than calculating 50, 45, and so on. This compensates for changes in the forecast quantity. If, for example, the forecast doubles, safety time will not have to be changed, and a safety-stock quantity will not have to be recalculated.

There are some situations where safety stock and safety time do not act in the same way. If an item has an intermittent demand, for example, a demand of 500 the current week, 0 for the next nine weeks, and 500 in week 11, safety stock and safety time will act differently. A safety stock of 50 on this item will keep 50 on hand all the time. A safety time of one week will not keep a quantity on hand all the time, but will allow the on-hand balance to drop to zero when there are no requirements. Safety time will schedule the order one week before the demand.

Lead Time

Lead time is the time required from the release of an order to the time it is received at the store, stockroom or DC. For logistics, lead time starts from the moment you determine that you need product to the time inventory is available to fill customer orders to be picked.

For logistics, lead time is comprised of several components:

1. *Order release and picking at the supply source*: The time required to release, pick, and pack the items to be shipped.

2. *Loading*: The time needed to load trucks or railcars.

3. *In transit*: The time it takes to get from supply sources to stocking locations.

4. *Unloading and put away*: The time it takes to unload trucks or railcars and put product away.

Two aspects of lead time are critical to understand: (1) lead times are only approximate, and sophisticated techniques for calculating and determining them do not help, and (2) lead times for distribution purposes are more relatively fixed than lead times for manufacturing or purchasing, although there are exceptions.

Lead times are estimates of how long the different activities listed above will take. For example, most companies are able to pick and load all within the same day, even within hours. In such a situation, the lead time for operations will be one day, so it doesn't make any sense to attempt to refine the lead time any further.

The in-transit lead time depends on the type of transportation and how far the product has to go. For example, a railcar shipment from a supply facility in Chicago to New York generally requires one week. Therefore, the in-transit part of the lead time will be one week; it doesn't make much sense to try to refine this to a more precise number. It is important to keep an eye on the in-transit lead time and try to keep it short, but exerting a great deal of effort to determine exactly what the lead time should be down to the fraction of a day won't yield much of a return.

Also, actual in-transit lead time is not always consistent. One time it may be slightly more than a week, another time it may be somewhat less. The difference varies according to level of service that the transportation company provides, the weather, etc. However, delays are exceptions and, unless they become the norm, the lead time should not be made longer to compensate. The lead time that should be used with DRP is the normal quoted lead time. This is the amount of time the transportation company says will be required to move the product from the supply source to the distribution point.

DRP uses a standard lead time, but generates reschedule messages to indicate when lead times must be compressed or extended. This is because DRP uses this one-week lead time on all planned orders shipped from Chicago to New York. The lead time shown with DRP must be an accurate representation of the normal lead time, or the system cannot portray reality. Once lead times are determined and given to DRP for planning purposes, they become fixed.

There are some situations where the lead time can be compressed. These are exceptional cases in which products are shipped via a faster and normally more expensive mode of transportation, for example, when a product is crucially needed because a planned shipment is delayed in transit, etc. In such a situation, the lead time will be compressed, although the shorter lead time is not used with DRP. The total lead time used with DRP is based on the normal mode of transportation, plus the time it takes to release, pick, pack, load, ship, receive, and put away an order.

Order Quantity

Four factors to consider when developing order quantities for distributing products are frequency of shipment, economic order quantity calculation, shipping unit, and total weight and cube.

1. *Frequency*: The frequency of shipment to a stocking location must be used to determine the order quantities for the items stored in the stocking location. If a store or DC receives only one shipment per month, the order quantity for the items must be in multiples of the quantity used each month (one month's supply, two months' supply, etc.). If, however, a store or DC receives a shipment every day, the frequency of shipment is not really important in determining the order quantity.

2. *EOQ*: The economic order quantity calculation is a method to calculate the theoretically most economic order quantity, and takes into

account the ordering and carrying costs. Under ideal circumstances, this order quantity will cost the least in number of orders and dollars over the course of a year. Several important aspects of the EOQ are:

a. The EOQ calculation is based on approximations. It assumes that the demand is the same each week, that there is a known cost for ordering, a known cost for carrying inventory, etc. These are just estimates, so any calculation based on these numbers will only be an estimate as well.

b. A precise calculation of the EOQ is not important. Any approximate EOQ will give nearly the same effect.

c. Too many people have blind faith that if each order quantity is calculated correctly by means of a formula, the sum of the order quantities will be correct. There is no reason why this should be true. In fact, the odds are very strong that it won't be. A constraint such as size of the storage location would not condone buying a new warehouse to stock "economical" order quantities. Or there may be a limit to the amount of money that management wants to invest in inventory, and there is no reason why the individual order quantities should happen to total this limit.

Order quantities don't take into account shipping frequency, and the EOQ formula itself has a fatal flaw in that it assumes a linear relationship between the amount of inventory and costs and the number of orders and costs. When a stocking location is filled, a new warehouse is needed. But until the present warehouse becomes so overcrowded that it is difficult to store material efficiently, there is no increase in the warehouse cost as inventory increases.

d. If you are moving inventory from location A to location B within the same company, most of the costs used to compute inventory carrying costs simply don't apply.

The perspective, then, on EOQ is that it is a helpful estimate in determining order quantities. It represents one factor—the balancing of ordering and carrying costs when you purchase the product. However, it is just an estimate and, therefore, only one of the factors to be considered in developing order quantities.

3. *Shipping unit*: For most products, there is a shipping quantity that makes sense from a material handling and storage point of view. These are quantities such as the amount that will fit on a pallet, on a

tier, in a storage container, etc. Any order quantity should be a multiple of these quantities. These shipping quantities, based on material handling and storage, are not necessarily the same as the selling quantities.

4. *Total weight and cube*: The total weight and cube, or volume, is a critical factor in freight costs to stocking locations. Freight rates for trucks and railcars are based on weight, and the cube is limited. The objective is to get optimum use of the car or truck by filling it with a mix of product that uses the available cube and, at the same time, gives the most weight.

Order quantities can be useful in achieving logistics goals. For example, let's consider the case where a small, heavy product is shipped every two weeks, and another product, which is light and bulky, is shipped every six weeks. The light, bulky product might take an entire railcar every six weeks because of cube. Yet, the small, heavy product does not utilize the entire cube when it is shipped every two weeks. By changing the order quantity of the light, bulky product to every two weeks, it can be used to fill the unused cube in the railcars at no additional cost. In addition, this may eliminate the extra railcars needed every six weeks.

There are some situations, like the above example, when the solution is obvious. But there are also a number of similar situations that are not as easy to see. Logistics people need some tools to recognize and manage the mix of products being shipped. DRP provides the tools; chapter 9 provides the details for its use.

Order Policies

The DRP examples so far have used what is called a "fixed order policy." Order policies are methods used to calculate the planned order quantities. Fixed order policy means that an order quantity has been specified and that planned orders are made equal to that quantity. This is the most common order policy.

A number of other order policies are also in use. For example, there are order policies in which the quantity is recalculated for each planned order. One simple calculation is lot-for-lot (sometimes referred to as "discrete order quantity") ordering. Lot-for-lot ordering means that the planned order quantity is made equal to the unsatisfied requirements. If 20 are needed, the planned order will be for 20. If 53 are needed, the planned order will be 53. This type of ordering makes sense where the setup and ordering costs are low. Usually, it not used for distribution items, since it means that the same item would be shipped to each stocking location each week. There are, however, some situations when this type of ordering can be used for fast moving, large volume items.

"Period order quantity" is another order policy that can be used with DRP. With period order quantity, a time period is specified instead of a quantity. All the requirements during that time period are added together to arrive at the planned order quantity. Period order quantity creates planned orders that equal a specified number of weeks or days of demand.

There are a number of situations in logistics where period order quantity can be used. Many times, the best way to specify the order quantity for a product in a stocking location is by the number of weeks of supply (e.g., one week or two weeks of supply). When period order quantities are used, the planned order quantities would equal requirements over the specified number of weeks.

More complicated order policies include "least total cost" (also known as "part period balancing"), "least unit cost," or the "Wagner-Whitin algorithm." These order policies attempt to compensate for some of the approximations in the EOQ calculation. They calculate the order quantity that balances the ordering and carrying costs for a demand that may differ week to week (50 one week, 25 the next, etc.). To put it another way, these order policies arrive at nearly the same number as an EOQ calculation if the demand is the same in each week.

A number of problems can occur with these order policies. One is that the balancing of ordering and carrying costs only applies if product is purchased. Moreover, it is only one of several factors that must be considered in developing an order quantity. Another is that because the order quantity is calculated by the computer, it is outside the control of the people using the system. That means the people using the system cannot be held accountable for any ordering or rescheduling because the computer has recalculated the order quantity. For these reasons, least total cost/part period balancing, least unit cost, and the Wagner-Whitin algorithm are not recommended.

It's easy to lose overall perspective when considering order quantity calculations. Conventional inventory management systems direct an inappropriate amount of attention at how much to order—once considered to be one of the most critical questions. With DRP, the important thing is what is needed and when it is needed. The right order quantity is useless if it doesn't arrive when it is needed. The real benefits come from making a valid plan and then executing it.

Additional Descriptive Information

The DRP displays in most companies include more descriptive information than the items explained above. Other information that may appear can have a great deal of value to the buyer, the planner, or supplier scheduler, and is available in most DRP packages. The additional descriptive information often includes item description, unit of measure, costs, including material cost, labor cost, and overhead cost, shelf life, buyer code, planner code, item type, inventory class, etc.

Action Messages

In addition to the DRP display, the logic in the system will search for, and detect, conditions that may require some action from the buyer, the planner, or supplier scheduler. For example, the DRP logic will look for and highlight any planned orders that are due for release. These are the planned shipments to the stocking location or the planned purchases from supply sources.

Action messages are also generated for shipments that are in transit, and are scheduled to arrive either too late or too early. In most cases, the planner or buyer will not act on these messages because there is generally no way to speed up or slow down the products that are in transit. These messages, however, are available to people and, in some special cases, they may choose to ship or request a shipment from the supplier through a faster mode of transportation because the shipment in transit will not arrive in time. If DRP is used to generate supplier schedules, action messages are generated for items to be shipped within a specified period negotiated with suppliers. In these instances, planners, buyers, and supplier schedulers attempt to work with the action messages for products not yet shipped. An example of this was given in chapter 4 in the supplier scheduling concept section.

The DRP logic also generates a number of miscellaneous action messages. These are messages for situations such as a negative on-hand balance, an order quantity that is too large, an on-hand balance that is below safety stock, etc.

These messages are all useful pieces of information, but people in logistics do not use them to the same extent as the master scheduler or the planner in manufacturing does. The master scheduler uses the action messages to help change the MPS. The planners in manufacturing and purchasing are usually able to speed up or slow down purchase orders based on when they are needed. Many distribution companies, however, do not print the action messages for in-transit orders that are arriving too early or too late unless the stockout is going to be serious.

One of the best, but sometimes most frustrating, features of action messages is the fact that DRP never forgets. Each time an item is planned with DRP, it is examined for all the action messages. Since the system never forgets, the action messages continue to appear until the problem is resolved. People working with DRP have said that it's like having your own policeman. But it can sometimes be frustrating to be continually reminded of the problems you have not yet resolved.

Using DRP

A buyer, a supplier scheduler, or a distribution planner using DRP works with the action messages and the display. The action messages may be a separate listing, or they may be listed on the display. If the messages are listed on the display, the planner will need some indication of which items have an action message and which do not. Most planners and buyers look only at the items with action messages and do not look at the remaining items. When DRP first runs for a group of items, the planners and buyers should review each item to make sure that the information DRP is using makes sense.

The planners and buyers are not the only people who look regularly at the DRP display; product managers, order entry and customer service personnel, salespeople, or anyone else interested in the status of a product also use the display. They can see when in-transit shipments are due to arrive, if an item is predicted to go on back order, and whether or not they can fill an unusually large customer order without jeopardizing the remaining customers. With the DRP display, people can intelligently answer customers' questions like when a product will be available, what quantity will be available, etc. For this reason, the DRP display needs to be available to those who need to know the information it provides.

There is also another important reason for making the DRP display available to the people in inventory stocking locations. These people have a tremendous amount of knowledge about the products and the customers. People in stocking locations, for example, have made tremendous contributions to the planning process. One distribution center manager looked at his DRP display and realized that the forecast for a key item didn't show the ordering pattern of a large customer who ordered every three weeks. The forecast showed a constant 50 a week, when this customer actually always ordered 70 units in the third week of the month. The DC manager called the distribution planner, who adjusted the forecast to show the way the actual customer orders were likely to occur.

The irony was that this situation had been going on for years, but the DC manager never had the visibility to see the forecast. As a result, he never really had a way to convey this information.

As you can see, the DRP display is a tremendous communications tool to make people at a stocking location that services customers a close part of the overall planning process. Everyone benefits when these employees get involved and feed information to buyers, manufacturing people, and to sales and marketing people.

Planning Horizon

The planning horizon is not part of the descriptive information of the DRP display. It is, however, an important part of the system since it determines how far DRP looks into the future. Anything beyond the planning horizon is unknown to DRP. This means that if you want information from DRP, the planning horizon has to extend into the future at least as far as the date you are investigating.

One approach is to make the planning horizon extend far into the future, say ten years. Although this approach will cover many situations, it has some limitations. Because DRP is quite specific, predicting events this far into the future is somewhat meaningless, as predictions are just not that accurate several years ahead. Another limitation is that all this information will be stored and manipulated each week. Storage and manipulation can be expensive, so most people opt for a shorter planning horizon.

The shortest planning horizon that will work with DRP is based on the total cumulative lead time. The total cumulative lead time is the span of time from the date the first raw materials or purchased items are ordered until finished products are delivered to the distribution centers or stores for sale. This includes the lead time for raw materials and purchased items, the lead time for manufacturing, and the lead time for distribution. Figure 6-9 shows the cumulative lead time for a tablet product.

In this example, the total cumulative lead time of 18 weeks covers procurement, granulation, compression and coating, packaging, and distribution lead times:

Cumulative Lead Time For a Tablet

								WEEK									
1	2	3	4	5	6	7	8	9	10	11	12	13	14	15	16	17	18

```
                                                          Distribution
                                                          Lead time 3
                                              Packaging
                                              Lead time 3
                                Compression
                                & Coating
                                Lead time 3
                  Granulation
                  Lead time 3
Procurement
Lead time 6
```

Figure 6-9

Assume for a moment that the planning horizon in DRP is 12 weeks, as shown in figure 6-10.

Under this scenario, the purchasing people always try to get deliveries from suppliers in less than the quoted lead times. Some of this purchased material will be late, and the manufacturing and logistics people will constantly be asked to make up the lost time. If they cannot make up the lost time, the MPS will be missed and customer service will suffer. This type of short lead-time scheduling can work occasionally, but it makes no sense as a normal method of operating.

Therefore, the minimum planning horizon for DRP should be at least as long as the longest cumulative lead time. There are a number of reasons why the planning horizon may need to be even longer, and many companies have other types of lead times that are longer. These are lead times for evaluating and purchasing new capital equipment, predicting

Cumulative Lead Time For a Tablet

											WEEK							
-6	-5	-4	-3	-2	-1	0	1	2	3	4	5	6	7	8	9	10	11	12

```
                                                              Distribution
                                                              Lead time 3
                                             Packaging
                                             Lead time 3
                                Compression
                                & Coating
                                Lead time 3
                   Granulation
                   Lead time 3
Procurement
Lead time 6
```

Figure 6-10

manufacturing and warehouse space requirements, predicting inventory investment levels, budgeting, etc. If these are longer than the cumulative material lead times, and they often are, the planning horizon for DRP should be long enough to provide visibility in these areas as well. Many companies today have planning horizons that run 18 to 24 months in the future. Many companies also run simulations several times a year that extend four to five years.

Master Production Schedule Display in Manufacturing

If you are a retailer, wholesaler, or distributor, you may wish to skip this next section. On the other hand, if you are interested in knowing how the "other half lives" and what manufacturers have to do to supply your needs, read on. Remember, knowledge is power.

Descriptive Information

The MPS display is quite similar to the DRP display. Both displays have a section showing descriptive information and a section showing time-phased information.

The descriptive information for the MPS display is much the same as the one for the DRP display. One difference is that the order quantity in the MPS display is for the information of the master scheduler only. It is not used to calculate planned orders; rather, as explained in chapter 5 in the manufacturing section, the MPS logic does not automatically generate master schedule orders. Rather, it shows where an order is needed. The master scheduler is responsible for actually creating and maintaining the orders.

Time-Phased Information

The time-phased information in the MPS display in figure 6-11 is reproduced from figure 5-2 in chapter 5.

Bear in mind that the distribution demands for the MPS items do not all have to come from the different DCs. It may be that the factory acts as the DC for the local area. In such a situation, the distribution demands are the demands from the other DCs, plus the forecast of material needed to supply the local customers.

Several methods are available to take the planned orders at the DCs and post them as distribution demands to the MPS display. The two most common are:

1. bills of distribution.

2. a computer program.

Either method can be used, and both are workable. One uses a bill of distribution; the other uses a computer program to link the DCs to the MPS. (See Appendix C for a detailed discussion of the two methods.)

Action Messages

The MPS displays the same type of action messages as those generated by the DRP display. These messages include MPS orders due earlier or later than scheduled, messages for orders that are due for release, and miscellaneous exceptions.

In addition, the MPS logic includes an action message that does not appear with DRP—"Not enough in the schedule to satisfy demands." With DRP or MRP, this message is unnecessary because the logic will create planned orders whenever there is not enough to satisfy the demands. But the MPS is manually set by the master scheduler rather than

Supply Source
Vitamin C Tablet 100/Bottle

On Hand Balance — 1700
Safety Stock   — 0
Lead Time   — 3 wks
Order Quantity — 1100

	Past Due	Week								
		1	2	3	4	5	6	7	8
Distribution Demands	300	300	150	750	450	300	300	0	0
Scheduled Receipts									
Projected On Hand	1400	1100	950	200	850	550	250	250	250
Master Schedule-Rcpt.					1100				
Master Schedule-Start		1100							

Figure 6-11

by the system. Therefore, an action message is needed to notify the master scheduler that he should consider adding to the MPS.

Using the MPS Display

Master schedulers use the MPS display in much the same ways as distribution planners use the DRP display. Typically, master schedulers work with the action messages and the MPS display. The display may appear on a printout of the action messages, or it may appear on a CRT. If the action messages and the MPS display are combined then master schedulers generally need some indication that shows them which items have action messages and which do not. There are some situations, however, where this is unnecessary. For example, sometimes nearly all items have action messages. In other cases, the number of items master scheduled is small enough so that master schedulers have no difficulty reviewing each item once a week.

The rescheduling action messages are important to the master scheduler because they point to the situations where orders are due to arrive earlier or later than when they are needed or when more should be added to the MPS. This enables the master scheduler to work by exception and concentrate on the items where the MPS may need to be changed. Although master schedulers do not have to change the MPS just because there is an action message, they should review the situation and decide what course of actions makes the most sense.

Even though the review of the MPS is done by the master scheduler, the process of evaluating and changing the schedule is one that affects many people within the company. And, the evaluation and discussion prior to making a change to the MPS, often involve other people in the company. To see why this is so, let's work through an MPS example. We'll assume that the forecast for a number of items at the DCs is increased significantly. Figure 6-12 shows the MPS display before the change in forecast (distribution demands), as well as the same display after the change.

As you can see in figure 6-12, after the change in forecast, the MPS at the bottom is no longer sufficient to cover what is needed. The 1,100 due in week 4 are needed two weeks earlier, and more product must be added to the MPS. A master scheduler looking at this display would first verify that the numbers make sense.

The master scheduler would then develop a first-cut MPS to satisfy the demands. The first-cut MPS might look like the one in figure 6-13.

The master scheduler has rescheduled the order due in week 4 so that it is now due in week 2. In addition, the master scheduler has added two orders (one due in week 3 and one due in week 6). Notice that the first two MPS orders are already overdue at the start. That is because the 2,200 bottles shown in the past-due week should have been started before the current week.

Before the master scheduler can make the change to the MPS, he must verify that it can be done. To do this, the master scheduler will have to go to production and inventory control to determine if there is enough material and packaging to begin the production of 2,200 bottles of this product right away. He will also have to check on material for the third order of 1,100 due to start in week 3. The master scheduler must then go to manufacturing to determine whether there is enough capacity to manufacture 2,200 bottles, and if the bottles can be made available in less than normal lead time. In addition, the master scheduler must calculate whether there is sufficient capacity to add another lot of 1,100 bottles starting in week 3.

For the purpose of this example, let's assume that the master scheduler finds that material is available today to fill 1,100 bottles, but there are

Supply Source
Vitamin C Tablet 100/Bottle

BEFORE CHANGE IN FORECAST
On Hand Balance — 1700
Safety Stock   — 0
Lead Time   — 3 wks
Order Quantity — 1100

	Past Due	Week							
		1	2	3	4	5	6	7	8
Distribution Demands	300	300	150	750	450	300	300	0	0
Scheduled Receipts									
Projected On Hand	1400	1100	950	200	850	550	250	250	250
Master Schedule-Rcpt.					1100				
Master Schedule-Start		1100							

AFTER CHANGE IN FORECAST
On Hand Balance — 1700
Safety Stock   — 0
Lead Time   — 3 wks
Order Quantity — 1100

	Past Due	Week							
		1	2	3	4	5	6	7	8
Distribution Demands	450	700	1050	750	500	450	150	300	150
Scheduled Receipts									
Projected On Hand	1250	550	-500	-1250	-650	-1100	-1250	-1550	-1700
Master Schedule-Rcpt.					1100				
Master Schedule-Start		1100							

Figure 6-12

Supply Source
Vitamin C Tablet 100/Bottle

FIRST-CUT MASTER PRODUCTION SCHEDULE
On Hand Balance — 1700
Safety Stock   — 0
Lead Time   — 3 wks
Order Quantity — 1100

	Past Due	Week							
		1	2	3	4	5	6	7	8
Distribution Demands	450	700	1050	750	500	450	150	300	150
Scheduled Receipts									
Projected On Hand	1250	550	600	950	450	0	950	650	500
Master Schedule-Rcpt.			1100	1100			1100		
Master Schedule-Start	2200			1100					

Figure 6-13

not enough bulk tablets to fill 2,200 bottles. So the second batch of 1,100 bottles will have to wait for a week while a batch of bulk tablets, now in production, can be rushed through production. We'll also assume that material can be obtained for the third order of 1,100 bottles by the time it is scheduled to start in week 3.

In manufacturing, the master scheduler found that there is enough capacity to fill 1,100 bottles starting this week, 1,100 bottles starting next week, and 1,100 bottles starting in week 3. Overtime will be required, but the capacity is available. In addition, the first batch of 1,100 bottles can be completed in two weeks instead of the normal three weeks, by working two shifts on Saturday. But the people in manufacturing also made it clear to the master scheduler that this is the best that they can do without cutting other products out of the schedule.

Based on this information, a second-cut master schedule is developed, as shown in figure 6-14.

The second-cut MPS still won't satisfy the demands from the DCs. Therefore, the master scheduler has to go to the logistics planners and to marketing to determine if something can be worked out temporarily to reduce the distribution demands for this product. One way would be

Supply Source
Vitamin C Tablet 100/Bottle

SECOND-CUT MASTER PRODUCTION SCHEDULE
On Hand Balance — 1700
Safety Stock   — 0
Lead Time   — 3 wks
Order Quantity   — 1100

	Past Due	Week							
		1	2	3	4	5	6	7	8
Distribution Demands	450	700	1050	750	500	450	150	300	150
Scheduled Receipts									
Projected On Hand	1250	550	-500	-150	-650	0	950	650	500
Master Schedule-Rcpt.				1100		1100	1100		
Master Schedule-Start	1100		1100	1100					

Figure 6-14

to temporarily reduce the quantities of this product being shipped to the different DCs. The normal lot sizes for the vitamin C product being shipped to the different DCs cover several weeks of supply. By reducing these lot sizes temporarily, shipments of this product could be made more frequently. The smaller shipments, however, will be made during a time when stock at the supply source is tight. The remaining shipments could be made at a later date when more of the product is available.

Marketing can also help by not pushing items during the period when the MPS is unable to meet the predicted distribution demands. For example, if there is a promotion planned for this product, it would make sense to either substitute another product or reschedule it by a few weeks.

Let's assume that the master scheduler, working with the distribution planners and the people in marketing, has been able to reduce the distribution demands somewhat. The revised MPS display now looks like the one in figure 6-15.

In spite of the master scheduler's efforts to work with manufacturing, production and inventory control, logistics, and marketing, there are still two weeks when the demands from distribution cannot be met by the supply source. During these weeks, the distribution planners will be

Revised MPS Display
Supply Source
Vitamin C Tablet 100/Bottle

On Hand Balance — 1700
Safety Stock   — 0
Lead Time   — 3 wks
Order Quantity   — 1100

	Past Due	Week 1	2	3	4	5	6	7	8
Distribution Demands	450	700	900	400	500	450	500	500	150
Scheduled Receipts									
Projected On Hand	1250	550	-350	350	-150	500	1100	600	450
Master Schedule-Rcpt.				1100		1100	1100		
Master Schedule-Start	1100		1100	1100					

Figure 6-15

relying on the safety stock in the distribution centers to cover the demand until the next week. In this example, the DCs are stocking an average of two weeks' safety stock.

There are two major points in this example:

1. Master production scheduling is a process that may involve *all the operating departments* in a company.

2. The MPS must show what is really going to happen—not what someone would like to happen.

Recap

To sum up, master production scheduling is a process administered by the master scheduler. DRP gives us an opportunity we never had before since it is the key input to the MPS; and it integrates logistics with manufacturing and purchasing in a manufacturing company. If logistics, manufacturing, and purchasing operations work together and communicate effectively, they can make detailed plans and execute them throughout the internal supply pipeline.

The most important thing about the MPS is that it must be accurate; it must truly show what will be produced and when it will be produced. The reason is that almost all other schedules are driven by the MPS. The purchasing schedules, the manufacturing schedule, the capacity requirements planning reports, the financial projections, and a number of other reports are all based on the MPS. If the MPS is wrong, all these schedules are wrong as well.

Even some of the schedules not driven by the MPS can be affected. For example, the planned shipments to the distribution centers are not driven by the MPS, but if the MPS is inaccurate, the planned shipments may not be made on time. The MPS is thus the essential linkage and interface between distribution inventories and manufacturing inventories.

Supplier Scheduling in Retail/Wholesale

The process of supplier scheduling is similar in many respects to master production scheduling within a manufacturing company. One way to conceptualize the process is to consider the supplier as the outside factory and often it is. The only difference is that the evaluation and negotiating process is done with the outside supplier as opposed to the internal supplier in a manufacturing company. Chapter 4 covers the process of supplier scheduling in significant detail: what it is, how to organize for it, and how to pilot and cut over with suppliers.

One other area holds a great deal of promise. For example, if your supplier is a manufacturer already using DRP and/or MRP II, he will welcome your willingness to do supplier scheduling and sharing information. You will have to do very little of the education, if any. He will know immediately what the potential of supplier scheduling offers and will enthusiastically embrace it.

This is the wave of the future. As more retailers, wholesalers, and distributors begin to use the DRP management process, they will find a very receptive group of manufacturers who are eager to do business that way. The level of professionalism in Class A manufacturing companies using DRP and MRP II is very high, and they want to develop customer-supplier partnerships.

PEGGING

A planner, master scheduler, or buyer using the DRP display or the MPS display often needs to know the source of the demands. For example, a master scheduler may have demands from the DCs that exceed the MPS. In such a situation, the master scheduler wants to see where these demands originate. Likewise, a buyer or planner using the DRP display for a purchased or manufactured item may have demands that exceed the purchase orders or the manufacturing orders for the item. Again, under these circumstances, the buyer or planner wants to see the source of the requirements.

This source information is called "pegging"—a listing of the demands of an item that shows where they are coming from by date and quantity. Figure 6-16 shows the pegging information for the MPS display used in figure 6-15:

Supply Source
Vitamin C Tablet 100/Bottle

On Hand Balance— 1700
Safety Stock   — 0
Lead Time   — 3 wks
Order Quantity — 1100

	Past Due	Week 1	2	3	4	5	6	7	8
Distribution Demands	450	700	900	400	500	450	500	500	150
Scheduled Receipts									
Projected On Hand	1250	550	-350	350	-150	500	1100	600	450
Master Schedule-Rcpt.				1100		1100	1100		
Master Schedule-Start	1100		1100	1100					

Pegging Information

Week	Quantity	Location	Week	Quantity	Location
P.D.	400	New York	2	400	Montreal
P.D.	50	Toronto	2	500	Chicago
	450			900	
1	500	Los Angeles	3	400	New York
1	200	Vancouver		400	
	700				

Figure 6-16

In figure 6-16, the pegging information is listed for the past due week and the next three weeks. In most systems, pegging is listed for some part of the planning horizon. In some companies, pegging is cut off beyond a specified number of weeks; while in other companies, pegging is listed to the end of the planning horizon. This is true in both logistics and manufacturing, and at the retail/wholesale level.

In logistics, most people cut off pegging information after 12 weeks. The reason is that the logistics planners rarely use this information very far into the future. In manufacturing, though, most people display pegging farther into the future because the information is used to plan for manufactured and purchased items. Many times these items have long lead times, and the planners are solving problems on current orders that are not due to arrive for some time. In retail/wholesale environments, pegging rarely goes beyond two to four weeks.

Although it is possible to display all the pegging information to the end of the planning horizon, most people find that for the few number of times pegging is used that far into the future, it is not worth displaying the information.

A master scheduler using the display in figure 6-16 would be most concerned about weeks 2 and 4. These are the periods in which the master schedule is not large enough to satisfy the demands from logistics. The master scheduler will want to know what DCs are creating the demands in weeks 2 and 4. Using pegging, he or she can obtain this information. Pegging shows that the demands in week 2 come from the Montreal and Chicago DCs. With this information in hand, the master schedulers and logistics planners can zero in on the problem and find a solution.

When used in this way, pegging is an extremely valuable tool and a time saver for both the master scheduler and the logistics planners. It enables them to spend their time solving problems rather than trying to determine where the problems will occur. The alternative to pegging is to look at each distribution center to see which one generated the requirements.

In the DRP display for a manufactured or purchased item, pegging lists the parent item number rather than the location. The pegging information for a manufactured or purchased item might look like the display shown in figure 6-17.

Pegging also exists for items in stores and distribution centers, in which case it lists the customer orders as in figure 6-18.

To conclude, pegging is essential to close the demand-supply loop. It

Pegging Information for a Manufactured or Purchased Item

Week	Quantity	Parent Item
P.D.	270	Vitamin C 1000/bottle
P.D.	390	Vitamin A 1000/bottle
	660	
1	500	Vitamin E 1000/bottle
1	750	Vitamin D 1000/bottle
	1250	

Figure 6-17

Use of Pegging for Items in Stores and DCs

Week	Quantity	Customer Number	Order Number
1	500	03784	A23529
1	250	45239	A23568
	750		

Figure 6-18

provides the visibility needed to move from one level to the next. It is especially critical at the retail level because buyers and planners often deal with large numbers of locations. For example, planners and buyers for Wal-mart must deal with more than 2,300 stores, supported by 13 DCs. Without pegging, making decisions on inventory availability and purchasing is nearly hopeless.

FIRM PLANNED ORDER

There are a number of situations when a buyer, planner or master scheduler wants a planned order to consist of a quantity or a date different from that assigned by the order-planning logic in DRP. A buyer may not have enough of a product in a supply source or may want a smaller-than-normal lot size shipped to a store. A logistics planner may want an item to be shipped to a DC before it is actually needed in order to fill a half-empty truck or railcar.

Regardless of the reason, the people using the system need a mechanism for overriding the dates and quantities of planned orders. The firm planned order (FPO) is such a means for accomplishing this task. An FPO is a planned order created by a human being rather than by a computer; the computer does not add, delete, or change a firm planned order in any way.

Firm planned orders are similar to planned orders in that they are still in the planning stage, and have not been released to manufacturing or placed with suppliers. They are similar to scheduled receipts in that they are not created or changed by the computer. Instead, planners maintain them. Rescheduling action messages from the computer are given for firm planned orders just as they are for scheduled receipts.

To illustrate the use of the firm planned order, we'll start with the master schedule display in figure 6-16 and use a firm planned order to solve the problems in week 2, where the demands from the DCs exceed the MPS.

The pegging information shows that the demand in week 2 is coming from the Montreal and Chicago DCs. Now let's look at the DRP display for Montreal as shown in figure 6-19.

Supply Source
Vitamin C Tablet 100/Bottle

On Hand Balance— 1700
Safety Stock   — 0
Lead Time   — 3 wks
Order Quantity   — 1100

	Past Due	Week 1	Week 2	Week 3	Week 4	Week 5	Week 6	Week 7	Week 8
Distribution Demands	450	700	900	400	500	450	500	500	150
Scheduled Receipts									
Projected On Hand	1250	550	-350	350	-150	500	1100	600	450
Master Schedule-Rcpt.				1100		1100	1100		
Master Schedule-Start	1100		1100	1100					

Pegging Information

Week	Quantity	Location	Week	Quantity	Location
P.D.	400	New York	2	400	Montreal
P.D.	50	Toronto	2	500	Chicago
	450			900	
1	500	Los Angeles	3	400	New York
1	200	Vancouver		400	
	700				

Figure 6-16

Montreal Distribution Center
Vitamin C Tablet 100/Bottle

On Hand Balance — 270
Safety Stock   — 220
Lead Time   — 2 wks
Order Quantity   — 400

	Past Due	Week 1	2	3	4	5	6	7	8
Gross Requirements		120	110	135	125	115	120	130	115
Scheduled Receipts			400						
Projected On Hand	270	150	440	305	580	465	345	615	500
Planned Orders			400			400			

Figure 6-19

There are two planned orders in the Montreal DC—one in week 2 and one in week 5. The planned order in week 2 is creating part of the problem at the supply source.

Now let's look at Chicago.

Chicago Distribution Center
Vitamin C Tablet 100/Bottle

On Hand Balance — 350
Safety Stock   — 150
Lead Time   — 1 day
Order Quantity   — 500

	Past Due	Week 1	2	3	4	5	6	7	8
Gross Requirements		125	115	105	110	105	100	115	110
Scheduled Receipts									
Projected On Hand	350	225	610	505	395	290	190	575	465
Planned Orders			500					500	

Figure 6-20

The Chicago DC in figure 6-20 also has two planned orders. Like Montreal, the one in week 2 is contributing to the problem at the supply source.

The master scheduler and the logistics planner look into the planned orders in week 2 to see that if by reducing the order quantity, it is possible to provide enough of the product to supply the two DCs until week 5 or 6, when product again becomes available at the supply source.

Taking this approach, the master scheduler and logistics planner decide to enter two firm planned orders for the Montreal DC (see figure 6-21).

One firm planned order is 250 in week 2. This will relieve some of the demand on the supply source. By planning to ship 250 to the Montreal DC instead of the normal 500, the supply source is relieved of 150.

The second firm planned order is for 400 in week 5. The reason for the second order is that the logistics planner and master scheduler are planning to allow the on-hand balance to drop below the safety stock of 220 in week 6.

The logistics planner believes that the projected inventory is sufficient

Planned Orders
Montreal Distribution Center
Vitamin C Tablet 100/Bottle

On Hand Balance — 270
Safety Stock   — 220
Lead Time   — 2 wks
Order Quantity   — 400

	Past	Week							
	Due	1	2	3	4	5	6	7	8
Gross Requirements		120	110	135	125	115	120	130	115
Scheduled Receipts			400						
Projected On Hand	270	150	440	305	430	315	195	465	350
Planned Orders									
Firm Planned Orders			250			400			

Figure 6-21

to keep the distribution center off back order, because week 5 will be the first time the supply source will begin to have available product.

In the DRP display in figure 6-21, the firm planned orders are displayed on a separate line. Some systems show firm planned orders on the planned orders line with some letter or symbol (200F, 200*, etc.), indicating that the order is a firm planned order.

As the next step in the evaluation of supply and demand, the master scheduler and logistics planner begin to work on the Chicago DC. In this case, they decide to enter a firm planned order for 300 in week 2. This order reduces the demand on the supply source. In addition, because of the firm planned order for 300 in week 2, the planned order for 500 that was in week 7 is moved up to week 5 (see figure 6-22).

Now, let's look at the MPS display and consider the effects of all these firm planned orders as shown in the new display in figure 6-23.

As we can see, the master scheduler and the logistics planner have done their jobs. The demands from the distribution system match and are in sync with the MPS. In most situations, it is unacceptable to consider a problem completely resolved when there is a negative projected on-hand balance in the MPS report. Often, there are negative projected on-hand balances in the report while the master scheduler is still in the process of solving the problem. And there are also situations where a product is rejected or cannot be produced, and the master scheduler may have to contend with negative projected on-hand balance for a while. But, in general, the master scheduler should not consider his job done until the problem is solved.

Analysis of the Example

To recap the preceding example, two points are of particular interest. First, the example demonstrates the fundamental need for people to be able to impose their will on the system. The type of reasoning, decisions, and value judgments used to resolve problems cannot be programmed into a computer. The only way to satisfactorily resolve such problems is to give the people using the system some simple, but powerful, tools. In using their creative abilities to develop and agree on a solution to a particular problem, they can then use the firm planned order, in this case, to implement their solution.

Secondly, firm planned orders are the way to handle a variety of distribution problems. By making the system show what will really happen (i.e., what will be shipped and when), the logistics and manufac-

Firm Planned Orders
Chicago Distribution Center
Vitamin C Tablet 100/Bottle

On Hand Balance — 350
Safety Stock   — 150
Lead Time   — 1 day
Order Quantity   — 500

	Past Due	Week							
		1	2	3	4	5	6	7	8
Gross Requirements		125	115	105	110	105	100	115	110
Scheduled Receipts									
Projected On Hand	350	225	410	305	195	590	490	375	265
Planned Orders						500			
Firm Planned Orders			300						

Figure 6-22

Supply Source
Vitamin C Tablet 100/Bottle

AFTER FIRM PLANNED ORDERS AT THE DISTRIBUTION CENTERS
On Hand Balance — 1700
Safety Stock   — 0
Lead Time   — 3 wks
Order Quantity   — 1100

	Past Due	Week							
		1	2	3	4	5	6	7	8
Distribution Demands	450	700	550	400	500	950	650	0	150
Scheduled Receipts									
Projected On Hand	1250	550	0	700	200	350	800	800	650
Master Schedule-Rcpt.				1100		1100	1100		
Master Schedule-Start	1100		1100	1100					

Figure 6-23

turing information will be accurate. If the planned and firm planned orders are used to plan truck and railcar for scheduling and loading, the orders must accurately represent what will be shipped and when it will be shipped. The firm planned order gives the ability to make this information correct.

In a very real sense, the firm planned order touches on a fundamental issue—it gives people the ability to have the final say in what will be done. This is necessary if people are to be held accountable. They cannot be expected to sit back and blindly take orders from a computer. They have to understand what the computer is recommending to them and why. But they must also have the wherewithal to impose their will on the system where necessary.

Some employers believe that the way to handle problems is to develop a computer program complete with parameters, factors, and weighting values to automatically allocate products when the supply source is unable to meet the demands of the stocking locations. In actual practice, such sophisticated computer programs have not worked well. This is no surprise to those who make their living managing distribution inventories—such dependency on the computer is totally out of touch with the real world.

The most common approach with DRP is to allow people to use their creativity, judgment, and ability to reason as a means for developing solutions to problems.

Finally, the firm planned order can be used to handle a number of situations in logistics in addition to the one explained in the example above. These include:

1. Planning transportation scheduling and loading.

2. Allowing for stock buildups in distribution centers or other stocking locations in advance of:
   a. Promotions.
   b. Special sales offers.
   c. Seasonal sales.

3. Allowing for stock buildups in distribution centers or other stocking locations for:
   a. Anticipation of labor strikes.
   b. Creating a new distribution center.
   c. Relocating or eliminating a distribution center.

Chapters 8 and 9 explain how each of the above is accomplished using DRP and firm planned order.

USING DRP TO MANAGE A LARGE NUMBER OF PRODUCTS

Some companies have a large number of items to be managed in their stocking locations. Let's take the actual case of a company that has 25,000 stockkeeping units maintained in six distribution centers. This represents a total of 150,000 stockkeeping units to be managed in this network. Assuming that only 5 percent of the items are in short supply at the supply source at a given point in time, on the average, logistics planners are confronted with the need to allocate approximately 1,250 items on a routine basis. Obviously, something must be done to help people cope with the volume of work represented by this situation. In practice, companies confronted with such problems have used the computer to help them manage such volumes.

The approach that works best is a situation in which the computer is programmed to work by exception. Anytime there is insufficient inventory on hand for distribution at the supply source, the computer generates an exception message. In addition, logic is programmed into the software so that the computer presents the logistics planners with various scenarios on how they can solve the problem.

The recommended approach works as follows: First, the computer takes out the safety stock and replans. Second, it looks at the results of the requirements once the safety stocks are discarded. If the total requirements are still larger than available stock at the source, the computer will go through a second set of logic that drops the order quantity rule and replans. The results are evaluated, and if the requirements are still higher than availability, the computer will recommend allocating whatever is available at the source on a pro rata basis based on the sales forecast and distance for each of the distribution centers.

Using the computer to present different scenarios makes good sense. It is important, however, to recognize that the computer should only be used to make recommendations as opposed to allocating the inventory on behalf of the planner. There is a subtle difference between the two. The computer does the detail work; the planner evaluates the alternatives and makes the final decision, as opposed to abdicating the responsibility for automatically allocating inventory to the computer.

When the need arises to remove order quantities and safety stock quantities, the computer program should recognize the situation and flag it for the buyers and distribution planners. This will remind them that as soon as inventory becomes available in sufficient quantities at the supply source, order quantity rules and safety stock quantities should be reinstated, since the inventory is now available.

In companies where several thousand items are replenished weekly—retailers and wholesalers, for example—it makes sense to build logic in the software of DRP that extracts only those products needing replenishment in the next one to three weeks. That way, because users only look at those products that require action, they eliminate the need to review a great number of products where no action is required.

CONCLUSION

This chapter covered the nuts and bolts aspect of a DRP system and the type of information used on a day-to-day basis by those on the firing line. Although such information does not have top-management appeal, it is essential for the smooth functioning of daily operations.

Chapter 7

Forecasting

The DRP Connection

To succeed, every company must plan, execute, and control its operations. Planning helps you make decisions about implementing programs to achieve your company's sales and profit objectives. Many times planning relies on forecasts. With regard to inventory, planning decisions are oriented toward deciding what's needed, where it's needed, how much is needed, and when it's needed. Based on this information, you decide whether to make or buy more product.

Thus, forecasts are an important component of effective inventory management. Despite this, many companies don't formally develop them. And, of those that do, many don't do as well as they should. Or could.

Although forecasts have always been a part of reordering decisions, the people doing the reordering may be unaware that they are actually forecasting. My experience has been that if a forecast is necessary, and it isn't provided by a formal system, it will be provided informally; that is, somebody will make a best guess based on his own idiosyncratic understanding of how the business works. That's why it's important to make forecasting part of the formal system. When it is, people will make the right kinds of forecasts, and everyone will be working from the same set of numbers. Most importantly, DRP will work much better within your company.

This chapter begins by discussing the forecasting process, with special emphasis on the role of people. Next, the chapter documents common complaints about forecasting and discusses the number of forecasts that are necessary, the responsibility and accountability for forecasting, and the nature of the inputs to forecasting. It talks about the components of a forecasting system and how forecasting and DRP work together. The chapter concludes by urging you to strive to eliminate the need to forecast. A few leading edge companies have already lessened their reliance on forecasts significantly through customer connectivity marketing. (See chapter 1).

This chapter does not include a discussion pertinent to the mathematics or statistics of forecasting techniques. That is beyond the scope of this book.

If You're Just Starting Out

Some people believe that DRP will not work in their environment until they get forecasting under control. Closer investigation reveals that this is not true. DRP will *especially* help you manage even when the forecasts are "not so great." Use the material in this chapter to improve your ability to forecast, but don't let it prevent you from making a decision to implement DRP and gain immediate benefits from it. Experience shows that the worse the forecast, the more you need DRP and vice versa. DRP, through its rescheduling capabilities, goes a long way toward compensating for forecasting errors.

What DRP Requires from a Forecast

Ultimately, DRP needs an estimate of the amount of a specific product that is expected to be demanded by customers from a specific location during a specifically defined future period. For example, what is the expected demand in cases for product 0882-5622-49 at the Atlanta DC during the month of June? Later sections will discuss this product.

Common Complaints About Forecasting

The list below is a summary of some common complaints about forecasting:

• There is a total lack of integration. Everybody uses a different forecast. The results are not even close to being consistent.

- Nobody is held accountable for forecast accuracy.

- Everybody is hung up on the statistical techniques instead of the forecasting process.

- Forecast accuracy varies from just poor to simply terrible. Since no feedback loops exist, however, no one really has an idea of how good or bad the forecasts are.

- Our system doesn't provide easy ways for a person to provide intelligence to the forecasts at meaningful levels.

- Nobody understands the underlying statistical methodology.

- Our business is promotion-oriented. No system can help us.

- We can't even capture demand—there's no way we can forecast.

- We have a lot of phase ins and phaseouts. Therefore, we never collect enough history to have a reasonable basis for forecasting.

The nature of the problems listed above can be further summarized as:

- There are too many forecasts, and none of them are any good.

- Feedback and accountability are lacking.

- Proper inputs are lacking.

How Many Forecasts Do You Need?

I can't state this any more simply: You only need a single forecast—it's difficult enough to get one good one. Typically, an organization has multiple forecasts for a very simple reason—different groups within the company have different needs. Existing forecasts aren't at the right level—they are either too low or too high. Or, they aren't in the proper unit of measure. Or, there's some other irreconcilable difference such as not believing another's forecast. One group can't use the other group's forecasts, so they derive their own.

One client company—a retailer—works with three forecasts. The buying organization uses one for making commitments to sources. It consists of high-level forecasts expressed in units. But, as they are more relevant to the way product is manufactured rather than the way it is sold, the forecasts are of little use to any other group.

The marketing organization develops forecasts as a by-product of promotional planning. These forecasts at the item level are expressed in dollars. Moreover, they are oriented to a specific advertising area. Unfortunately, it is difficult to map an advertising area to a geographic area serviced by a replenishment location. Thus, they, too, are of limited relevance to other groups.

Finally, the people who are responsible for replenishing stocks in the warehouses and retail stores derive forecasts. Their forecasts for a specific item at a specific location are expressed in units.

What do you think the probability is that any of these forecasts total the same number? Here's a clue: They don't make probabilities that small. And, the differences in the totals look close when compared to the differences in the mix.

The point here is that each group should be able to look at forecast information with a unique eye. Even so, there must be only one forecast. It can be derived from the top down, from the bottom up, or from a combination of the two. Extend it and display it any way that's necessary. But, don't derive more than one. If you do, you're asking for trouble because accountability for the forecast will be a charade. In addition, it will be practically impossible to arrive at the same destination at the same time, as different functions will be marching to a different drumbeat.

Responsibility and Accountability

Marketing's job is to develop and implement programs for increasing sales and/or share of market. But, if the nature and the projected impact of the programs aren't adequately communicated throughout the rest of the organization, the likelihood of success is low. On the one hand, the more information marketing can provide, the better. On the other hand, it doesn't make sense for marketing to develop detailed forecasts for all products. If it did, it might get little else done. So, who should create the forecast? How should it be done? And who should be held responsible and accountable for the results?

The forecast must represent a consensus. The demand planner is responsible for collecting information relevant to forecasting from all sources and for analyzing it. The following represents an approach that has proven successful with many clients.

Start by stratifying your products. For example: Group together all of your high-volume products, all low-volume products, all products that are bought by a large number of customers, and all those purchased by a low or medium number. While you can probably think of more strata applicable to your individual company, use these four groupings to help you determine who is responsible for what within your company.

High Volume to a Few Customers

This strata contains products that you really can't afford to run out of. The difficulty is that they're not always easy to forecast because, although volume is high, demands tend to be infrequent. Fortunately, since there's only a few customers, "closeness to the customer" makes economic sense.

The best way to derive forecasts for these kinds of products is for the demand planner to consider input from your salespeople. They're the ones from your company who are closest to the customer. If they don't know what's going on with them, nobody else will either. This guidance could be detail level, (depending on the number of products) or it could be high level. If it's high level, the demand planners should reduce it to the detail level.

These are situations in which customer connectivity marketing can have dramatic results.

Low or Medium Volume to a Few Customers

Medium or even low volume doesn't necessarily imply that forecasting will be difficult. The frequency of demands is a much more important indicator. But when demand is attributable to only a small number of customers, it will almost certainly be sporadic. Unlike the first strata discussed, "closeness to the customer" doesn't make economic sense for these kinds of products. And because of the infrequency of demands, a statistical approach usually generates disappointing results.

The best thing to do in forecasting these kinds of products, if you must keep them in the product line, is to place them under the guidance of an experienced demand planner. Supplement this when feasible by soliciting input from other people who have less costly opportunities to be close to the customer, such as service technicians. Again, this is the kind of situation in which customer connectivity marketing can be of great benefit.

High Volume to a Broad Customer Base
These kinds of products are usually the easiest ones to forecast. Volume is high, and since there are many different customers, demands tend to be frequent. Thus, statistical forecasting and/or focus forecasting works well. Use history as a basis for developing detail forecasts and/or for "reducing" higher-level ones to detail level.

The demand planners should be responsible and accountable for the detail statistical forecasts, including reducing them from higher levels when necessary. Marketing should be responsible and accountable for reviewing high-level forecasts and for providing any and all relevant intelligence about promotions, trends, and other impacts.

Low or Medium Volume to a Broad Customer Base
These products normally represent 80 percent of the total items, and about 20 percent of the total dollar volume. The infrequency of demand will have a much more severe impact on forecast performance than volume. Reasonable forecasts can be attained by deriving higher-level forecasts from a statistical model or focus forecasting. Marketing should be responsible for reviewing the high-level forecasts and for providing all relevant intelligence about promotions, trends, and other impacts. Demand planners should be responsible and accountable for reducing them to detail level.

The Proper Inputs

Lack of proper inputs is a major reason why many forecasting systems fail to achieve their potential. This section explains the proper inputs and contrasts them to the traditional ones.

Importance
When properly done, statistical forecasts can minimize the demand planners' efforts in reviewing forecasts. This is especially true for low-, medium-, and high-volume products sold to a broad customer base. You'll achieve best results if the history upon which the statistical forecasts are based reflects reality. If it doesn't, your demand planners will spend a disproportionate amount of time reviewing and fixing forecasts. More importantly, the credibility of the entire forecasting system will be damaged, perhaps fatally. No one will believe the numbers; and this will signal the beginning of the end of formal forecasts within your organization.

Problems with Traditional Inputs

For many companies today, the quality of historical data is suspect. There are many reasons for this. Consider the actual sales figures displayed in figure 7-1.

Month	Actual Sales
January	150,500
February	165,300
March	142,600
April	184,200
May	120,900
June	180,600

Figure 7-1

In many companies, this type of information is commonly used as the source of data for statistical forecasting and as the basis for management interaction. Yet, very often, it causes major problems.

The reason is simple. An organization seldom achieves a 100 percent level of service. As a result, past actual sales seldom reflect the true demand for a product. For example, as shown in figure 7-2, demand, or orders received, in April and May far exceed product availability, resulting in back orders. It's not difficult to imagine that very different forecasts would be derived depending upon which set of numbers formed the basis—actual sales or orders received.

Capturing actual demand isn't easy for many businesses. For exam-

Month	Actual Sales	Orders Received	Monthly Variance
January	150,000	151,000	(500)
February	165,300	164,800	500
March	142,600	142,900	(300)
April	184,200	205,200	(21,000)
May	120,900	150,000	(29,100)
June	180,600	130,200	50,400

Figure 7-2

ple, during extended periods when product is out of stock, some customers may reorder the same product several times until they finally receive it. Cancellations aren't easy either. Did a customer really intend to buy from you? Or was he simply covering his bases and/or price shopping? If he was, it makes sense not to include the order in the demand. If he canceled because you couldn't service him, it probably should be included.

Usually, there's no obvious answer to these questions. The important thing is to recognize the impact that these kinds of problems can have and do something about it, if possible, by developing some filters within your own order-entry system.

Another factor that can distort the input data is the length of the month. For example, demand history is typically collected in monthly increments. Likewise, forecasts are usually derived for a monthly increment. Not considering differences in the number of sales days in each month can be quite misleading to the statistical model. And, the resulting forecasts may be seriously distorted. Figure 7-3 demonstrates how deceptive this data can be.

Month	Actual Sales	Sales Days	Average Daily Sales
January	2,003,400	21	95,400
February	2,182,700	23	94,900
March	1,720,800	18	95,600
April	2,092,000	22	95,100
May	1,910,000	20	95,500
June	2,094,000	22	95,200

Figure 7-3

Effective Use of Order Processing
As discussed earlier, it's important for your order-entry system to recognize and capture true demand. It's ironic, but many of them in use today aren't capable of doing so. Thus, many companies have found that when they implement a new forecasting system, they must also upgrade the order-entry system. Unfortunately, many don't discover this until after they have implemented the new forecasting system. And, although it usually isn't too late to fix the problem, it is cheaper and faster to correct the problem at the outset.

For example, consider a customer in the Boston area who orders a widget. The Boston DC is out of this particular item, but it is resourceful, and determines that the New York City warehouse can ship the product on time. Boston makes the requests and the customer is satisfied.

Now, consider a customer who orders a deluxe widget. You're out of deluxe widgets but offer to supply him immediately with a standard one. He accepts.

Finally, a customer requests an immediate shipment of a widget. You're out of stock, so you inform him that you'll be able to ship one to him early next month. He is unhappy with the situation, but since you're the only supplier for this product at the moment, he has no choice but to accept.

Let's discuss the way most organizations would treat these situations today, and then look at the actions these organizations should have taken.

In the first instance, most companies would post a shipment to New York's history. But this action overstates what actually happened, and it perpetuates Boston's out-of-stock problems. The solution is to make the order-entry system smart enough to post a demand to Boston even though New York actually makes the shipment.

In the second example, most companies would post a demand for the standard widget. Again, this can cause confusion. Make order entry smart enough to post the demand to the deluxe widget. Otherwise, you'll perpetuate the deluxe widget's out-of-stock situation and overplan for the standard one.

In the last example, the solution is to make order entry smart enough to post the demand to the current month instead of to the next one. Your customer wanted it now. He's only accepting it next month because you couldn't service him properly.

Impact of Promotions on Demand History
Under most circumstances, you should only use a statistical forecast to forecast regular business. That is, management interaction, rather than statistics, should be used to communicate the impact of promotions. Thus, the history used as the basis for statistical forecasts also should reflect only regular business. That's why the forecasting system you use should store at least two separate kinds of demand history—one that

contains regular demand and one that allows you to specify what you want it to contain.

When You're Starting Out

When you begin to formally forecast, the quality of your demand history may be suspect: You'll have collected shipments instead of history, the history will be affected by promotions, etc. Don't let that stop you. There's very little that you can do about it. Start with what you have and work hard to improve it. Recognize that you will accumulate a mixture of demand and shipments and be able to create a valid history over time.

GENERAL GUIDELINES

Keep as much history about demand for a product as is feasible. Two years should be the minimum. To save space, store information about detailed demand (product/DC/customer) somewhere other than the forecasting system itself. This information will allow you to reconfigure the demand-history database when necessary, such as when you close a DC or open a new one. Customers can be reassigned, so you can effectively use all relevant information about demand just as if a customer had always been serviced by that DC.

Store at least two different forecasts for each month: the one resulting from the statistical model or focus forecast, and the one resulting from any management interaction. Meaningful comparisons can be made later if necessary.

Forecasts should be calculated over at least an 18-month horizon. This will cover most long lead-time products and it is also a long enough period to assist in the budgeting process. Don't overlook budgeting— this is an important part of closing the operations/finance loop. And forecasting has a significant impact on budgeting.

Finally, a forecast should correspond to a monthly increment. It should be updated using statistics or focus forecasting only once per month unless it is a "hot" high-fashion item or a new record that has just hit the charts. Then weekly or biweekly forecast updates may make sense. Of course, intelligence should be added to the forecasts as needed. Don't wait until the end of the month to provide this important information.

Components of a Forecasting System

When you hear the word "forecasting" or the term "forecasting system," what do you automatically think of? If you're like most people, it brings to mind thoughts of statistics and mathematics, a black box number cruncher devised by statisticians instead of by business people. Unfortunately, this view is the norm, not the exception. There are actually four components to a forecasting system, and the number-crunching part is no more important than any of the other three.

The four components of a forecasting system are listed in figure 7-4. We'll pay particular attention to the relative importance of each component. You might be surprised how they rank.

    – Statistical Component
    – Management Interaction Component
    – Feedback Component
    – Information Organization Component

Figure 7-4

Statistical Component

This is the component most people think of when they hear the word forecasting. Statistical forecasting emphasizes the use of mathematics and statistics to derive a forecast of the future. This forecast is based solely on what has happened in the past. In fact, all statistical approaches to forecasting assume that what has happened in the past will help forecast what will happen in the future. Sometimes, this is not the case. If the past can't always be used to forecast the future, the statistical forecast is of limited value.

Detail Versus Higher-level Forecasts
There are basically two ways to derive SKU-level forecasts. The most fundamental is to forecast all the individual items on the basis of their own history (see figure 7-5). This method uses the history that corresponds to each DC. If this method is used, forecasts will be affected by the peaks and valleys experienced at each DC.

	Jan	Feb	Mar	Apr	May	Etc.
LA	67	41	50	64	54	. . .
CH	33	22	41	49	46	. . .
NY	54	57	68	39	55	. . .
VANC	47	21	25	47	59	. . .
TOR	57	66	71	37	62	. . .
MTL	60	86	63	20	15	. . .
TOTAL	318	293	318	256	301	. . .

Figure 7-5

An alternative is to derive a higher level forecast and then reduce it to the SKU level. This reduction may be done on the basis of historical or projected percentages. Examples of higher-level forecasts include an item across all locations where it is stocked (sometimes referred to as an item national forecast), a product line, a product family, and others.

Reducing Higher-level Forecasts
As mentioned earlier, DRP operates at the SKU level. Therefore, a higher-level forecast must be reduced to the SKU level before it's useful to DRP. The next section provides some insights into reduction methods.

Developing Forecasts for DRP
To reduce a higher-level forecast, calculate the historical percentage of national business attributable to each DC. The interval over which to calculate the percentage can vary. Depending upon the attributes of the product, six months to two years is a suggested time frame.

For example, assume that the annual national forecast derived for a product is 5,000 cases. When the last 12 months of historical demands for each SKU are added up, the sum is 4,550 cases. You distribute the forecast by calculating the percentage that each DC contributed to the history. Then, you multiply this percentage by the forecast of 5,000 to yield the reduced SKU forecasts (refer to figure 7-6).

Reconciling Differences Among Forecasts
The methodology just described is also useful for reconciling differences between two forecasts. For example, marketing might provide a higher-level forecast that's different from the sum of the detail forecasts. Most software packages make it easy to proportionally distribute the

Distribution Center	History	Percent of Total	New Forecast
Los Angeles	1200	26.4	1320
Chicago	1150	25.3	1265
New York	1300	28.6	1430
Vancouver	250	5.5	275
Toronto	150	3.3	165
Montreal	500	10.9	545
Total	4550	100.0	5000

Figure 7-6

difference between the forecasts over the DCs. Normally, this is acceptable, but you don't have to do this—do what you think best represents what will really happen. You might, for example, put the difference into two forecasts—Los Angeles and Chicago—because that's where you think the difference will be sold.

What you do with the difference isn't the issue. The issue is that you must reconcile the individual forecasts by DC with marketing's forecast. If you do this, then everyone is working from the same set of numbers.

Techniques for Deriving Forecasts
There are many techniques for calculating statistical forecasts. If any two techniques you are comparing both have statistical validity, the difference between the forecasts yielded by each will not be significant. For example, if you derived forecasts for 100 products using two different statistical techniques, in 80 percent of the cases the differences in the forecasts derived between the two methods would be insignificant. In 10 percent of the cases, technique X would be better than Y; in the other 10 percent, Y would be better than X. The point is newer, more sophisticated techniques aren't the answer to forecasting problems.

Two popular and sophisticated techniques for deriving statistical forecasts are least squares and exponentially smoothed moving averages. It is beyond the scope of this book to discuss the techniques in detail, but you should be aware of their existence since many commercially available software packages use them. One technique, however, does warrant further discussion—focus forecasting.

Focus Forecasting

Focus forecasting[1] is a simulation approach to forecasting. It takes advantage of computing capabilities that didn't exist until very recently. The system tries many different "models," and then selects the "best one," that is, the one that would do the best job of predicting what has already occurred.

Figure 7-7 lists only a few examples of focus forecasting models or strategies. These are by no means all that you should consider. In fact, the number of strategies evaluated are limited only by your imagination and by any relevant computing constraints. Some commercially available focus forecasting software packages include more than 20 strategies.

Whatever we sold during the last quarter is what we'll sell during the next quarter.

Whatever we sold last year during the coming quarter will be what we'll sell this year during the coming quarter.

Whatever the average was during the last two quarters is what we'll s.ll during the coming quarter.

Figure 7-7

Focus forecasting uses each strategy to simulate what it would have predicted to occur. In other words, "If we had been using this model, how well would it have performed?" It keeps track of which model came the closest to predicting what actually occurred. It then recommends that that model be used as the basis for forecasting. With focus forecasting, the technique chosen for the next product could be an entirely different one (see figure 7-8).

The Catch-22 of Statistical Forecasting

Statistical forecasting creates a catch-22 situation. The techniques that you use must be complex enough to generate meaningful results. On the

---

[1] For a detailed discussion of focus forecasting, please refer to Bernard T. Smith *Focus Forecasting: Computer Techniques for Inventory Control* (Essex Junction, VT: Oliver Wight Limited Publications, Inc., 1984).

It's June 1989. We need to derive forecasts for the next twelve months, beginning with the third quarter of 1989. Let's evaluate the three strategies we noted above and select the one that "would have done the best job of predicting what's already occurred."

	1988	**1989**
January	280	101
February	336	126
March	218	151
April	181	188
May	228	129
June	134	192
July	234	
August	223	
September	281	
October	214	
November	106	
December	42	
Total	2477	

Strategy One—Whatever we sold during the last quarter is what we'll sell during the next one.

Last quarter actual was 509 (188 + 129 + 192)
Last quarter prediction was 378 (101 + 126 + 151)
Percentage error was 25.7% (378 / 509)

Strategy Two—Whatever we sold last year during the coming quarter will be what we'll sell this year during the coming quarter.

Last quarter actual was 509 (188 + 129 + 192)
Last quarter prediction was 543 (181 + 228 + 134)
Percentage error was 6.7% (543 / 509)

Strategy Three—Whatever the average was during the last two quarters is what we'll sell during the coming quarter.

Last quarter actual was 509 (188 + 129 + 192)
Last quarter prediction was 550 (234 + 223 + 281 + 214 + 106 + 42) / 2
Percentage error was 8.1% (550 / 509)

Strategy two would be selected: it yielded the smallest percentage error of all strategies evaluated.

Figure 7-8

other hand, unless people understand how a number was calculated, they have trouble relating to it. There's no easy solution to this dilemma, which is why focus forecasting approaches have gained such popularity today.

Management-Interaction Component

This is the second component of a sound forecasting process. In the real world, things often change too quickly for you to be able to rely solely on statistical forecasts. The combination of a statistical forecast with consensus input from multiple business people is the best and most sensible approach to deriving forecasts. I refer to the need for and the process of providing this information as management interaction.

Importance of Management Interaction

Consider a product that has been a marginal performer. Now, however, marketing believes it can implement new programs and gain significant market share. Be careful! The statistical-forecasting module won't know about the new programs and it will continue to forecast the usual level of business because that's what the history indicates is proper. And, if that is the case, chances are there won't be enough product to satisfy the incremental demand.

Marketing must, therefore, tell the rest of the organization about the projected impact of its programs. Otherwise, the programs most likely will not succeed. Countless times companies spend good money planning promotions only to discover too late that there's not enough product available. Of course, they tend to blame the forecasts, but it's usually their own fault.

The predictions may be expressed at a higher level or at a detail level, either in units or currency. If you provide predictions at higher levels, the software you use must be capable of reducing the impact to the detail level. In addition, if the predictions are expressed in currency, the software must also be capable of converting it to units. Finally, make sure that the software you use makes it easy to convert a forecast for any group of SKUs.

Marketing Intelligence

What is marketing intelligence? It is information provided about promotions and other programs designed to influence the prevailing level of business.

The impact of promotions must be provided to the forecasting system. Unlike statistical forecasts, which are typically monthly oriented, this information is much more effective if it's provided in weekly increments. Listed below are factors to consider when predicting the impacts of promotions.

- Expected magnitude of increase in demand for products being promoted. This should be time-phased if the length of the promotion is longer than one week.

- Length of the promotion period.

- Impact on the items being promoted *before* the promotion begins. In other words, if customers know in advance about a promotion, how will this impact demand before the promotion period begins.

- Impact on the items being promoted *after* the promotion ends. In other words, have customers bought before they really need product because of the promotion? If so, how long will it be before they buy again?

- Impact on complementary products. For example, consider a company promoting a spreadsheet software program. The company is not promoting how-to books that help people who use the package. Nonetheless, it would seem likely that if more spreadsheet packages are sold, more books would be sold, too. These kinds of opportunities need to be considered when designing a promotion.

- Impact on competitive products. If only one specific spreadsheet package is being promoted, it is likely that sales of competing products may decline during the promotion. This, too, needs to be factored into the promotional campaign.

Many companies don't explicitly consider the factors listed above during their planning processes. Naturally, they suffer the consequences.

Other Aspects

Promotions aren't the only reason that marketing intelligence is important. Anytime, and, for any reason the existing demand history doesn't reflect the expected conditions of the market, it's important to convey to the forecasting system the following information:

- A mature product is losing market share to a competitive product. Marketing programs have been developed in an attempt to reverse this trend. Remember, the history reflects declining demand, so unless you tell DRP about the plans to regain market share you won't. That is because DRP will not provide levels of inventory that are sufficient to service the additional customers.

- You're trying to take market share away from a competitive product. You design marketing programs such as increased advertising, a lower price, etc. Again, this won't happen unless you tell DRP about your intentions.

- You've chosen to deemphasize a stellar product. Unless you tell DRP about the plans, it will continue to think that it's a stellar product, and will plan inventory accordingly.

Document Your Assumptions: It's important that you document the assumptions upon which marketing intelligence was developed. A record will help immensely in the future when someone ponders why demand jumped dramatically two years ago. In addition, you'll be able to better explain why a large forecast error occurred.

Forecasts for New Products
A demand planner is usually responsible for providing forecasts for new products. Generally there are few new products. In almost all cases, a forecast for an existing but similar product can be cloned. That is, it can provide the basis for the new item's forecast.

This makes sense because there's not enough history—there may not be any—to derive a statistical forecast. Marketing's primary role here is similar to its role for promotions—a responsibility for signing-off on the estimates.

Feedback Component

Forecasting is a control process just like statistical quality control. You must constantly monitor adherence to standard. You can't maintain control unless you monitor it. That's what the third component of the forecasting process—feedback—is all about. It helps you determine when the forecasting process is out of control, and signals when you should take the appropriate action to regain control of the system. Despite it's importance, feedback is the component that is almost always missing from homegrown forecasting systems. It is also the component forecasting software packages most often ignore.

Monitoring the Process
The forecasting software must provide the capability of determining when performance is out of tolerance. Typically, two periods of time are relevant. One is the most recently completed period. The other is a longer period of time, such as the last 12 to 18 months.

A demand filter can be used to test tolerance for the most recently completed period. Tests for biases can be used for longer periods of time, but before any tests can be performed, it's necessary to understand the importance and relevance of the forecast error.

Measuring Forecast Error
It is relatively easy to calculate forecast error, which is simply the difference between the actual demand in the period most recently completed and the forecasted demand for the same period. Figure 7-9 shows an example of forecast-error calculation.

Actual demand for March: 300 cases
Forecasted demand for March: 350 cases
Forecast error: 50 cases

Figure 7-9

Demand Filter
An effective demand-filtering process will help to maintain the validity and credibility of your inputs to the forecasting system. Essentially, a demand filter is a mechanism for flagging large forecast differences, also known as forecast errors.

What's the definition of large? Large can be anything you want it to be. It can, for example, be any error that is greater than a specified percentage. It's a good idea to assign different hurdles for different strata of products. For example, you probably want to exert tighter control over fast-moving, high-margin products (see figure 7-10).

A demand filter only flags exceptions. You must determine what caused the large error and develop a solution.

The most effective demand-filtering process is one that forms a bridge between the order-entry system and the system that captures demand history for use in forecasting. Such a bridging capability en-

```
Demand Filter Hurdles
    Class "A": Errors of +/-  15%
    Class "B": Errors of +/-  50%
    Class "C": Errors of +/- 100%

SKU XYZ is an "A" item
    Actual Demand:      200
    Relevant Forecast:  251
    Percentage Error:   25.5%
This SKU would be flagged

SKU ABC is a "B" item
    Actual Demand:       30
    Relevant Forecast:   22
    Percentage Error:   26.7%
This SKU would not be flagged

SKU DEF is a "C" item
    Actual Demand:        5
    Relevant Forecast:    3
    Percentage Error:   40.0%
This SKU would not be flagged
```

Figure 7-10

ables you to flag unusually large customer orders at the time of order entry and pass judgment before customer orders are processed.

Modifying the Demand History

Don't be afraid to modify the demand history. Suppose, for example, the demand filter was tripped. You look for the underlying reason and determine that a customer placed a large one-time order. Therefore, you don't expect this behavior to recur. You would filter this demand out of the demand-history data that you feed into the forecasting system. If you don't filter it, the system will respond to it.

Another good example of the need to modify historical data concerns pipeline fill for new products. Usually, it appears that initial demand was very high. In reality, it is just inventory that filled the pipeline. You need to modify the historical data so that it will not adversely influence your forecasts.

Some companies react negatively to this advice. The demand history you supply to forecasting need not bear any relationship to what really happened; it should reflect what could have or should have happened or even what you wish would have happened. And although it is important to record and save what actually happened, demand history is actually more valuable for purposes of sales and financial analysis than it is for purposes of forecasting.

Biased Forecasts

A forecast model is said to produce unbiased forecasts if the resulting forecast errors are as likely to be positive (under forecasted) as they are to be negative (over forecasted). As explained above, a demand filter examines the forecast error that corresponds to a single period. This, however, does not reveal anything about the nature of the errors over time. Thus, tests for forecast biases must examine a series of errors.

Various statistical techniques are available for detecting biases. None of them is simple, nor completely foolproof. Although a discussion of these techniques is beyond the scope of this book, an easy way to look for biases is simply to produce graphical output that displays a series of errors. Examine the output for a string of consecutive positive or negative errors. If you find such a string, consider using a different kind of forecast model.

Biased forecasts are typically not a problem if you're using focus forecasting. The selection of a new model every month with focus forecasting usually prevents biases.

Information-Organization Component

The fourth and final component of a forecasting system—information organization—relates strictly to the software you're using. It should allow you to organize and summarize information on many levels. Flexibility is the key.

Focus Your Efforts

Traditionally, many organizations have focused the majority of their resources, especially dollars, on the statistical component of their forecasting system only to have a poor return on their investment. Many companies have learned the hard way, after spending thousands of dollars on software, that you can't effectively use a forecasting system unless you manage the key inputs and outputs. Focus your efforts where they can have the largest impact on the overall process of forecasting.

Also, make sure people are involved in the forecasting process. Put procedures in place to detect and flag problems. Determine what caused the problem. Then fix it. You'll be surprised by the results.

Finally, always remember a key principle of forecasting: The only thing that you can be sure about a forecast is that it is going to be wrong. More important than hitting the number is to (1) have a formal process in place that helps you improve forecast accuracy, and (2) have a formal planning system like DRP that helps you respond faster to changes. In many instances (as shown in chapter 5) DRP can help to eliminate the need for forecasting altogether.

PROVIDING FORECAST INFORMATION TO DRP

Finally, forecasts are only a means to an end. They must be supplied to DRP to be functional. The following section deals with the interface between forecasting and DRP. Specifically, it describes the conversion of monthly forecasts to a weekly orientation, the influence of month-to-date demand, and the influence of known future actual demands.

Converting from Monthly to Weekly

Forecasts are monthly oriented, such as a forecast "for the month of June." DRP, however, works in weekly, sometimes daily, increments. How can this gap be bridged?

Most software packages provide various alternatives. The gap, however, can be bridged very simply. For example, if there are four planning weeks in a month, post one-fourth of the monthly forecast quantity to each week. A more complicated method backfires.

Forecast for the Month of June: 500 Cases
Planning Weeks Contained in June 4

Forecast for week ending 06/03: 125

Forecast for week ending 06/10: 125

Forecast for week ending 06/17: 125

Forecast for week ending 06/24: 125

Occasionally, a company reports that this simple scheme doesn't make sense because it always makes 80 percent of its shipments in the last week of the month. Even though this may be true, it's probably not how this company desires to conduct business. It should therefore break down the weeks evenly—it's even difficult to get a reasonably accurate forecast that's monthly oriented.

Influence of Month-to-Date Demand

Consider the accuracy of your monthly oriented forecast. Then, think about the accuracy that's associated with taking that forecast and rather arbitrarily spreading it across weeks in that month. Supposing that the forecasting system you use always supplied perfect monthly forecasts, it's still very likely that the breakdown to weeks would not be perfect.

Therefore, you might consider keeping track of month-to-date demand. As you get farther into a month, flag unusual conditions that may require adjusting the forecasts for the remaining weeks. Your software should provide the option to do this automatically.

The key is to have software that can give you the information to help you decide what you want to do, without defaulting automatically to the computer. Remember, 99 times out of 100, the inventory needed to support the original forecast is already in place. Furthermore, a one-week deviation is usually insufficient to draw any conclusions. Let DRP handle the required changes. Experience shows that in a network of multiple inventory stocking locations you will oversell the forecast in some locations and undersell it in others. Often, the overall net impact for all locations is insignificant.

Influence of Future Actual Demands

Some customers order in advance. For example, they'll place an order today for product they don't want shipped for two more weeks. This information about future actual demands should be introduced into the DRP planning process. It should supplement the weekly forecast breakdown and, in some cases, replace it.

The process of considering actual future demands is referred to as "forecast consumption." Although there are many different methods for forecast consumption, I only advocate one for companies operating multiple inventory stocking locations. This particular forecast consumption logic compares the actual demand in a period to the forecast for that

	Week One	Week Two	Week Three	Week Four
Forecast	125	125	125	125
Demand	150	80	0	0
Use	150	125	125	125

Figure 7-11

period. Then, it chooses the larger of the two for use in the DRP calculations (see figure 7-11).

Obviously, since the actual demand in week 1 exceeds the forecast, it would be foolish not to use this information for planning purposes.

CONCLUSION

The trend in the past 30 years has been to look for the forecasting panacea, a technique that generates a perfect forecast. One tractor manufacturer, for example, uses econometric models, correlation analysis, and a calculation of the disposable income of farmers. At the conclusion of the process, this company only produces a forecast in total dollars, which is usually overridden by the general manager or sales manager.

Unfortunately, there is no perfect forecasting technique. Nevertheless, techniques must be used, and can be successful if tempered with good judgment. The four most important elements in forecasting are:

1. Assigning the responsibility for developing forecasts.

2. Maintaining accurate data on both shipments *and* actual sales demand.

3. Maintaining good communications, and implementing a communications policy as a normal part of running the business.

4. Measuring the forecast.

Last, but not least, strive for every opportunity available for customer connectivity marketing. By offering your customers value-added services, you eliminate the need for forecasting. You also open a window of significant opportunity that can change the way you do business. The reason is simple—customer connectivity marketing is the last frontier. He who gets there first will ultimately shift the balance of power in his marketing channel. Nothing can compare in terms of increasing profitability and market share.

Chapter 8

Solving Logistics Problems

Common Approaches

The day-to-day process of managing a logistics operation is filled with challenges. This chapter describes various techniques that can be used to surmount them. The most common solutions to distribution problems using DRP discussed in detail in this chapter include:

- Seasonality, promotions, and special sales offers.

- Stock build-ups and depletions.

- Creating a new distribution center.

- Phasing out a distribution center.

- Rearranging the distribution network.

- Creating regional distribution centers (RDCs).

- Controlling obsolescence.

- Handling back orders.

SEASONALITY, PROMOTIONS, AND SPECIAL SALES OFFERS

Seasonality, promotions, and sales offers are a way of life in many companies. Unfortunately, a good deal of money can be made or lost on them depending on how they are handled. The types of seasonality, promotions, and special sales offers discussed here have one thing in common—there is a period of time when the items sell at a rate that is greater than the rate at which they can be manufactured. That means some manufacturing has to be started in advance of the peak selling season, and those items have to be stocked.

The objectives in this situation are (1) to use the stock built up before the peak selling season, combined with the manufacturing capacity, to meet the peak sales demand; and (2) to meet the peak sales demand without creating and carrying unnecessary inventory or causing unnecessary manufacturing inefficiencies.

In manufacturing, solutions to problems related to seasonality, promotions, and special sales offers begin with master production scheduling. Let's look at the distribution demands by month for a product, as well as the company's manufacturing capacity. The distribution demands are calculated by totaling the demands from DRP for all the DCs (see figure 8-1).

In figure 8-1, the product is very seasonal, with 40 percent of the sales for the year occurring from October through December. The maximum capacity in manufacturing is 2,800 a month except for the month of July, when the plant will be shut down for vacation. Over the course of the year, there is enough manufacturing capacity (32,200)

Distribution Demand & Manufacturing Capacity Profile

Month	Distribution Demands	Manufacturing Capacity
January	1800	2800
February	1775	2800
March	1790	2800
April	1750	2800
May	1600	2800
June	1650	2800
July	1500 (Two-week shutdown)	1400
August	1850	2800
September	1975	2800
October	3000	2800
November	3500	2800
December	3900	2800
TOTALS	26,090	32,200

Figure 8-1

to meet the distribution demands for the year (26,090). In the period from October through December, though, the demands from distribution exceed the manufacturing capacity, and some of the manufacturing will have to be done earlier and stocked for the peak selling season.

Working with these numbers, the master scheduler developed a proposed production plan for this product (see figure 8-2).

For the purposes of this example, the product shown is the only product in the family. Since there is only one item in the family, the MPS is the same as the production plan. The master scheduler worked with manufacturing to develop the production plan for this product. It is based on a two-shift operation (1,865 per month) from January to June. The plan of 1,400 in July results from the two-week shutdown for vacation.

From August through December, the plan is based on a three-shift operation (2,800 per month). This will give 500 more than the demands from distribution. This is an acceptable tolerance of two percent for the production plan when compared to the distribution demands, since the management of this company allows the master scheduler a 5 percent tolerance.

Notice that the inventory builds up to a peak of 2,500 in September, just before entering the peak selling season. Then it drops to 500 at the end of December because 500 is the difference between the distribution demands (26,090) and the production plan (26,590).

Proposed Production Plan

Month	Distribution Demands	Production Plan	Manufacturing Capacity	Inventory Build-up
January	1800	1865	2800	65
February	1775	1865	2800	155
March	1790	1865	2800	230
April	1750	1865	2800	345
May	1600	1865	2800	610
June	1650	1865	2800	825
July	1500	1400 (Shutdown)	1400	725
August	1850	2800	2800	1675
September	1975	2800	2800	2500
October	3000	2800	2800	2300
November	3500	2800	2800	1600
December	3900	2800	2800	500
TOTALS	26,090	26,590	32,200	

Figure 8-2

The second part of this problem is what to do with the inventory buildup. The inventory could be stored at the supply source or the DCs, or both, depending on several factors.

Space: If the supply source has the space and the distribution centers do not, it makes sense to store the inventory buildup at the supply source and ship it to the DCs as needed. On the other hand, if the supply source does not have the space, and the DCs do, then it makes sense to store the buildup at the DCs.

In many cases, both the supply source and the distribution centers have available space, and some of the buildup can be stored at each. Other times, it can vary by distribution center. Some DCs may have the space and others may not. Therefore, it makes sense to store the inventory for the DCs that are short of space in the supply source, and to store the rest at the distribution centers that do have space available.

The distribution planners have the responsibility for working with the DC managers to verify that they have the space to handle whatever inventory buildup is planned for storage at each distribution center. Chapter 10 explains techniques for verifying these space requirements.

Storage: This is a second factor in deciding how to store the inventory buildup over the course of the year. If the inventory buildup is stored at the supply source and then shipped to the DCs as needed, the shipping level will be fairly low until the peak selling season, at which point it will increase dramatically, possibly overloading the shipping and receiving people. This must be considered since the people at the DCs will be picking and shipping to customers at the same time as they are expected to receive and store a large number of shipments.

As in the situation with warehouse space, planners have the responsibility for working with the DC managers to verify that distribution centers can handle the shipping and work load during the peak season. The way to verify labor and equipment requirements will also be explained in chapter 10.

Overloading transportation: If a company owns its own trucks or railcars, it makes more sense to ship at a nearly constant rate. A planner can verify whether or not the method of transportation is overloaded by using the DC transportation planning report (see chapter 9). This report shows the weight, cube, and number of pallets planned for shipment to the different DCs throughout the planning horizon.

Safety stock: It is prudent to keep a certain level of safety stock at the supply source. With some of the safety stock stored at supply sources, it can be sent to any of the distribution centers. If, however, all the safety stock is located at the DCs, and the distribution center forecasts are wrong, it is very expensive to transfer that safety stock from one distribution center to another. Nobody makes money shipping the same product twice.

The fact is there are any number of situations and any number of ways to handle inventory buildups. DRP provides the tools to evaluate the different methods of storing the inventory buildup. It then provides the tools to implement whatever decisions are made. The people using the system evaluate and decide what should be done; DRP provides the framework to implement these decisions.

If the decision is to store all the inventory buildup at the supply source, nothing more has to be done. The planned orders from the DCs will be at a lower level during the first part of the year. The planned orders will then show an increased level of shipments near the end of the year. This is exactly what will occur if the inventory buildup is stored at the supply source. Figure 8-3 shows a monthly summary taken from the DRP display for this item at the New York DC.

Summary From DRP Display
New York Distribution Center

On Hand Balance — 650
Safety Stock — 100
Lead Time — 5 days
Order Quantity — 300

	MONTH											
	1	2	3	4	5	6	7	8	9	10	11	12
Gross Requirements	540	530	540	525	480	495	450	555	590	900	1050	1170
Scheduled Receipts												
Projected On Hand	110	180	240	15	135	240	90	135	145	145	295	25
Planned Orders		600	600	300	600	600	300	600	600	900	1200	900

Figure 8-3

In most companies, logistics planners work from a DRP display showing weekly time periods throughout the planning horizon. This example shows a monthly summary because it makes the same point with fewer numbers.

If the decision is to store some of the inventory buildup at the distribution centers, firm planned orders must be used to alter the existing schedule of shipments.

Logistics planners alter the shipping schedule depending on the current constraints. For example, the constraint is storage space at the supply source. This has been determined by using the projection of warehouse space requirements (see chapter 10). In this example, the supply source is unable to store more than 1,000 of this item. The rest has to be stored at the DCs.

The first thing the logistics planner does is to go to the MPS display for this product to see what additional shipments should be made. The master scheduler needs to increase shipments to the DC so that the projected on-hand balance for this item remains at 1,000 or less:

MPS Display
Monthly Summary

	MONTH											
	1	2	3	4	5	6	7	8	9	10	11	12
Distribution Demands	1800	1775	1790	1750	1600	1650	1500	1850	1975	3000	3500	3900
Scheduled Receipts												
Projected On Hand	65	155	230	345	610	825	725	1675	2500	2300	1600	500
Master Schedule	1865	1865	1865	1865	1865	1865	1400	2800	2800	2800	2800	2800

Figure 8-4

Pegging is used to identify shipments at later dates and move them up. In month 8, the logistics planner needs to ship more than 675. Let's assume that the pegging shows two orders of 300 (New York and Los Angeles) and one order of 100 (Vancouver), which could be moved up. The logistics planner could move these orders by using firm planned orders.

In the New York DC, the new display looks like the one in figure 8-5.

Summary From DRP Display
New York Distribution Center

On Hand Balance — 650
Safety Stock   — 100
Lead Time   — 5 days
Order Quantity   — 300

	MONTH											
	1	2	3	4	5	6	7	8	9	10	11	12
Gross Requirements	540	530	540	525	480	495	450	555	590	900	1050	1170
Scheduled Receipts												
Projected On Hand	110	180	240	15	135	240	90	435				
Planned Orders		600	600	300	600	600	300					
Firm Planned Orders								900				

Figure 8-5

MPS Display
Monthly Summary

	MONTH											
	1	2	3	4	5	6	7	8	9	10	11	12
Distribution Demands	1800	1775	1790	1750	1600	1650	1500	2550	1275	3000	3500	3900
Scheduled Receipts												
Projected On Hand	65	155	230	345	610	825	725	975				
Master Schedule	1865	1865	1865	1865	1865	1865	1400	2800	2800	2800	2800	2800

Figure 8-6

Figure 8-6 shows how the first planned orders in New York, Los Angeles, and Vancouver change the MPS display.

The logistics planner continues to the next time period (month 9), then the next, and so on until after the peak selling season.

But storage space isn't the only constraint the logistics planner has to worry about. Let's assume that mode of transportation is the problem. Let's also assume that the company operates its own fleet of trucks and wants to use them whenever possible. Near the end of the year the fleet will be unable to handle the volume of shipments. Therefore, the logistics planner will attempt to smooth out the level of shipments.

To achieve its goal, the planner could use the DC transportation planning report (explained in detail in chapter 9) to show the shipments by weight and cube. The logistics planner also has to check with the master scheduler to ensure that the inventory will be on hand when he plans to ship it. Figure 8-7 shows the plan that the logistics planner and the master scheduler developed.

The schedule of shipments is much more level than that shown earlier in figure 8-3. And, from July through November, the distribution center is used to stock the item in anticipation of the peak selling season:

Summary From DRP Display
New York Distribution Center

On Hand Balance — 650
Safety Stock   — 100
Lead Time   — 5 days
Order Quantity — 300

	MONTH											
	1	2	3	4	5	6	7	8	9	10	11	12
Gross Requirements	540	530	540	525	480	495	450	555	590	900	1050	1170
Scheduled Receipts												
Projected On Hand	110	180	240	15	135	240	390	735	745	745	295	25
Planned Orders		600	600	300	600	600						
Firm Planned Orders							600	900	600	900	600	900

Figure 8-7

The example here is one where the peak selling season is due to the seasonality of the product. Even so, exactly the same methods are used to handle promotions and special sales offers. The only difference is that such offers tend to have a shorter peak selling season. The peak selling season in this example lasted for three months, but promotions and special sample offers may only last several weeks. However, exactly the same methods apply and can be used.

Certain commercially available software packages enable you to mass load firm planned orders after you decide on the buildup plan. In other words, they enable you to deploy inventory before it is needed. Without such capabilities, you must use a time-phased safety-stock quantity for the inventory buildup period. This allows you to achieve similar results.

To summarize the points of this example:

1. DRP and master production scheduling provide the tools to evaluate how to build stock in anticipation of a peak selling season.

2. DRP and master production scheduling provide the tools to implement whatever solution is decided.

3. Because the solution is implemented within the DRP system, it becomes visible to everyone. The shipments, the inventory buildup, projected freight costs, the material and capacity required, etc. become apparent to logistics, manufacturing, store management, and to people in the DCs supporting the stores.

STOCK BUILDUPS AND DEPLETIONS

There are a number of situations when inventory must be built up and depleted, and it cannot be stored at the supply source. These situations include plant shutdowns because of renovations or vacations, installation of new equipment, or upcoming union contracts. In such cases, most people use some kind of temporary outside storage to hold their inventory buildup and then deplete it.

In many instances, the plant will be closed and products cannot be made. This means that planning this inventory buildup and depletion must be handled correctly. If the wrong inventory is stockpiled or not enough is stockpiled, customer service will suffer, and a great deal of money can be lost.

This example is similar to the inventory buildup designed to handle seasonality, promotions, and special sales offers. The difference is that an outside storage area must be used, and the area must always be restricted to the situations mentioned earlier. In some cases, the size of the inventory buildup for seasonality, promotions, or a special sales offer may require an outside storage area. In those cases, the method explained in this section can be used to handle the problem.

There are basically two aspects to the problem of stock buildups and depletions:

1. How to use DRP to control and buildup inventory in the stockpile.

2. How to use DRP to control the depletion of the stockpile.

In this example, because a company is renovating its plant, it needs to shut down manufacturing for two months. Customers are not going to stop ordering during the shutdown, so the company must continue to supply its distribution network. In addition, because of the renovation at the plant, the supply source will be unavailable. Consequently, all the inventory must be moved from the supply source to the temporary storage area, and the DCs will be supplied from that location.

The first action is to establish the new storage area, the stockpile, in the system. It is not possible to begin stockpiling the inventory within DRP until a stocking location exists within the system. An item number is created for each item to be stored there. These numbers are linked to the supply source using either of two methods: bills of distribution or a special computer program (see Appendix C for more details). When these links have been created, the distribution network will appear as shown in figure 8-8.

**Revised Distribution Network
Including a New Stockpile Location**

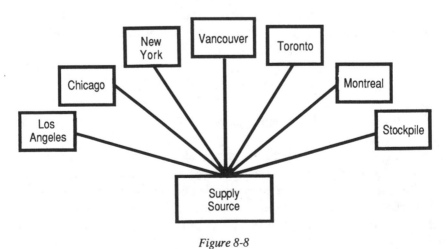

Figure 8-8

All the distribution centers draw from the supply source, and the stockpile draws from the supply source as well. Once this distribution network is set up, inventory buildup can begin, using exactly the same methods explained earlier to build up inventory in anticipation of a peak selling season. Production planning and master scheduling are used to visualize the distribution demands, evaluate the manufacturing and purchasing capacity, and develop production plans and master production schedules which will provide enough of a product to satisfy the day-to-day needs of the distribution network as well as to begin stockpiling inventory. Let's assume that the summary shown below represents the MPS developed for one of the items being stockpiled:

MPS Display
Monthly Summary

	MONTH											
	1	2	3	4	5	6	7	8	9	10	11	12
Distribution Demands	2300	4700	3400	4200	1900	5000	2700	3200	4100	2100	3500	3900
Scheduled Receipts												
Projected On Hand	2300	2200	3400	3800	6500	6100	3400	200	200	200	200	200
Master Schedule	4600	4600	4600	4600	4600	4600	0	0	4100	2100	3500	3900

Figure 8-9

The MPS for this product is zero during the seventh and eighth months, when the shutdown is scheduled to occur. The MPS for the first six months is large enough to handle the distribution demands during the same period of time, the distribution demand over the two-month shutdown, and a safety stock of 200.

The projected inventory builds to a peak of 6,500 during May. This inventory must be moved to the temporary storage area by the end of June to make room for the renovation.

The logistics planner then enters firm planned orders at the stockpile location to show this movement out of the supply source and into the stockpile. In this case, the supply source is unable to store more than 3,000 of this product. When the projected inventory for this item becomes higher than 3,000, plans will have to be made to move the excess to the temporary storage area. But the logistics planner should not start using the outside storage area until necessary because of the cost. For this reason, the first firm planned orders to move this product from the supply source to the stockpile occurs during the month of March. A summary of the DRP display for this product at the stockpile location appears in figure 8-10.

Monthly Summary From DRP Display
Stockpile Location

On Hand Balance — 0
Safety Stock   — 200
Lead Time   — 1 wk
Order Quantity   — 1000

	MONTH											
	1	2	3	4	5	6	7	8	9	10	11	12
Gross Requirements												
Scheduled Receipts												
Projected On Hand	0	0	400	800	5000	6100	6100	6100	6100	6100	6100	6100
Planned Orders												
Firm Planned Orders			400	400	4200	1100						

Figure 8-10

Figure 8-10 shows the firm planned orders that the logistics planner entered to transfer stock from the supply source to the storage area. These cause the MPS summary to change. The logistics planner keeps the projected inventory for this item at or below the 3,000 that can be stored at the supply source. In addition, by the end of June, he transferred all stock from the supply source to the stockpile location, as shown by the zero projected on-hand balance for June.

In the months after June, the projected on-hand balance becomes a negative 5,900 (see figure 8-11) because the distribution demands in July and August show against the supply source when, in fact, they will be supplied from the stockpile.

MPS Display
Monthly Summary

	MONTH											
	1	2	3	4	5	6	7	8	9	10	11	12
Distribution Demands	2300	4700	3800	4600	6100	6100	2700	3200	4100	2100	3500	3900
Scheduled Receipts												
Projected On Hand	2300	2200	3000	3000	1500	0	-2700	-5900	-5900	-5900	-5900	-5900
Master Schedule	4600	4600	4600	4600	4600	4600	0	0	4100	2100	3500	3900

Figure 8-11

The correct solution is to show the distribution demands for the months of July and August against the stockpile location. If this is done, the summary from the DRP display for the stockpile location would look like the one in figure 8-12.

Monthly Summary From DRP Display
Stockpile Location

On Hand Balance — 0
Safety Stock — 200
Lead Time — 1 wk
Order Quantity — 1000

	MONTH											
	1	2	3	4	5	6	7	8	9	10	11	12
Gross Requirements							2700	3200				
Scheduled Receipts												
Projected On Hand	0	0	400	800	5000	6100	3400	200	200	200	200	200
Planned Orders												
Firm Planned Orders			400	400	4200	1100						

Figure 8-12

Now the summary from the display correctly shows how the demands will actually balance against the stockpile. The remaining projected on-hand balance of 200 is the planned safety stock. If the distribution demands for the months of July and August are shown against the stockpile location, the summarized MPS display appears as shown in figure 8-13.

Not all commercially available software packages have the capabilities to show the demands correctly as illustrated in figures 8-12 and 8-13. The situation depends on what methods are used to link the distribution centers to the supply source and what features are available in the software.

If bills of distribution are used to link the items at the DCs to the supply source, a feature called Effectivity Dates or a feature called Deviations Tied to an Order can be used to show the requirements correctly. These features, and the method used to show these requirements correctly, are explained in Appendix C.

If a computer program is used to link the items at the DC to the supply source, it must have some logic to account for situations in which a distribution center is supplied from one facility for a time (e.g., the supply source), and then supplied from another facility for a time (e.g., the stockpile). (Appendix C also includes an explanation of how this logic would show the demands correctly.)

Revised MPS Display
Monthly Summary

	MONTH											
	1	2	3	4	5	6	7	8	9	10	11	12
Distribution Demands	2300	4700	3800	4600	6100	6100	0	0	4100	2100	3500	3900
Scheduled Receipts												
Projected On Hand	2300	2200	3000	3000	1500	0	0	0	0	0	0	0
Master Schedule	4600	4600	4600	4600	4600	4600	0	0	4100	2100	3500	3900

Figure 8-13

CREATING A NEW DISTRIBUTION CENTER

There are a number of reasons for creating a new DC. Probably the most common reason is that a business expands and it is economical to have a new DC. For example, the business in a particular area may be serviced from two DCs, and it now seems appropriate for a new, single DC to handle the area.

Another instance is an area being serviced from the supply source. In this case, the supply source acts as a DC. As the business in this area grows, it may make sense to open a DC and no longer service the customers from the supply source.

When a new DC is created, an item number must be created for each of the items to be stocked. In addition, DRP needs planning information, such as the lead time, order quantity, safety stock, etc. for each of the items, as well as a bill of distribution or table entry showing the supply source for the item.

Generally, when a new DC is created, demand at one or more of the existing DCs is affected. In some instances, though, demand may not be affected, as in the case when a company enters a new market or opens a DC in a new country. When demand at other DCs is affected by the new DC, planning must be done for items at the new DC, as well as for the other DCs.

The technique for planning the items at the new DCs is to load a forecast starting on the date the DC is scheduled to open. Figure 8-14 shows what the DRP display would look like for an item at a new DC.

As you can see, the forecast for this three-way lamp in the Houston DC starts in week 4. Week 4 is the first time the new Houston DC will be able to open for business. There is a firm planned order for 150 due to be shipped in week 2 to this DC. This was created by the logistics planner indicating an intention to stock up prior to opening for business. There is a system-generated planned order due to be shipped in week 6. These orders are creating distribution demands on the supply source.

Now let's look at this three-way lamp in the Chicago DC, which has been supplying the Houston area. (See figure 8-15).

The forecast drops by 25 a week beginning in week 4. This is indicative of the fact that the Houston DC will be servicing those customers starting in week 4. In this example, only the Chicago DC is affected. In other situations, several DCs could be affected, in which case the forecasts for the items would have to be changed.

DRP Display
Three-Way Lamp
Houston Distribution Center

On Hand Balance — 0
Safety Stock   — 50
Lead Time   — 2 wks
Order Quantity — 150

	Past Due	Week							
		1	2	3	4	5	6	7	8
Gross Requirements					25	25	25	25	25
Scheduled Receipts									
Projected On Hand	0				125	100	75	50	175
Planned Orders							150		
Firm Planned Order			150						

Figure 8-14

DRP Display
Three-Way Lamp
Chicago Distribution Center

On Hand Balance — 350
Safety Stock   — 150
Lead Time   — 1 day
Order Quantity — 300

	Past Due	Week							
		1	2	3	4	5	6	7	8
Gross Requirements		105	105	105	80	80	80	80	80
Scheduled Receipts									
Projected On Hand	350	245	440	335	255	175	395	315	235
Planned Orders			300				300		

Figure 8-15

When other DCs are affected, it may also be necessary to reevaluate the order quantities and safety stocks. Since the demand on the DC has changed, these numbers may have to be updated, too.

By using the above method of creating new DCs, all logistics planners have to do is create a new DC with DRP, and then change the forecasts. The logic of DRP and master production scheduling or supplier scheduling handles the rest. Demands from the new DC, and the reduced demands from the affected DCs are posted to the supply source. Master schedulers or supplier schedulers can evaluate this and determine whether their master schedules are sufficient to cope with the opening of the new DC. If not, their schedules may be changed, or the date for shipping the product from the new DC may be changed. Also, firm planned orders can be used to ship enough of the product to the new DC to supply the customers until more of the product is available.

PHASING OUT A DISTRIBUTION CENTER

At one time or another, companies inevitably phase out DCs. A common reason is a geographic change in sales mix, such as losing several large customers or experiencing a shift in sales from the East Coast to the Midwest. A second reason may be strictly competitive; a company not doing well in an area may decide not to do any more business there. A third reason may be based on a new direct delivery program being instituted with new suppliers.

If handled improperly, a phaseout can be quite costly. If it is planned poorly, you may end up with surplus stock that must be disposed of or transported to another DC.

Phasing out a DC involves planning the maneuver, then disposing of any leftover inventory. The objective of the phaseout is to have as little inventory as possible remaining. But regardless of how well the planning is done, it is likely that some inventory will be left over. The amount of inventory remaining also depends on how much time the planners have to work on phasing out the DC. If the planners have three or four months to set up and execute a plan, it is unlikely that there will be any significant amount of inventory left over. If they only have a few weeks, significant amounts of inventory will have to be disposed of or moved.

Planning the Phaseout

Phasing out a distribution center is handled in a very similar process by which a DC is created. It starts by changing the forecasts in the affected DCs.

As an example, let's consider the New Orleans DC, which is being phased out, and the Houston DC, which will service the customers from the New Orleans area. Figure 8-16 shows the DRP displays for the three-way lamp at both DCs.

Several aspects of the two displays are of interest. One is that the forecast for the New Orleans DC drops to zero in week 6 and remains there. This is the DC that will not be in operation after week 5. The second is that there is a scheduled receipt for 100 due in week 2. This is different from the order quantity of 150 used in the past, and it is just large enough to satisfy the demands to the end of week 5. The logistics planner, knowing that the DC is closing, created an order just large enough to satisfy the remaining forecast.

In this case, the logistics planner changed the order policy to lot-for-lot on the item in the New Orleans DC shown in figure 8-16 because it is being discontinued at this DC. This way only what is needed will be ordered.

The planner also set the safety stock to zero.[1] Since the three-way lamp is being discontinued at this DC, the planner wants the inventory to be down to zero in week 5. If a safety stock remains on the item, the logic in DRP tries to retain the safety stock quantity, even though it would never be used.

For the item at the Houston DC, the forecast increases by 25, starting in week 6 because the Houston DC will be servicing the customers in the New Orleans area.

The appeal of this approach is its simplicity. Once the above-mentioned actions are taken, the logic of DRP calculates and displays the plan. The distribution requirements are posted to the supply source, which is then evaluated by the supplier scheduler or master scheduler. The projected on-hand balance for the items in the New Orleans DC is the inventory that must be disposed of or moved elsewhere.

---

[1] Removal of the safety stock normally takes place one lead time before the shutdown of the DC. Certain commercially available software packages enable you to specify a date when to remove safety stocks. If this is not possible, it is the responsibility of the planner to remove them.

DRP Display
Three-Way Lamp
Houston Distribution Center

On Hand Balance — 120
Safety Stock   — 50
Lead Time   — 2 wks
Order Quantity   — 150

	Past Due	Week							
		1	2	3	4	5	6	7	8
Gross Requirements		25	25	25	25	25	50	50	50
Scheduled Receipts									
Projected On Hand	120	95	70	195	170	145	95	195	145
Planned Orders		150				150			

DRP Display
Three-Way Lamp
New Orleans Distribution Center

On Hand Balance — 25
Safety Stock   — 0
Lead Time   — 2 wks
Order Quantity   — lot-for-lot

	Past Due	Week							
		1	2	3	4	5	6	7	8
Gross Requirements		25	25	25	25	25			
Scheduled Receipts			100						
Projected On Hand	25	0	75	50	25	0			
Planned Orders									

Figure 8-16

Disposal

Remaining inventory in a closed DC can be disposed of through several methods. The simplest way is to transfer it to another DC or to the supply source. Another approach is to discount the products to sell them off.

To illustrate how an item can be disposed of, let's take another product, a ceiling-mounted lamp in the New Orleans DC (see figure 8-17).

In figure 8-17, the requirements for this product will not use up the on-hand balance, and there will be 165 remaining in inventory that must be disposed of or moved. Depending on the amount of time the planner has to phase out this DC, there could be many leftover products.

If the planner decides to transfer this inventory to another distribution center, he can use firm planned orders. First, he decides which DC in the inventory will receive the products, and then enters firm planned orders for the remaining quantity. These firm planned orders will be deviations from the normal distribution channels, since they are shipments from the New Orleans DC rather than from the supply source. (This method is explained in Appendix D.)

DRP Display
Ceiling-Mounted Lamp
New Orleans Distribution Center

On Hand Balance — 340
Safety Stock — 0
Lead Time — 2 wks
Order Quantity — lot-for-lot

	Past Due	Week 1	2	3	4	5	6	7	8
Gross Requirements		35	35	35	35	35			
Scheduled Receipts									
Projected On Hand	340	305	270	235	200	165	165	165	165
Planned Orders									

Figure 8-17

DRP Display
Ceiling-Mounted Lamp
New Orleans Distribution Center

On Hand Balance — 340
Safety Stock   — 0
Lead Time   — 2 wks
Order Quantity   — lot-for-lot

	Past Due	Week							
		1	2	3	4	5	6	7	8
Gross Requirements		35	35	35	35	35	165		
Scheduled Receipts									
Projected On Hand	340	305	270	235	200	165	0	0	0
Planned Orders									

Figure 8-18

Once the firm planned orders are entered, the DRP display for the items in the discontinued DC will be similar to the display for the ceiling-mounted lamp at the New Orleans DC (see figure 8-18).

The large gross requirement in week 6 comes from the firm planned order needed to transfer the remaining inventory to another distribution center. Using firm planned orders in this way, the transfer of the remaining inventory can be planned at both the discontinued DC, and the DC that will be receiving the additional inventory.

In some situations, planners may want to transfer the remaining inventory back to the supply source rather than to another DC. The supply source then is treated as a DC, and a firm planned order is created for delivery to the supply source from the discontinued DC. Some software packages will allow for this; others will not. It is beneficial to examine the particular software package prior to such a transfer to ensure that the system can handle it. If your software cannot handle such transfers, you should try to modify it. If this cannot be done on time, a scheduled receipt could be created to cover the shipments of remaining inventory to the supply source. The disadvantage of this method is that the system does not show the transfer until it is actually entered as a scheduled receipt. As a result, you cannot plan the transfer in advance using the information in the system.

Rearranging the Distribution Network

There are a number of situations when the distribution network needs to be rearranged. These include consolidating several DCs into one or breaking a DC apart into several new acquisitions.

Each of these problems can be solved using the tools explained earlier for creating or phasing out a DC. These changes to the distribution network, regardless of how complex they may appear, are just combinations of creating and phasing out DCs. What is important is to reflect the changes as they are taking place. Your bill-of-distribution module must be kept current for DRP to help you make the transition from one distribution deployment strategy to another. It is very desirable to have a procedure describing who is authorized and who is accountable for maintaining the network.

Creating Regional Distribution Centers (RDCs)

Sometimes it makes sense to create regional distribution centers (RDCs). These are large DCs that service satellite distribution centers in the nearby geographic area. For example, a West Coast RDC might be located in San Francisco. This RDC could service customers in the San Francisco area, as well as servicing the DCs in Los Angeles, Portland, Seattle, Salt Lake City, and Phoenix. The San Francisco RDC is supplied from Chicago, and the West Coast satellite distribution centers are supplied from San Francisco.

Any number of reasons for creating RDCs basically fall into two categories—economics and customer service. Economic reasons include better freight rates, lower warehousing costs, and lower inventories. Better freight rates can be obtained when there is a large volume of product moving from one point to another, such as from the supply source to the RDC. The smaller shipments can then be sent from the RDCs to the satellite DCs. Because these shipments are smaller, they don't have the advantage of the lowest freight rates, but they travel shorter distances, which reduces the overall shipping costs.

Lower inventories are possible because more safety stock can be held at the RDCs and less at the satellite DCs. Safety stock is used to handle demands that are above forecast until the supply source is able to resupply the DC. If an RDC can resupply a satellite DC overnight, that

DC doesn't have to carry as much safety stock as if it were resupplied from Chicago, which may require one to two weeks.

The RDC, however, still has to carry the safety stock for the satellite distribution centers. Nevertheless, there is an inventory savings here. The safety stock that an RDC carries is less than the sum of the safety stocks for the satellite DCs. The reason is that forecast deviations in satellite DCs tend to cancel one another. One satellite may be selling more than forecast, and another may be selling less. These negate each other from the perspective of the RDC. The supply is sufficient for all DCs, although without the RDC each DC would have to carry enough stock to handle the deviations on its own.

Reduced inventories and economies of scale lower warehousing costs. Reduced inventories mean lower warehousing costs because the volume to be stored is decreased. The economies of scale arise because it is cheaper to store items at the RDCs than at the smaller DCs. Mechanized or semimechanized material-handling and order-picking systems are volume oriented. Even if the same amount of inventory is stored in the distribution network, the fact that much of it is stored in a large, centralized RDC rather than the smaller, more expensive satellite DC creates some savings.

For example, consider a situation in which 40,000 pallets of a product are stored at four different DCs. In this case, each DC stores approximately 10,000 pallets. If a large RDC is created to store 20,000 of these pallets more cheaply than can be done in the separate DCs the company could realize significant cost savings.

The second reason for creating RDCs is to provide better customer service. An RDC makes it possible to justify smaller satellite DCs or possibly renting public warehousing services that are closer to the customers, therefore providing faster customer service. It is also possible to justify the volume supplied to the small satellite DCs from an RDC, if it is not economically feasible to ship to them from the supply source. In fact, a number of companies have closed down their DCs and have begun using public warehousing services instead. These warehouses are actually satellite DCs supplied by RDCs.

This is not to say that establishing RDCs will always reduce inventory, lead to better freight rates, provide lower warehousing costs, or yield better customer service. It depends on the situation. If savings can be realized in freight, safety stock, and warehousing, and the plan is well-executed using DRP, the savings will be realized. The same holds for customer service.

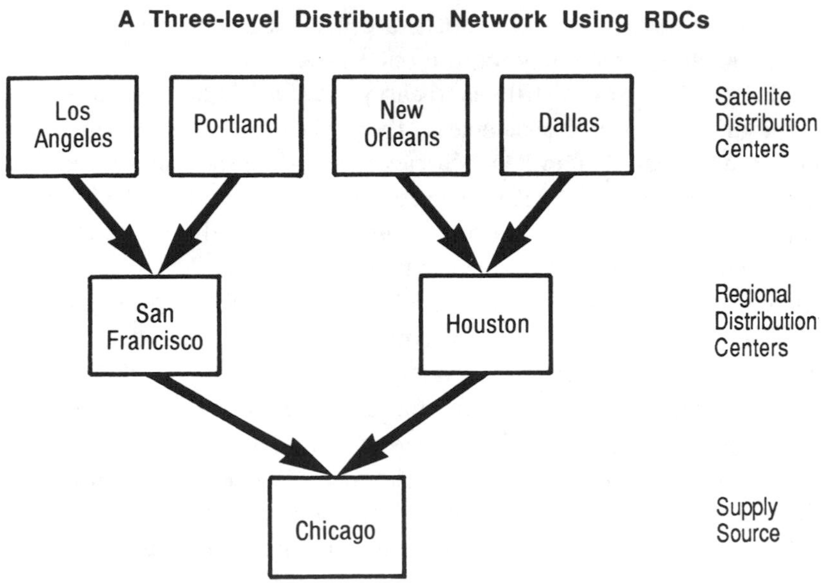

A Three-level Distribution Network Using RDCs

Figure 8-19

Using DRP to Manage RDCs

It is very simple to handle RDCs with DRP. The only step is to show a DC supplied from an RDC as opposed to being supplied from the supply source. Figure 8-19 shows a distribution network as represented within DRP. (Note: this is actually a sample from a larger distribution network—a subset is used for purposes of illustration.)

To show how DRP works with RDCs, let's look at the DRP displays for the Los Angeles and Portland satellite DCs, and also the DRP display for the San Francisco RDC (figures 8-20 and 8-21).

In this case, the demands from the satellite DCs are appearing as gross requirements at the San Francisco RDC. In addition, in the San Francisco RDC, a forecast of 30 per week is showing in the gross requirements quantity. This forecast of 30 a week exists because the San Francisco RDC services the customers in the Bay Area. The pegging for the San Francisco RDC would show the total demands from the satellite distribution centers, as well as the forecast of 30 per week to handle the customers in the San Francisco area.

Now, let's look at the DRP displays for the New Orleans and Dallas satellite DCs. (See figure 8-21, which also shows the DRP display for the Houston RDC.)

DRP Display
1¹/₂ oz. Nutmeg
San Francisco
Regional Distribution Center

On Hand
  Balance   −800
Safety Stock −250
Lead Time   −2 wks
Order
  Quantity   −500

	Past Due	Week							
		1	2	3	4	5	6	7	8
Gross Requirements		205	280	30	30	455	30	280	205
Scheduled Receipts									
Projected On Hand	800	595	315	285	255	300	270	490	285
Planned Orders				500		500			

DRP Display
1¹/₂ oz. Nutmeg
Los Angeles
Satellite Distribution Center

On Hand
  Balance   −160
Safety Stock −75
Lead Time   −2 days
Order
  Quantity   −250

	Past Due	Week							
		1	2	3	4	5	6	7	8
Gross Requirements		80	75	90	80	100	95	85	90
Scheduled Receipts									
Projected On Hand	160	80	255	165	85	235	140	305	215
Planned Orders			250			250		250	

DRP Display
1¹/₂ oz. Nutmeg
Portland
Satellite Distribution Center

On Hand
  Balance   −90
Safety Stock −50
Lead Time   −2 days
Order
  Quantity   −175

	Past Due	Week							
		1	2	3	4	5	6	7	8
Gross Requirements		50	45	60	55	40	50	60	45
Scheduled Receipts									
Projected On Hand	90	215	170	110	55	190	140	80	210
Planned Orders		175				175			175

Figure 8-20

DRP Display
1½ oz. Nutmeg
New Orleans
Satellite Distribution Center

On Hand
  Balance   −140
Safety Stock −75
Lead Time   −2 days
Order
  Quantity   −200

	Past Due	Week							
		1	2	3	4	5	6	7	8
Gross Requirements		70	75	65	80	65	70	80	85
Scheduled Receipts									
Projected On Hand	140	270	195	130	250	185	115	235	150
Planned Orders		200			200			200	

DRP Display
1½ oz. Nutmeg
Dallas
Satellite Distribution Center

On Hand
  Balance   −85
Safety Stock −40
Lead time   −2 days
Order
  Quantity   −125

	Past Due	Week							
		1	2	3	4	5	6	7	8
Gross Requirements		35	45	30	40	45	35	30	40
Scheduled Receipts									
Projected On Hand	85	50	130	100	60	140	105	75	160
Planned Orders			125			125			125

DRP Display
1½ oz. Nutmeg
Houston
Regional Distribution Center

On Hand
  Balance   −880
Safety Stock −200
Lead Time   −2 wks
Order
  Quantity   −400

	Past Due	Week							
		1	2	3	4	5	6	7	8
Gross Requirements		240	165	40	240	165	40	240	165
Scheduled Receipts									
Projected On Hand	880	640	475	435	595	430	390	550	385
Planned Orders			400			400			

Figure 8-21

Again, the demands from the satellite distribution centers are diminishing and appear as gross requirements at the regional distribution center. In addition, a forecast of 40 per week is included because the Houston RDC services the customers in the Houston area.

The planned orders from the RDC show as distribution demands on the MPS display for this item at the supply source. (In this example, the supply source is a factory.) Figure 8-22 shows an example of the MPS display at the supply source.

An important point is that DRP can work with any number of levels in the distribution network. In this case, we have satellite distribution centers, regional distribution centers, and a supply source. We could also have several levels of RDCs supplying one another. Whether they are practical and profitable is another issue; the point is, DRP can portray this situation realistically.

In general, it is better to use bills of distribution to link the satellite distribution centers to the RDCs, and the RDCs to the supply source. The reason is that the bill-of-distribution logic in DRP software packages will keep track of the different levels and ensure that the satellite

MPS Display
Chicago Supply Source

On Hand Balance — 950
Safety Stock — 0
Lead Time — 4 wks
Order Quantity — 1000

	Past Due	Week							
		1	2	3	4	5	6	7	8
Distribution Demands		0	400	500	0	900	0	0	0
Scheduled Receipts									
Projected On Hand	950	950	550	50	50	150	150	150	150
Master Schedule-Rcpt.						1000			
Master Schedule-Start		1000							

Figure 8-22

distribution centers are planned before the RDCs, and that the RDCs are planned before posting distribution demands to the supply source.

If bills of distribution are not used to link the distribution centers, some scheduling will have to be done in running DRP. The satellite DCs will have to run DRP and then be used as demands to the RDCs. The RDCs will then run DRP and send their distribution demands to the supply source. If there is any problem in running DRP at any of the locations, the entire network could be delayed. One way to handle this situation is to allow several hours or a day between the satellite DRP, the regional DRP, and the MPS run at the supply source. This gives each of the locations time to correct any problems, but it also prolongs the process.

CONTROLLING OBSOLESCENCE

Many companies are plagued with the problem of obsolescence. Dairy products, canned foods, drugs, camera film and other types of products have expiration dates. For some products, federal regulations require that these expiration dates be printed on the product, and if the products are not sold or used by the expiration date, they must be destroyed.

Obsolescence can also be a problem in products that are not regulated by expiration dates but have short life cycles. In high demand today, items in cosmetics, fashion, video games, for example, can experience a dramatic reduction in demand a few months from now.

Unfortunately, obsolete inventory is often discovered when it is too late. By the time it is found, the expiration date has passed or the demand for the item has dropped. Sometimes this happens during the annual "physical inventory surprise," in which many companies lose hundreds of thousands of dollars as they write off obsolete inventories.

Whether an item is expiration dated or has a short life cycle, we need a system that will identify and highlight potentially obsolete inventory. DRP fits the bill because it can be used to see potentially obsolete inventory while there is still time to do something about it.

As stressed throughout this book, DRP is a valid simulation of reality. As such, it can be used to identify any number of problem areas, including obsolete inventory. The DRP logic only needs to detect such inventory and generate an appropriate action message.

There are several ways in which DRP can identify and report potentially obsolete inventory. One is to develop a system in which the inventory is stored as a total, and this total is further defined by a lot number indicating the expiration date. This is very similar to systems where a total on-hand balance is maintained and defined by inventory location. DRP logic can then include a section that checks the expiration dates against the date the on-hand balance will be used up. Any lots that have expiration dates earlier than the date the on-hand balance will be used up should have an action message generated for potentially obsolete inventory.

This method can identify potentially obsolete inventory in advance, but it will only identify items that have exceeded their expiration dates. It does not identify overstock situations, in which items will not pass their expiration date, but there is too much inventory in the distribution center. These situations are a function of the quantity used in comparison to the forecast, not the expiration date. In addition, the commercially available DRP software packages typically do not contain this logic.

Overstock Situations

Another method not as complete is simpler and will also identify overstock situations. This method, which works very well, uses the planned orders in DRP.

If, for example, there is a forecast of 100 per week, a safety stock of 200 (two weeks), and an on-hand balance of 2,000, DRP can plan an order due to be received in the distribution center in 18 weeks.

There are any number of reasons why there are 18 weeks of inventory at a distribution center. One is that the forecast was revised downward. At one time, the 2,000 on hand may have been only 6 weeks of supply.

There is a way to identify potential obsolescence with DRP. When there are no planned orders for an item at a distribution center for some specified number of weeks, there is the possibility of obsolescence. These situations should be brought to the planner's attention through an action message. If the item has an expiration date, the planner can have the people at the distribution center check it. If the date will pass before the stock is used up, some plans can be made to transfer the item to another DC. If the item is one with a short life cycle, some plans can be made to promote it or move it to another location.

It is up to you to decide when an action message should be generated, and the number of weeks vary by product. For example, if an item has a six-month life, it may make sense to have an action message generated when there are no planned orders for three months.

This method assumes something close to first in, first out (FIFO) in handling inventory. In other words, if a skid of material is left in the back of the distribution center and never touched, this method will not pick it up as potentially obsolete inventory. If, however, the people in the distribution center do a reasonable job of FIFO, potentially obsolete inventory will be picked up and highlighted. Most people choose a number of weeks that is somewhat less than the life of the product.

A valuable by-product of this method is that it helps to identify slow-moving products. It may make sense to discontinue these products, and this method will highlight them.

HANDLING BACK ORDERS

Back orders are handled in a similar way as customer orders (i.e., in addition to the forecast.) This is because back orders have to be satisfied, and the forecast in the future has to be satisfied as well. The back orders generally appear in the past-due time period and are treated as gross requirements (see figure 8-23).

DRP Display
Three-Way Lamp
Houston Distribution Center

On Hand Balance — 0
Safety Stock   — 200
Lead Time   — 2 wks
Order Quantity   — 600

	Past Due	Week 1	2	3	4	5	6	7	8
Gross Requirements	50	100	100	100	100	100	100	100	100
Scheduled Receipts									
Projected On Hand	-50	-150	350	250	750	650	550	450	350
Planned Orders	600		600						

Figure 8-23

DRP is planning to satisfy the 50 on back order, as well as the forecast for 100 each week.

CONCLUSION

In this chapter, we covered a number of important issues that affect the management of a logistics operation. Some occur very infrequently, such as opening or phasing out a distribution center. Others, like seasonality, promotions, etc. are very common. DRP develops a process for dealing with all of these issues in a formal manner, thus giving its users more control in the planning and execution phases.

Chapter 9

Transportation Planning

Taking Advantage of Cost-saving Opportunities

THE MISSING LINK

To be complete, a logistics planning system must recognize the importance of scheduling both inventories and transportation from supply sources to distribution points. That is because in the world of logistics, certain fundamental requirements must be satisfied. Given a network of DCs that are supplied from one or several supply sources, logistics people need to schedule and manage inventories in the network and also schedule shipments to DCs.

In many companies, the cost for transportation is the largest single logistics cost. In fact, in some companies, transportation costs represent more than half the total costs of logistics. From 1974 to 1980, transportation costs rose faster than any other element of cost within logistics. Since deregulation, opportunities have opened up to curb transportation costs, but without the proper tools for effectively scheduling inventories and replenishing stocking locations, companies are unable to fully realize the possible savings now available in the transportation arena.

With DRP, it is possible to implement accurate transportation loading and scheduling. Transportation planning is used with shipments from the supply source to the DCs, and from DC to DC if this type of shipping is done. This planning will be effective because DRP is an accurate, detailed simulation of a logistics operation. As such, it can be used to show what items are planned to be shipped and when shipping should take place.

219

To illustrate the kinds of savings that can be achieved from planning and managing transportation, consider a company that ships 20 million pounds of different products each year from its Chicago plant to its Los Angeles DC. Railcars are used to ship the product. In this example, each railcar can be loaded with products up to 100,000 pounds, and each railcar contains 2,600 cubic feet of volume. Let's also assume the company negotiated the rate structure shown in figure 9-1:

Chicago to Los Angeles Rate and Weight Structure	
Car Weight	Avg. Cost Per Cwt.
0 to 50.000	8.00/cwt.
50.000 to 75.000	6.40/cwt.
75.000 to 90.000	6.20/cwt.
90.000 to 100.000	5.40/cwt.

Figure 9-1

The rate structure in this case, as in most cases, is designed to provide an incentive to ship the maximum weight of the railcar. For example, a railcar weighing 50,000 pounds costs $4,000, while a railcar weighing 100,000 pounds costs $5,400. This represents a 33 percent savings on a hundredweight (cwt.) basis.

Despite the economies of scale, most companies today do not have the tools in place to use the most advantageous rate structures. This is because they are unable to visualize future shipments to the various DCs. Obviously, if they could, they would realize significant savings. For example, if they saw that this week they would be sending a half-full railcar or truck, they could begin to pull products up from next week. By shipping some products a few days earlier than originally planned, they could now fill the railcar or truck. This would be done by pulling the right products up, products to be sold in the next few days or week, rather than just shipping any products that happen to be available at the time. Another example would be a company that has the visibility to use both the weight and cube of a railcar or truck by adjusting the mix of product to be shipped.

But let's go back to the sample company. It has enough volume to ship

200 railcars a year to Los Angeles for a total cost of $1,080,000. What typically happens, however, because of a lack of visibility, railcars are not filled to the maximum and the company uses and pays for more than 200 railcars. Figure 9-2 shows what actually happened over the course of a year.

Actual Volume For One Year				
No. Cars Shipped	Avg. Weight Per Car	Total Weight	Cost Per Cwt.	Total Costs
30	45.000 lbs.	1.350.000 lbs.	8.00	108,000
39	60.000 lbs.	2.340.000 lbs.	6.40	149,760
40	84.000 lbs.	3.360.000 lbs.	6.20	208,320
133	97.000 lbs.	12.901.000 lbs.	5.40	696,650
242	286.000 lbs.	19.951.000 lbs.	5.83*	1,162,730

Figure 9-2

This company actually spent $82,730 or 7.7 percent more than necessary. Also the average fill rate was 91.6 percent. (Fill rate is the ratio of what was actually loaded to what yields the best freight rate.) In this case, the average weight per railcar for the year was 82,442 pounds. The best freight rate starts at 90,000 pounds, so the average fill rate was 91.6 percent (82,442 divided by 90,000).

According to industry standards, 91.6 percent is considered a very good ratio. But, in point of fact, this company actually shipped 42 cars more than necessary. In addition to paying the extra freight cost on the railcars, it also lost money on loading and unloading the additional cars. Since no additional freight was actually loaded or unloaded, and an additional 42 cars were ordered, moved, packed, and checked, more work went into moving the same volume of freight.

DRP can dramatically change the situation. One company went from a fill rate of 59.8 percent before DRP to a fill rate of 94.2 percent using DRP over a two-year period. These savings were achieved by logistics planners working with a transportation planning report. This basic report takes the information that already exists with DRP and displays it for the logistics planner (see figure 9-3).

The most striking aspect of this report is its simplicity. The report in figure 9-3 requires very little extra information in addition to what is

DC Transportation Planning Report

Week	Distribution Center	Number of Pallets	Weight	Cube
1	Los Angeles	95	390,000	9,800
2	Los Angeles	80	340,000	8,040
3	Los Angeles	110	420,000	10,730
4	Los Angeles	98	405,000	10,380
5	Los Angeles	100	392,000	10,060
49	Los Angeles	90	370,000	9,475
50	Los Angeles	134	440,000	10,960
51	Los Angeles	115	425,000	10,785
52	Los Angeles	96	395,000	10,120

Figure 9-3

already available with DRP. DRP contains the planned shipments by date and quantity for all the items to all the different DCs. These are known as planned orders. To make this information into a transportation planning report, all that is necessary is to extend these planned order dates and quantities by factors for weight (in pounds), volume, (cubic feet), and quantity per pallet or other suitable shipping unit. Many companies already have this information. For those who do not, the job of developing it is usually a simple one. The information is then displayed by distribution center by week.

In reality, DRP helps logistics planners develop the transportation capacity requirements by extending planned orders to be shipped to inventory stocking locations. This uses the same type of calculation that is performed in manufacturing for developing capacity requirements to support master production schedules.

USING THE DC TRANSPORTATION PLANNING REPORT

The logistics planner scans the transportation planning report to find the number of railcars or trucks required each week. In this case, the objective is to have railcars loaded with 90,000 to 100,000 pounds. In week 1, the plan looks good; four railcars will be needed and each will be loaded with approximately 97,500 pounds (390,000 pounds/four railcars). Next, the planner checks the cube of the railcars since each car can only hold 2,600 cubic feet. In week 1, each railcar will be loaded to an average of 2,450 cubic feet (9,800 cubic feet/four railcars). The planner then checks the number of pallets. In this type of car, a maximum of 25 pallets can be loaded. The average for week 1 is 23.8 pallets/railcar (95 pallets/four railcars). So in week 1, the logistics planner has a good schedule that will fill up four railcars.

In week 2 the weight is low for four railcars (340,000 pounds versus an available of 400,000 pounds). In week 3 the weight is high for four cars (420,000 pounds versus a possible 400,000 pounds). In this situation, the logistics planner checks to see if it is possible to move some freight from week 3 to week 2. To do this, he selects items that can be moved up, and then checks to ensure that moving the items does not violate the restrictions in week 2.

The planner first identifies the limits of what should be moved. In this example, the planner needs to move at least 20,000 pounds, but not more than 60,000 pounds, out of week 3. It is necessary to move at least 20,000 pounds to reduce the weight in week 3 below 400,000 pounds, the maximum for four railcars. If the weight in week 3 is reduced by more than 60,000 pounds, the remaining weight will be less than 90,000 pounds per railcar and the best freight rate will be lost.

The cube of the items to be moved into week 2 from week 3 should be at least 330 cubic feet but less than 2,360 cubic feet. Less than 330 cubic feet will not unload enough cube out of week 3, since week 3 is already overloaded. More than 2,360 cubic feet will not fit within the cube of four railcars (2,600 cubic feet/railcar times four railcars equals 10,400 cubic feet less 8,040 cubic feet already in week 2 equals 2,360 cubic feet available).

In addition, the number of pallets must be considered. The number of pallets moved into week 2 should be less than 20 but more than 10. It should be less than 20 because the maximum for four railcars is 100 pallets, and 80 are already scheduled in week 2. At least 10 pallets must be moved out of week 3 because it is overloaded by that amount.

To summarize, the logistics planner is looking for items to move from week 3 to week 2 that fit within the limits shown in figure 9-4:

Weight, Cube, and Pallet Capacity Limitations

	Weight	Cube	Pallets
More Than	20,000	330	10
Less Than	60,000	2,360	20

Figure 9-4

**Details to the
DC Transportation Planning Report**

LOS ANGELES DISTRIBUTION CENTER

Week	Item Number	Quantity	Order Type	Pallets	Weight	Cube
2	D3467-46	4,000	Planned	10	35,000	740
2	A4538-19	6,700	Planned	25	50,000	1,280
2	H3297-29	7,000	Firm Plnd.	20	80,000	2,650
2	S6730-94	2,500	Planned	10	90,000	1,010
2	N4510-01	3,900	Planned	10	70,000	1,300
2	T3256-98	1,500	Firm Plnd.	5	15,000	1,060
				80	340,000	8,040
3	A3468-26	5,600	Planned	15	50,000	1,740
3	H4388-69	7,200	Firm Plnd.	20	55,000	1,490
3	V3498-10	9,000	Planned	18	45,000	1,700
3	R6638-04	8,500	Planned	11	82,000	1,710
3	B4315-18	9,300	Planned	14	68,000	1,480
3	Y3519-92	6,800	Planned	18	68,000	1,300
3	E7842-31	4,500	Planned	9	37,000	850
3	T3346-48	1,900	Planned	5	15,000	460
				110	420,000	10,730

Figure 9-5

In looking for products that meet the criteria, the planner uses a listing of the details from the transportation planning report. This resulting list can be another hard copy report or a CRT display (see sample CRT display, figure 9-5).

As you can see, week 3 has three items that fit within these limits. The limits are marked with an asterisk in figure 9-6.

It is also possible to combine several items to meet the limits. In this case, there are two items that can be combined to provide the necessary weight, cube, and number of pallets (see figure 9-7).

Display Showing Limits Candidates to Fill a Railcar

Week	Item Number	Quantity	Order Type	Pallets	Weight	Cube
3	A3468-26	5,600	Planned	15	50,000	1,740**
3	H4388-69	7,200	Firm Plnd.	20	55,000	1,490**
3	V3498-10	9,000	Planned	18	45,000	1,700**
3	R6638-04	8,500	Planned	11	82,000	1,710
3	B4315-18	9,300	Planned	14	68,000	1,480
3	Y3519-92	6,800	Planned	18	68,000	1,300
3	E7842-31	4,500	Planned	9	37,000	850
3	T3346-48	1,900	Planned	5	15,000	460
				110	420,000	10,730

Figure 9-6

Additional Candidates to Fill a Railcar

Week	Item Number	Quantity	Order Type	Pallets	Weight	Cube
3	E7842-31	4,500	Planned	9	37,000	850
3	T3346-48	1,900	Planned	5	15,000	460
				14	52,000	1,310

Figure 9-7

At this point, the logistics planner must determine if any of the products within the limits will be available to ship in week 2 instead of week 3 as originally planned. This can be determined by meeting with the master scheduler, the buyer, or supplier scheduler and discussing each of the items. The master scheduler, buyer, or supplier scheduler uses his schedule display to indicate whether or not enough of the item will be available in week 2.

For example, let's take one item and look at manufacturing's MPS display. The item is the first one listed—A3468-26—which fits within the limits. Looking at the MPS display, the master scheduler sees that the projected on-hand balance in week 2 (15,600) is greater than the 5,600 that the logistics planner wants to move up from week 3. Therefore, 5,600 of this product could be shipped in week 2 rather than week 3:

Supply Source
A3468-26
Liquid Soap

On Hand Balance — 5200
Safety Stock — 0
Lead Time — 3 wks
Order Quantity — 15,000

	Past Due	Week							
		1	2	3	4	5	6	7	8
Distribution Demands		2550	2050	5600	1450	2300	8100	750	2550
Scheduled Receipts		15000							
Projected On Hand	5200	17650	15600	10000	8550	6250	13150	12400	9850
Master Schedule-Rcpt.							15000		
Master Schedule-Start			15000						

Figure 9-8

The situation is not always this simple. Sometimes there may not be enough product projected to be on hand at the supply source. In such a situation, it may be possible to change the MPS or supplier schedule to satisfy the needs of logistics. This is not usually done, however. Generally, there are a number of items that can be moved from other weeks to help with transportation scheduling. In the example above, there are three individual items and one combination of items that can solve the logistics planner's problem.

Once the logistics planner and the master scheduler agree on which items to be moved, firm planned orders are used to implement the solution. In this case, the logistic planner or the master scheduler creates a firm planned order for 5,600 in week 2. When this is done, the transportation planning report, the detail display, and the MPS display appear as shown in figures 9-9 through 9-11.

Four aspects of these examples apply to DRP in transportation capacity requirements planning:

1. The logistics planner has the tools to plan transportation and loading.

2. The logistics planners and the master schedulers are thrust into a situation where they need to work closely together and help each other solve problems.

3. DRP is truly a simulation of what is going to happen. Both planned and firm planned orders show what is going to be shipped and when it must be shipped. Therefore, the shipping information is available for other uses.

4. Because the information is accurate, it can be used to develop transportation freight budgets, to negotiate freight rates, and to justify over-the-road equipment like trucks and railcars.

DC Transportation Planning Report

Week	Distribution Center	Number of Pallets	Weight	Cube
1	Los Angeles	95	390,000	9,800
2	Los Angeles	95	390,000	9,780
3	Los Angeles	95	370,000	8,990
4	Los Angeles	98	405,000	10,380
5	Los Angeles	100	392,000	10,060

Figure 9-9

Details to the
DC Transportation Planning Report

LOS ANGELES DISTRIBUTION CENTER

Week	Item Number	Quantity	Order Type	Pallets	Weight	Cube
2	D3467-46	4,000	Planned	10	35,000	740
2	A4538-19	6,700	Planned	25	50,000	1,280
2	H3297-29	7,000	Firm Plnd.	20	80,000	2,650
2	S6730-94	2,500	Planned	10	90,000	1,010
2	N4510-01	3,900	Planned	10	70,000	1,300
2	T3256-98	1,500	Firm Plnd.	5	15,000	1,060
2	A3468-26	5,600	Firm Plnd.	15	50,000	1,740
				95	390,000	9,780
3	H4388-69	7,200	Firm Plnd.	20	55,000	1,490
3	V3498-10	9,000	Planned	18	45,000	1,700
3	R6638-04	8,500	Planned	11	82,000	1,710
3	B4315-18	9,300	Planned	14	68,000	1,480
3	Y3519-92	6,800	Planned	18	68,000	1,300
3	E7842-31	4,500	Planned	9	37,000	850
3	T3346-48	1,900	Planned	5	15,000	460
				95	370,000	8,990

Figure 9-10

Supply Source
A3468-26
Liquid Soap

On Hand Balance — 5200
Safety Stock   — 0
Lead Time   — 3 wks
Order Quantity   — 15,000

	Past Due	Week							
		1	2	3	4	5	6	7	8
Distribution Demands		2550	7650	0	1450	2300	8100	750	2550
Scheduled Receipts		15000							
Projected On Hand	5200	17650	10000	10000	8550	6250	13150	12400	9850
Master Schedule-Rcpt.							15000		
Master Schedule-Start				15000					

Figure 9-11

Recognizing Back-haul Opportunities

Many companies move a lot of products to a stocking location, and nearby there is a supplier or several suppliers that ship to the supply source. This represents an opportunity if the company operates its own fleet of trucks, or if it is close to justifying such a fleet.

If transportation planners are aware of these back-haul opportunities, they can take advantage of them by having the trucks deliver products to the stocking locations, and then load purchased material or products from suppliers for the return haul to the supply source.

But the transportation planners have to know when these opportunities exist; they must know the approximate weight, cube, and timing of shipments from suppliers to supply sources.

DRP is a way to make such opportunities visible. As explained before, the planned shipments to stocking locations are stored in the system. This information is used to develop the transportation planning report. In addition, the planned shipments to the supply sources exist in the system. These are the planned orders for purchased material or purchased products.

For example, suppose a particular material is purchased from a supplier located in the same city as one of the DCs. The planned orders to that DC represent the shipments from the factory to that city. The planned orders for the raw material represent the planned shipments from the city to the factory.

By storing the weight and cube of the raw material, and coding the suppliers located near DCs, the same type of transportation planning report can be presented as that used for shipments to the distribution center. The only difference is that the report shows planned shipments to the factory.

With the two reports, the planner can compare the outbound planned weight and cube with the inbound planned weight and cube and determine whether or not the opportunity for back haul exists.

It is also possible to combine the information from these two reports into a single report or CRT display.

Opportunities for Shipment Consolidations

Users of DRP are also taking advantage of the transportation planning information when a given DC is serviced from several manufacturing facilities. DRP is of great value in these situations because consolidation opportunities can be planned and scheduled, taking into consideration shipments from one or more supply sources to the same DC in a given day or week.

DRP AND SHIPPING SCHEDULES

In a number of distribution companies, an established shipping schedule indicates which shipments are to be made to different stocking locations on specific days of the week. For example, a shipping schedule might reveal that shipments to the Los Angeles DC should be made every Tuesday and Friday, shipments to Chicago every Monday, and shipments to Montreal every Wednesday.

Once the shipping schedules are set in the system, they must be adhered to religiously. Any deviation will create more or less inventory in the pipeline, and reduce efficiency and credibility with the users. Most forms of inventory have a common denominator—time. In many instances, inventory only exists because more or less time is required to ship, assemble, manufacture, or purchase.

If customers are willing to wait two weeks to get a product as opposed to one or two days, you can do business with much less inventory. If a supplier's product is only a phone call away, chances are you can carry little or no inventory.

Shipping schedules deal with shipping time. Therefore, shipping schedule dates must be respected if inventory levels are to be stabilized.

Typically, the shipping schedule is not changed from day to day or week to week. In fact, in many companies the shipping schedule is fairly rigid for the following reasons:

1. Only a limited number of shipping doors or rail docks are available.

2. Loading dock space is limited.

3. Manpower and equipment are limited.

4. The schedule is dependent on the work load at the distribution centers.

The limitations in doors, dock space, people, and equipment at either the shipping or receiving locations cause many companies to level the load by assigning a fixed shipping schedule. There are other ways to accomplish this goal, however. For example, a company might set its capacity at 40 trucks per day and not be concerned with their destination or source. In a number of cases, however, it is easier and more convenient to simply set a fixed shipping schedule. As the conditions change, the shipping schedule may also be changed, although schedules are generally adhered to.

One problem with a fixed shipping schedule is that the planned orders created for shipping from supply source to stocking locations may not agree with the set shipping schedule. For example, DRP may plan an order due to be shipped in day 7 and the shipping schedule for Los Angeles is set for days 1, 5, and 9 (see figure 9-12).

In such a situation, DRP is not a true simulation of reality. The planned order for 200 in day 7 will not actually be shipped in day 7. Instead, this product should be shipped in day 5. If this product is postponed until the next shipment, in this case day 9, the Los Angeles DC will be out of stock and on back order.

But if the planned order will be shipped in day 5, DRP should show it in day 5 and not in day 7 in order to be a valid simulation of will happen. By showing the planned order when it will be shipped, DRP is correct for this item, and the distribution demands will appear in the MPS

Los Angeles Distribution Center
Green Beans 16oz Can

On Hand Balance —120
Safety Stock   —40
Lead Time   —1 wk
Order Quantity   —200

	Past Due	Day 1	2	3	4	5	6	7	8
Gross Requirements		40	40	40	40	40	40	40	40
Scheduled Receipts		200							
Projected On Hand	120	280	240	200	160	120	80	40	200
Planned Orders								200	

Shipping Schedule   XX   XX

Figure 9-12

display supplier schedule in the correct week. The master scheduler or buyer will now see that the 200 need to be on hand in day 5, two days earlier than the normal logic of DRP would calculate for this product.

As you can see, in this situation, there is a conflict. The product does not have to be shipped until day 7, for arrival in day 8. But the shipping schedule is for days 1, 5, and 9. Which is correct?

The correct answer is reality; that is, what is actually going to happen. If the order is going to be shipped in day 5, then it should be shown in day 5. If, however, the shipment is earlier than when normal logic would call for, then the planner must be alerted to the change. In this situation, the planned order should be moved to day 5, which is when it will be shipped, and an action message should be given to the planner indicating that the order is due to be shipped earlier than absolutely needed. This way, the planner is able to see what the system is doing. The modified version of the DRP display for this item appears in figure 9-13.

Some people may question the need to generate an action message to show the planner that the logic of DRP has moved the planned order

Los Angeles Distribution Center
Green Beans 16oz Can

On Hand Balance — 120
Safety Stock   — 40
Lead Time   — 1 wk
Order Quantity   — 200

	Past Due	1	2	3	4	5	6	7	8
Gross Requirements		40	40	40	40	40	40	40	40
Scheduled Receipts		200							
Projected On Hand	120	280	240	200	160	120	280	240	200
Planned Orders						200			

Shipping Schedule   XX   XX

ACTION MESSAGE
Planned order 200 Day 5 not needed for shipment until Day 7

Figure 9-13

date. Such thinking fails to recognize that people are responsible for operating the system, not the computer. And if people are accountable for operating the system, they need to be able to see what the system has done and the real need dates of the orders. In some situations, there may not be enough stock to satisfy the distribution demands. When this happens, the planner needs to know what is needed for each distribution center.

The best way to change the planned orders is by using the computer, although it is possible for a person to make the changes, provided the number of changes is small enough to be managed manually with firm planned orders. In most situations, the volume of the changes is large enough to justify using the computer.

The process is the same for both. The planned orders are calculated based on the date the items are needed at the DCs. The shipping schedule is then considered, and all planned orders that are not scheduled to ship on one of the shipping dates are adjusted by moving the planned orders to the next available shipping date. This does embody a tradeoff. The decision to ship earlier will create additional inventory in the distribution pipeline before it is needed. The results, therefore, must be compared to the costs and advantages of maintaining a fixed shipping schedule. DRP can be used to simulate both conditions.

Two different methods can be used with the computer to adjust the planned order dates to agree with the shipping schedule. One is to allow the DRP logic to plan orders and also take the shipping schedule into account before creating and storing the planned orders. The other method is to have a separate computer program that is run after DRP has created and stored the planned orders. This program adjusts the planned order dates based on the shipping schedule, and updates the distribution demands if they have been posted to the MPS or supplier schedule. Appendix E explains the logic of both of these methods.

DOS AND DON'TS IN TRANSPORTATION PLANNING

A sound logistics system must schedule both inventories and transportation. The following guidelines will help you take full advantage of DRP in planning transportation from supply sources to your distribution centers.

1. If you deliver to your DCs using a shipping schedule, make sure you show it and plan for it within the system. Do not do an "end run"

around the system. If you do, you will end up lying to yourself and other system users. Eventually, credibility will be lost, and the informal system will take over.

2. If it is company policy to ship only full truckloads to the distribution centers, then you must plan for it within DRP. First, use DRP to determine how much weight and cube need to be shipped to the DCs. If it is not enough to fill a truck or a railcar, use the information from the system to advance planned shipments from future days or weeks. Remember, DRP has already calculated your next shipping priorities to the DCs. Use this information and whatever decision you reach, communicate it to the system and the users.

Caution! Do not delay planned shipments to the DCs simply to reach the desired weight and cube. This is the quickest way to destroy your priorities and your credibility with distribution center people and customers. If you use a transportation lead time of one week and it is realistic, then stick with it through thick and thin, and ship on time. If you don't, you are, in effect, playing with transportation lead time, increasing inventories, and reducing reaction time.

It is advisable to preselect high-volume products that will qualify for advance shipments to make the weight and cube. Communicate this list to all interested users. Do not permit deviations from this list of fillers without prior approval. If you do, people will pick any product close at hand and ignore DRP priorities, which again is tantamount to going around the system.

3. Anytime future planned shipments are advanced to make weight and cube, it is vital to consider the possible impact on the supply source. There is a logistics/supply source trade-off here, which must be evaluated before the final decision is made.

4. If you are managing thousands of products and shipping to multiple locations, you may need some computer support to help manage your transportation plan. The computer can be extremely helpful in sorting the information, searching for future planned shipments, and making recommendations. Although you should definitely take advantage of the massive data manipulation capabilities of the computer, do not forget that computers cannot make decisions, and they cannot be held accountable for results. The computer should only recommend

action based on parameters you have established. In the final analysis, only you can make the final decision.

Conclusion

DRP has proven to be a very powerful tool for transportation planning. Users of DRP have achieved excellent savings in the transportation area. If you use DRP for transportation planning as recommended in this chapter, and avoid the pitfalls, you will undoubtedly reduce costs in transportation.

Chapter 10

Financial Planning and Budgeting Simulation

Beyond Traditional Accounting

As stressed throughout this book, DRP is more than just a way to schedule products and transportation—it is an accurate, detailed simulation of a logistics operation, and, as such, it can be used for other types of planning. One of the most important uses of DRP is in financial planning and budgeting. Because it is a detailed simulation, DRP can also be used to plan warehouse space requirements. DRP can be valuable to a logistics organization in the following ways:

1. Financial planning and budgeting
   a. Predicting inventory investment by location.
   b. Predicting transportation costs to the distribution centers.
   c. Predicting warehouse space requirements.
   d. Predicting labor requirements and equipment needs.

2. Simulation
   a. Simulating different distribution networks.
   b. Simulating different sales patterns.
   c. Simulating new product introductions, acquisitions, and mergers.
   d. Simulating different modes of transportation.

Financial Planning and Budgeting

Companies that use DRP do a more effective job of financial planning and budgeting. In the past, logistics managers had to rely on historical factors and their own knowledge of the business. And, in most cases, logistics costs were usually figured as a percentage of sales. For example, logistics costs for a company may have been running at 6 percent of sales. In this situation, people may expect the logistics managers to either hold that percentage or improve on it.

But, any number of factors change and affect the logistics costs. The distribution network may be handling a new product with a different weight or cube. Sales may shift from one geographic area to another. A change in customer service policies may require faster deliveries in some areas. New DCs may be added, or existing distribution centers may be closed. Each of these events has the potential to change logistics costs significantly. Yet, in contrast to DRP, the historical method for predicting logistics costs will be unable to predict the effects caused by these changes.

Predicting Inventory Investment by Location

Inventories are a major asset in all companies. In fact, they are the largest asset in many companies. They are also usually the most manageable asset, with the exception of accounts receivable, since others, like buildings and machinery, cannot be turned into cash so readily.

DRP contains all the information needed to accurately predict future inventory levels. For example, it contains a projected on-hand balance for every item at every stocking location. This projection extends to the end of the planning horizon and shows the future on-hand balance of each item at each location. The resulting balance can be extended by the actual and/or standard cost of the item and summarized to yield the projected inventory value by location.

DRP also contains the scheduled receipts and planned orders for each item to the end of the planning horizon. These are the quantities that will be in transit, and can be costed out and summarized to give the in-transit inventory projection.

An example of such an inventory projection for a single item appears in figure 10-1.

Inventory Projection at Standard Cost

Distribution Center	400	200	1,200	1,000	800	600	400	1,400	1,200
In Transit		1,200				1,200	1,200		
Total	400	1,400	1,200	1,000	800	1,800	1,600	1,400	1,200

DRP
100 Watt Light Bulbs
Houston Distribution Center

On Hand Balance– 100
Safety Stock   – 70
Lead Time   – 2 wks
Order Quantity – 300
Actual or
   Standard Cost – $4.00 each

	Past Due	Week							
		1	2	3	4	5	6	7	8
Gross Requirements		50	50	50	50	50	50	50	50
Scheduled Receipts		300							
Projected On Hand	100	350	300	250	200	150	100	350	300
Planned Orders						300			

Figure 10-1

This type of display is not usually printed for all items because it is too detailed. Instead, the information is condensed for all items and listed in a summary report. Figure 10-2 shows such a report.

In this report, the projected inventory is listed for each of the different DCs, as well as the supply source and the in-transit inventory. Other variations are possible, however. It is possible, for example, to show the summary report by product group. It is also possible to list the summary report both ways. The detail exists within the system; how it is organized for presentation is up to the users.

For example, if the details of the Dallas projected inventory for May 24 are needed, a special report, or CRT display, could be produced to list all the inventory projections by item for the Dallas DC for the specified

Inventory Projection
$(000)

WEEK OF	New Orleans	Dallas	Los Angeles	Port-land	DC Totals	In Transit	Supply Source	Grand Total
Current Week	1,210	850	1,600	300	3,960	500	2,400	6,860
May 3	1,050	740	1,565	450	3,805	300	2,050	6,155
May 10	980	700	1,320	620	3,620	300	1,800	5,720
May 17	960	950	1,150	550	3,610	550	1,200	5,360
May 24	1,040	910	1,640	510	4,100	400	2,350	6,850

Figure 10-2

week. The sample report shown in figure 10-3 illustrates what such a display might look like.

Of course, the inventory projections from DRP are only as good as the information on which they are based. If the sales forecasts, purchase plans, production plans, purchase schedules, and master production schedules, etc. are incorrect, the inventory projections will also be incorrect. If sales are coming in at 20 percent below forecast, for example, yet the company doesn't revise the sales forecast, the purchase plan, or the production plan, the inventory projections will be wrong. The system is a management tool—it only produces information based on the data people enter into it.

Detail Display of Inventory Projection
Dallas DC
Week of May 24

ITEM	PROJ. ON HAND	ON HAND COST
100 Watt Bulb	300	1,200
150 Watt Bulb	200	1,100
500 Watt Bulb	600	3,000

TOTAL		910,000

Figure 10-3

If the sales forecast is lowered, but the purchase plan and production plan are left unchanged, the inventory projections from DRP will show the increasing inventory at the source location due to a purchase plan or production plan that is greater than the sales forecast. This is the buildup that can occur if the purchase plan or production plan are met, but sales occurs at a rate similar to the new forecast.

Information on sales forecasts, purchase plan, and production plans will seldom be perfect. The essence of good planning is to take the best information available and plan with it until better information can be developed. Good planners do not gaze into a crystal ball to determine what's going to happen a year or more into the future, and then sit back and wait for it to happen. Instead, they continually revise and evaluate information based on the changing situation. (The same type of financial predictions explained for a distribution network can also be developed when operating an MRP II system in a manufacturing company. The projected on-hand balance for components, subassemblies, etc. can be extended by the cost. These topics, however, are beyond the scope of this book.)

Once the company has a valid plan, it can be used for controlling the financial side of the business, since the operating and financial people use the same plan. That means that the financial people can have a plan to measure against. Moreover, it will be a realistic plan, not just one of historical comparisons. If inventory is higher than predicted, the reason will be that more product was purchased or produced than listed in the plan or because sales were lower than the plan. With DRP, the reasons for not meeting the plan can easily be determined. If operating people use DRP to plan their operations well and work to the plan, the financial planning will be far better than ever before.

In the past, we spoke of inventory "levels" and treated inventory as a static element. The textbooks taught us that if we calculated the sums of the safety stocks, and one-half the lot sizes, we would know the expected inventory level. Of course, that didn't take into account any anticipated inventory ahead of peak seasons or inventory used to level production. Nor did it take into account in-transit inventory or the ever-changing situations in the real world of logistics. Sales are never exactly the same as the forecast, and suppliers sometimes do not deliver on time and/or at the right quantity. Therefore, in a logistics system that is supplied from its own manufacturing facility, it is often necessary to build inventory to level production or to hold inventory at the factory because there isn't enough to go around. At the resale/wholesaler levels, inventories often must be deployed and positioned ahead to supply a promotion, and then add to it. These real-world situations have to do not so much with inventory levels as with the flow of inventory. And that is where DRP is at its best.

Predicting Transportation Costs to the DCs

There are two reasons why it is extremely difficult to predict transportation costs without using DRP: varying transportation costs and different modes of transportation. Without formal planning systems, there is no way to gain the necessary information; some people even attempt to develop independent forecasting systems to predict transportation expenses. But because these systems are independent of the system that actually determines what and when product will be shipped, the result is two systems that are unconnected and give inconsistent information.

Chapter 9 examined how DRP is used to plan transportation weight and cube from supply sources to stocking locations. This information specifies the weight and cube to be shipped between two points in the distribution network. A program can then be written to extend this information by the freight rates to predict transportation costs. These rates should include the cost per cwt., plus weight and cube limitations based on the favored mode of transportation to a stocking location.

The report in figure 10-4 is a variation of the DC transportation planning report.

Transportation Cost Budget

Month	Distribution Center	Number of Pallets	Weight	Cube	Freight Cost
Jan	Los Angeles	95	390,000	9,800	15,600
Feb	Los Angeles	80	340,000	8,040	13,600
Mar	Los Angeles	110	420,000	10,730	16,800

Figure 10-4

The details to verify this summary can also be made available. The report or CRT display is similar to the details that back up the DC transportation planning report shown in figure 9-5 (see chapter 9). An example of these supporting details appears in figure 10-5:

**Details to the
DC Transportation Planning Report**

LOS ANGELES DISTRIBUTION CENTER

Month	Item Number	Quantity	Order Type	Pallets	Weight	Cube
Feb	D3467-46	4,000	Planned	10	35,000	740
Feb	A4538-19	6,700	Planned	25	50,000	1,280
Feb	H3297-29	7,000	Firm Plnd.	20	80,000	2,650
Feb	S6730-94	2,500	Planned	10	90,000	1,010
Feb	N4510-01	3,900	Planned	10	70,000	1,300
Feb	T3256-98	1,500	Firm Plnd.	5	15,000	1,060
				80	340,000	8,040

Figure 10-5

If you have opportunities for back haul as described in chapter 9, that information should be used as part of the budgeting process for freight. In the same way that figure 9-4 shows the movement of freight to a DC, back haul opportunities from a supplier located near a DC can be displayed in an identical format. The only difference is that such a report represents the freight coming to the supply source rather than the freight leaving. By comparing the two reports, a planner can factor the back haul opportunities into the freight budgets.

With this type of information, it is possible to have complete visibility into the transportation costs of a distribution network. Although the most obvious benefit is in the area of budgeting the costs, it is also possible to use the information yielded by DRP to negotiate freight rates, make changes to the operation of your own truck fleet, if you operate one, and indicate general areas for cost savings in the distribution network.

Predicting Warehouse Space Requirements

How much space will you need next year? Will you have enough, or will you need to build or rent space? Without DRP, it is difficult to answer these questions with any certainty. This is because what will be on hand at the DCs depends on many variables such as sales growth, geographical shifts in sales patterns, new product introductions, changes in the product size or weight, etc.

If logistics planners are unable to accurately predict space requirements by stocking location, it can be expensive and can result in a number of problems, including unnecessary material handling costs, product damage, recordkeeping problems, wasted time searching for products, and increased obsolescence.

In the same way that DRP can be used to predict inventory investment by location, it can be used to predict space requirements by stocking location. The projected on-hand balance extended by the space per product yields the total space requirements. The space per product is typically different for each item, and is the amount of space that item requires.

Predicting Labor Requirements and Equipment Needs

A logistics manager must be able to predict the manpower and equipment needs of the distribution network by location. Too much or too little manpower capacity can be expensive and create a number of problems. This is especially important in a business that is seasonal, since the peaks are important in planning the budget.

It is possible to predict the number of hours needed for labor and equipment by stocking location using DRP. This calculation reflects the hours needed to load and unload railcars and trucks. The planned orders for the DCs represent the shipments that have to be loaded and unloaded at the DCs. By extending these planned orders by the labor hours, capacity requirements can be generated and displayed.

This is the same process as capacity requirements planning in the manufacturing operation. Routings in a manufacturing company specify the operations to be performed, the equipment to be used, and the number of hours required. These routings are extended by the planned orders to yield capacity requirements, which are then summarized. An example of a capacity requirements planning report for a logistics operation appears in figure 10-6.

The demonstrated capacity at the top of the report is the standard measure of capacity. This is the actual number of hours of work completed. Typically, several weeks of history are used to develop the capacity number, and the calculation is also the capacity the supervisor agrees to provide.

Capacity Requirements Planning Display
Manpower at Supply Source

Demonstrated Capacity — 180 hrs/wk

	Past Due	Week							
		1	2	3	4	5	6	7	8
Capacity Requirements		171	178	184	181	176	180	191	178
Four Week Average					179				181

Figure 10-6

Although the report in figure 10-6 is for manpower at a stocking or supplier location, it can also be used for lift trucks or any other piece of material handling equipment. For shipping locations like RDCs or factories supporting multiple satellite distribution locations, this type of capacity planning report shows the capacity requirements for loading and unloading freight. It can, therefore, be used to budget and plan for manpower and equipment.

This type of planning is especially helpful in situations governed by seasonality. It can eliminate the need for logistics people to hire on short notice to cover seasonal peaks or other significant changes in the level of work. With DRP, they can see these situations developing ahead of time and plan for them accordingly.

At the satellite distribution locations, the situation is somewhat different. A capacity requirements planning report can be produced to show the requirements for unloading freight. This report does not show the hours and equipment required to pick orders. If the order-picking activity is significant as compared to the unloading activity, as it is in most DCs, it is necessary to show the capacity requirements in the report.

The best way to do this is to have standards for order picking and a forecast of orders to be picked. This forecast of orders is based on the sales forecast for the different items in the DC and the estimated rates of orders to be processed per day. For example, the forecast of orders can be converted to the number of line items to be picked using a conversion factor or algorithm. The number of line items are multiplied by the time standard required to pick an item. This yields the capacity requirements in manpower and equipment. These capacity requirements are added to the capacity requirements necessary for unloading shipments for supply sources. The result is the total capacity requirements at the DC.

With this information, the ability of the DC manager to see the probable work load in the future enables him to do a more professional job of operating the DC.

SIMULATION

For years, theoreticians have looked for a model to simulate various business situations. These models were based on a "macro approach," using exotic formulas and tables. For example, techniques such as linear programming were supposed to be able to optimize space, manpower, inventory, freight costs, equipment, etc. and give the right answer to some important logistics questions. For all its great promise, linear programming had very little practical application.

DRP, on the other hand, does not claim to yield a single "right" answer. It is not an optimization technique, and it isn't a technique superimposed from the top, making a great many assumptions. DRP calculates schedules and predictions at the most detailed level in the business for each item. Each of the detailed schedules is then totaled to give summarized results. DRP thus provides the information that people are using to run the business, and it also provides the information that is needed to simulate possible situations and examine their effects. The same system is used for operations as well as simulations.

Simulating Different Distribution Networks

Every logistics executive will occasionally be asked to review the current distribution network and evaluate proposed changes. There are any number of reasons for this, but the most common are the following:

1. Desire to improve customer service.

2. Introduction of new products, mergers, or acquisitions.

3. Desire to reduce costs.

4. Competitive pressures to have a DC in a particular location.

5. Geographical shifts in product sales.

The problem of evaluating a new distribution network is that every-thing changes. If, for example, a new DC is added to the network, it will affect the sales of other DCs. This, in turn, will affect the transporta-tion, warehouse space, operating costs, inventory, manpower and equip-ment needs at the DCs. Without DRP, a logistics executive has little in the way of formal planning systems to help in analyzing change.

With DRP, this problem can be solved easily. A company only has to change the network, run DRP, and analyze the results. To illustrate this concept, consider the case of a manufacturer of canned and frozen foods, which had experienced above-average growth and, therefore, had to reevaluate its distribution network. The network was comprised of six DCs, shown in figure 10-7, and had been in operation since 1970. At that time, 75 percent of the total sales volume passed through the company's three eastern DCs (New York, Philadelphia, and Atlanta). From 1970 to 1978, the company also experienced excellent growth in the western part of the country, and sales through the Los Angeles and Houston DCs represented 30 percent of the national total.

**1970 Distribution Network of Manufacturer
of Canned and Frozen Foods**

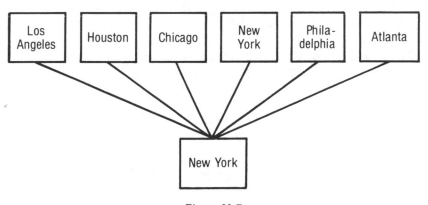

Figure 10-7

Because of the strong sales figure, the company experienced the following two problems:

1. Los Angeles and Houston were out of space and needed to hire more people.

2. The Houston DC was servicing customers as far as New Orleans, and the Los Angeles DC was servicing customers in Oregon and Washington state.

This manufacturer considered two alternatives. The first was to move the Los Angeles and Houston DCs to larger facilities. The second was to add two new distribution centers into the network. The first new DC would be located in Seattle to service Oregon and Washington state customers. The second new DC would be located in New Orleans to service Louisiana and nearby southeast customers.

In considering the first alternative, most of the information was already available; the company's current DRP reports and displays showed the transportation costs from the supply source to these two distribution centers. The current inventory space projections also showed the necessary size for Los Angeles and Houston. And the current capacity requirements planning reports showed the number of people and equipment needed in the two distribution centers. The only major costs that had to be estimated were the cost of the new buildings and the move.

The second alternative, however, required a simulation. The following steps show how this new distribution network could be simulated:

1. Reconfigure the distribution network to include two new distribution centers in Seattle and New Orleans. This would include adding items to be stocked in the new DCs, linking these items to the supply source, loading in-transit lead times from the supply source to the DCs, loading shipping quantities, etc.

2. Change the sales forecast in the effected distribution centers. In this case, the sales forecast in Los Angeles would change based on a DC in Seattle, and the sales forecast in Houston would change based on a DC in New Orleans.

3. Estimate the difference in transportation costs from the supply source to the new and existing locations by generating a new transportation planning report and comparing it to the current plan.

4. Estimate the difference in transportation costs from the distribution center to the customer. This could be difficult since there may be many different customers with different volumes and ordering patterns. Some people use zip codes or telephone numbers to evaluate the distance between the distribution center and the customer. This information can be used to estimate transportation costs from the DC to the customer.

5. Run DRP and analyze the results, including the predicted transportation costs, inventory, manpower and equipment needs, warehouse space, etc.

Typically, most companies would run such a simulation on a copy of the data base, rather than using the live data base. This allows the logistics planners to take their time in analyzing the simulation. It also allows them to make minor changes and run additional simulations. Since this manufacturer did not think it had a capability to simulate—yet it had just implemented DRP—it hired an outside consulting firm to do the study. Ironically, this consulting firm used the same DRP software package that the manufacturer had purchased.

Simulating Changes in Sales Patterns

Logistics managers want to know the impact on their distribution operations if sales increase by some percentage or if the pattern of sales changes. With DRP, they can do what-if analyses for various sales situations. For example, they could simulate a sales increase of 30 percent or a change in the sales pattern from the east to the Southwest.

In the case of the simulated sales increase or decrease, the following actions must be taken:

1. Change the sales forecast to show the increase, decrease, or shift in geographic pattern.

2. Run DRP and analyze the results. This may require some changes to the purchase and master production schedules, shipping quantities, etc., and then DRP might be run again.

Simulating New Product Introductions, Acquisitions, and Mergers

New product introductions, acquisitions, and mergers result in new products being handled by the distribution network. Often these changes are made without considering the potential impact on logistics, and, as a result, people wonder why a distribution center is out of space or costs are rising faster than anticipated.

DRP enables logistics planners to simulate the effects of these new products on the distribution network. All that has to be done is to add the new products, load the forecasts, purchase, and production schedules, run DRP, and analyze the information. The system will provide excellent information showing the implications of these changes on logistics and/or manufacturing.

Simulating Different Modes of Transportation

Often, there are opportunities to trade transportation cost and inventory investment. Sometimes, it makes sense to use a slower, cheaper form of transportation even though it increases inventory. Others times, it makes sense to use a more expensive form of transportation because it is faster and reduces inventory. The difficulty is that without DRP, it's hard to evaluate these options in aggregate for all items shipped to a given DC. If you ship $100,000 a month of merchandise from a DC and it takes half a month to get material to the DC, you will have $50,000 of in-transit inventory on the average. A faster mode, one week for example, would reduce the value of in-transit material by half.

With DRP, this type of situation can be easily simulated. It can be done by changing the in-transit lead times for the items, running DRP, and analyzing the results. The reports and displays from DRP will predict the transportation cost and inventory investment for each situation.

CONCLUSION

From this chapter, it should be clear that DRP is not simply a better way to control inventories. DRP is a detailed and accurate simulation of a logistics operation and can, therefore, be used for budgeting and financial planning, as well as for an almost unlimited number of other simulations. The planning and scheduling capabilities of DRP open new horizons for accountants. As a rule, accounting systems exist to record history, and do not have forward-planning capabilities.

Systems like DRP provide the financial executive with projections into the future, enabling the company to carry out simulations that have operational and financial implications. DRP can help answer the question "Can I do it?" while the accounting systems help to answer the question "Can I afford to do it?"

Chapter 11

Management Issues

Problems on the Road to Successful DRP

At this point, you might ask "Why don't more companies take advantage of DRP, when it can lead to vastly improved customer service and profitability?" The question has four major answers:

- Tunnel vision

- Hardware and software pitfalls

- The I'm-different/I'm-unique syndrome

- Lack of understanding of natural linkages

Let's look at each one to see what must be eliminated for a company to succeed with DRP.

TUNNEL VISION

Sources of the Problem

Tunnel vision is a trap in which people are taught to focus solely on their own functional area, oblivious to its relationship to other areas in the company. The seeds of tunnel vision are sown early in the educational system when people are taught to compartmentalize knowledge by taking up a "major." By the time they enter the business world, they've pigeonholed themselves in marketing, accounting, operations, human resources, logistics and other narrowly defined specialties. Most MBA programs aren't geared for training people to become industrial generalists; rather they prepare students to be specialists in administration, finance, marketing, engineering, and other disciplines.

Effects of Tunnel Vision

Regardless of the source, tunnel vision always results in confusion and destructive turf battles. Time and again, logistic, manufacturing, and purchasing executives explain what's wrong with their company by pointing to their colleagues down the hall or across the lot.

The logistics vice president complains that manufacturing is to blame for high costs and low customer service. The manufacturing vice president feels, in turn, that logistics is to blame for the company's woes, because it assumes that any amount of any product can be spun out the door at a moment's notice. And the head of purchasing points to both manufacturing and logistics, saying that they rely on his department to compensate for their own lack of planning.

The fact is in any company the whole is greater than the sum of the parts, and if any one department plays by its own rules, the entire organization suffers. Therein lies one of the key challenges and responsibilities of management—to make sure that people understand the idiosyncrasies of the flow of materials from suppliers to customers and to see that linkages between departments are established and maintained, so that the flow of information and product is uninterrupted at all times.

HARDWARE AND SOFTWARE PITFALLS

Many managers today believe that problems in purchasing, manufacturing, and logistics can be solved with the "right" hardware-software combination. Today's state-of-the-art hardware and software will provide extremely useful information and can handle complex scheduling problems. But people must be prepared to handle the new power at their fingertips; otherwise, the shock will be like going from a Piper Cub to the space shuttle. The best computer or most sophisticated software package can't tear down the fiefs that often exist within a company, nor correct tunnel vision. Many companies have invested millions of dollars in hardware and software, only to find that nothing has changed.

In fact, new systems often worsen the situation because people focus their attention on the mechanics of the tools, rather than on the new skills and mind sets necessary to put the tools to good use. The real answer lies in attitudinal and behavioral changes, which can only be achieved through education and retraining. Every dollar spent on matching the right skills with the right tools will have a far greater payoff than $10 worth of hardware and software.

For example, two years ago, a major distributor in the automobile-parts supply business invested in a new DRP software system. The goal was to give employees a new state-of-the-art system to improve customer service and reduce operating costs and inventories.

About $1 million and 18 months later, the company switched on its new DRP system. It crashed. What happened? The company failed to take the time to upgrade its workers' skills. Despite numerous discussions and recommendations, oriented toward taking the necessary steps to enhance the skills of their people, management did not pay attention. Instead, management focused most of its time and effort on the new software system. This resulted in a mismatch, and the company paid the price.

The real solution to successful hardware-software installation is to ask an age-old question, "What's in it for me?" Believe it or not, whenever you talk about introducing new systems in any company, this is the first question that pops up. This means that education must be one of the first steps in instituting a new system. The education must provide the understanding that people need to answer their own questions. People must see the benefits for themselves and their companies for a new system to work; they must understand how they fit into the new picture. Once they do, they participate actively and enthusiastically in the change process.

Many people have been performing the same job for a long time and, as a result, are set in their ways. Others have picked up bad habits over the years. Don't think for a moment that just because you decided to spend a princely sum of money to change your system that all the habits—good and bad—will simply disappear when you turn on the switch.

THE I'M-DIFFERENT/I'M-UNIQUE SYNDROME

In addition to a preoccupation with tools over skills, people have long argued that systems like MRP can't be used in their company because they're "different" and believe they have "unique" problems. Oliver Wight ran into that 15 years ago when he revealed the effectiveness of using MRP. To counter such arguments, he demonstrated that MRP works in almost any manufacturing setting, because all manufacturing companies are governed by what he called the "universal manufacturing equation":

- What am I going to make?

- What does it take to make it?

- What do I have?

- What do I need to get?

Today, I encounter similar arguments about DRP. "We're a retailer—how can we possibly use a system geared for manufacturing?" or vice versa. In working with retailers, wholesalers, and distributors, I have discovered that when you examine how they provide customer service, attempt to reduce operating costs, and control inventory investment, they are more alike than they are different. In fact, manufacturers who service customers through their own distribution centers, along with retailers, wholesalers, and distributors who buy from them, are all governed by the universal logistics equation described in chapter 5:

- What am I going to sell?

- Where will I sell it?

- What do I have?

- What do I have on order?

- What do I need to get?

Today, retailers, wholesalers, and distributors such as Sears, Mass Merchandisers, Bowman Distribution, AWC, ServiStar, and many others are proving that the universal logistics equation does govern the flow of materials in their businesses, and that DRP provides the necessary tools to solve each component on a routine basis.

LACK OF UNDERSTANDING OF NATURAL LINKAGES

This book begins with a discussion of how the components of a marketing channel form natural linkages. Too many managers see the components of the channel as discrete entities, and are therefore oblivious to the natural "pull." But does this pull mean that all businesses in the channel are idle until the ultimate customer makes a move?

Clearly not. Companies deliberately make an operational or financial decision to pump product into the marketplace before it's needed. In other words, the product is pushed through the channel. Three primary reasons for this approach are: (1) promotions and deals, (2) pricing, and (3) economies of scale in transportation and manufacturing. Although each one may represent a valid strategy, in many cases, the short-term gains are offset by disruption in other parts of the marketing channel. Before explaining when it is appropriate to push product, let's consider some of the more destructive consequences.

Penalties of Pushing Product

Promotions and Deals
Today, many companies use promotions and deals as a standard business practice, buying from one deal to the next and, in the process, displacing significant amounts of inventory. Generally done to take advantage of attractive pricing, it is a Faustian bargain. The price breaks are offset or even mitigated by additional costs incurred for transportation, warehousing, and manufacturing of products before they're needed. Moreover, promotions and deals create large demand "spikes" that send shock waves reverberating throughout the entire marketing channel. This is underscored by research conducted by Walter Salmon of the Harvard Business School, which indicates that promotions and deals increase inventories at the distributors' level by as much as 50 percent. In addition, they boost inventory carrying costs by as much as $1.2 billion a year.

Another negative aspect of operating in a promotion-and-deal mode is the rise of a new breed of intermediaries called "diverters," companies that buy when the deals are on, sit on the inventory, and then offer it at a very slight margin. Since diverters generally ship to a public warehouse, they incur virtually no overhead for handling the inventory. Although this might be a quick way to make a buck, it disrupts the marketing channel by making it almost impossible for the manufacturer to trace the location of his product. In the food and pharmaceutical industries, product traceability is critical for compliance with government regulations, and companies that cannot pinpoint the location of their products are vulnerable to significant liability suits in the event of a massive recall. Other companies, too, are affected by diverters in terms of warranties and control of their sales programs.

Pricing
Just as promotions and deals disrupt the normal flow of materials from manufacturer to ultimate customer, pricing also affects the smooth operation of the marketing channel. Many firms incorporate pricing into their annual strategic and business planning and, at predictable times throughout the year, will announce "surprise" price hikes. This, of course, causes customers to plan around the increased prices and to order in abnormally large quantities. The result? A tsunami surges through the marketing channel, washing away the orderly flow of materials. Customers skip the next order cycle, forcing all partners in the pipeline to cope with the feast-famine cycle.

Economies of Scale in Transportation and Manufacturing
At the outset, manufacturing and logistics always strive for long production runs and truckload consolidations to achieve economies of scale. This is because it rarely makes sense to move a case or single units from a factory to a distribution center or customer; rather, goods are moved in pallets or truckloads quantities. The trade-offs in lower transportation costs are balanced by the inventory carrying costs.

Manufacturing also needs to stabilize human and production equipment resources, to attain maximum productivity. This causes product to enter the industrial pipeline before it is actually needed. Other reasons to pump product upstream include space considerations at plants and distribution centers, and the need to compensate for long lead times in producing and distributing goods.

Overall Consequences of Pushing Product through the Channel

In planning for promotions and deals, manufacturing must build inventory in advance. This forces purchasing to commit significant capital for large quantities of material necessary to support production schedules.

In addition, manufacturing must commit capacity to support the effort. This type of inventory buildup is normally done over a period of several weeks, sometimes months. Logistics must then take the inventory and somehow deploy it before it is needed. The positioning of the inventory in the logistics pipeline is based on history and trends; in other words, a forecast. This means that transportation, warehousing, and inventory carrying costs are incurred for several weeks or months prior to their actual sales.

As the inventory buildups and deployments are made, based on forecasts, manufacturing inevitably responds to short-notice adjustments in production schedules in the middle of a promotion or deal. Logistics is caught in a game of inventory redeployment to compensate for "errors" in the forecast. This typically augments operating costs for manufacturing, material handling, shipping, and transportation.

When promotions and deals are over and the dust settles, people assess the situation and clean up the mess. For example, they must ask, "How much is left over at deal prices, sitting in the wrong distribution center? How much will it cost to move it again? Repackage it? Redeploy it?"

Sound familiar? Those who have lived through several of these episodes can add their own war stories. But the bottom line is always the same. Product has been made, sold, and deployed to customers. In most cases, customers are retailers, wholesalers, and distributors, and unless they sell the promotion or deal, additional costs will be incurred. Depending on the industry and type of product involved, manufacturers might be faced with significant amounts of returned goods. In some situations, to avoid additional inventory carrying costs, product will be heavily discounted (e.g., Christmas cards and gift wrap), thereby erasing the gains that the promotion or deal offered in the first place. Ultimately, the heavy discounting results in diminished margins for all partners in the channel.

Who is accountable, and who keeps tabs on the costs so everyone in the channel knows the score? It's not easy to do since costs are spread across companies, and, within a company, they're further spread across functional areas. In truth, very few promotions or deals end up making money for everyone in the pipeline; there are always winners or losers in this zero-sum game. This is why "everyday low prices" are gaining in popularity, and deals and promotions are beginning to disappear as a way of doing business.

Why Push?

If pumping product through the marketing channel only offers false economies and is so destructive to the overall flow of goods and materials, why do companies engage in it? To answer the question, we must inevitably look at the manufacturers. Historically, manufacturers have had extremely inflexible processes geared toward long production runs, very slow changeovers, and long procurement and manufacturing lead times. For the most part, manufacturers still operate in this fashion.

In addition to flexibility, it generally takes too long for information to circulate upstream across all members of the marketing channel, and back again to the manufacturer. If information could speed up, and if manufacturing operations were more flexible, the situation could change dramatically, and the need to push would practically vanish.

Until that time, however, it is acceptable to push inventory *as long as it matches the natural pull.* This balance can be achieved only if the retailer, wholesaler, and manufacturer respond quickly to changes in demand. When that happens, manufacturers don't have to make big runs and build large inventories in anticipation of incentive campaigns. Of course, inventory adjustment cycles will still be necessary to support sales and marketing efforts. But the adjustments will be shorter and smaller, and whatever push is necessary will result in small ripples rather than major waves in the channel. When you can combine flexibility with good information, push and pull can create a dynamic equilibrium in which customer purchases consume the inventory that has been pushed upstream, creating a beneficial situation for everyone in the pipeline.

CONCLUSION

By understanding the kinds of problems that companies encounter when they implement DRP, you will maximize your chances of success. You'll also find that by exploring each problem area, you will greatly enrich your understanding of the major concepts underlying your company's most powerful distribution tool.

The Proven Path

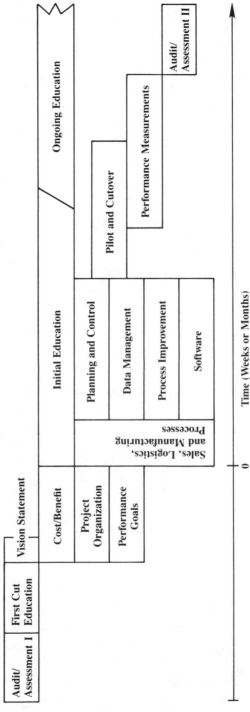

Time (Weeks or Months)

DRP Implementation Plan

The Proven Path encompasses 16 basic steps, regardless of whether you're implementing MRP II, JIT/TQC, or DRP, and whether you're using a Fast-Track approach or following a standard company-wide implementation.

Naturally, the time frame will vary from company to company depending on its size, complexity, and competitive posture.

The implementation steps are the same for a company-wide or a Fast-Track approach. Understanding and following each step with dedication leads to Class A results. The following pages explain each of the components in the Proven Path chart.

The explanations for MRP II, Just-in-Time/Total Quality Control (JIT/TQC), and DRP are each contained in a separate section, and each includes a detailed implementation plan. This detailed implementation plan is an improved version of the Oliver Wight Detailed Implementation Plan which has been used by thousands of companies over the last 15 years. What needs to be done is for you to tailor the plan to your company:

---

[1] The following document is an excerpt from *The Proven Path: A Roadmap to Class A Success—The Integrated Approach to MRP II, JIT/TQC, and DRP* Revised Edition (Essex Junction, VT: Oliver Wight Limited Publications, Inc. 1990)

1. Cross off any tasks you have already completed.

2. Add any tasks that are individual to your company's implementation.

3. Replace the generalized job titles in the plan with the names of the people in your company responsible for the different tasks.

4. Add dates. The general time frame is included in the explanation of each Proven Path element. It's up to you to develop the start and due dates for each element as well as the tasks within each element.

Appendix B is a sample of what a tailored implementation plan would look like.

Many companies today are simultaneously implementing several of these management tools, or overlapping the implementations. For example, a company may be implementing DRP and MRP II. The Proven Path approach makes it easy to integrate these implementations because the implementation approach is the same for all. To illustrate this, let's look at combining the detailed implementation plans for MRP II and JIT/TQC. This would involve the following:

1. Combine similar implementation tasks. Rather than writing a vision statement for MRP II alone, write one for MRP II and JIT/TQC. Rather than setting performance goals for MRP II alone, set them for both MRP II and JIT/TQC.

2. List separately those implementation tasks that do not overlap. For example, there would be an implementation task for the JIT Breakthrough Pilot and a task for the MRP II pilots (software, conference room, and live).

3. Modify the tasks in situations where simultaneous or overlapping implementations alter the tasks. One example of this is in the area of inventory record accuracy: some provision will have to be made for JIT/TQC point-of-use storage which might not be the case for an MRP II-only implementation. These tasks are clearly identified in the comments sections of the detailed implementation plans.

The same approach would be used to combine DRP and MRP II, or any other combination of these implementations.

There are a number of abbreviations used in the RESPONSIBLE column of the detailed implementation plans. The table below shows these abbreviations and their meaning:

Dept.	Department
Distr.	Distribution
Engr.	Engineering (either Design or Manufacturing)
Exec.	Executive
Mgmt.	Management
Mgr.	Manager
MIS	Management Information Systems
P&IC	Production & Inventory Control
Suprvsn.	Supervision

1. Audit/Assessment I (DRP)

DEFINITION: An analysis of the company's current situation, problems, opportunities, strategies, etc. The analysis will serve as the basis for putting together an action plan.

PURPOSE: To determine which tools are specifically needed, and in what order they should be implemented. For example, a company may believe that it needs a new MRP II system. This may be true, but the analysis may reveal that because of substantial inventories in the field, implementing a DRP system first will provide the greatest payback. Once DRP is up and running, the company can focus on the incremental gain from a new MRP II system.

This step and its companion, audit/assessment II, are critically important to ensure that the improvement initiatives to be pursued by the company match its true needs; that they will generate competitive advantages in the short run; and that they will be consistent with the company's long-term strategy.

WHO & HOW: Participants in this step include the executives, a wide range of operating managers, and in virtually all cases, outside consultants with Class A credentials in MRP II, JIT/TQC, and/or DRP.

The process is one of fact finding, identifying areas of consensus and disagreement, and matching the company's current status and strategies with the tools it has available for execution. The end result will be the development of an action plan to move the company onto a path of continuous improvement.

TIME FRAME: Several days to one month.[2] Please note: The audit/ assessment is not a prolonged, multi-month affair involving a detailed documentation of current systems. Rather, its focus and thrust is on what's NOT working well and what needs to be done to become more competitive.

---

[2] Time Frame as used in this document refers to elapsed time, not workdays of applied effort. In this specific instance, the number of workdays would typically range from two to eight.

2. First-Cut Education (DRP)

Definition: Key people must learn how the approaches work as specified by audit/assessment I: what they consist of; how they operate; and what is required to implement and use them properly.

Purpose: To provide a basic understanding of the approach to be pursued so the group can 1) complete a cost/benefit analysis, 2) provide the leadership necessary for the implementation, and 3) understand how to manage successfully when the new tools are available.

Who & How: A small group of executives and managers (perhaps a dozen people) attend a public seminar on the approach being considered.

Time Frame: One to four weeks.

Note: Some executives may go through first-cut education prior to audit/ assessment I. Either they will not be aware of the value of this step, or may want to become familiar with MRP II, JIT/TQC, and DRP prior to the audit/assessment. The order is not important; the critical issue is to make sure that both steps are done.

3. VISION STATEMENT (DRP)

DEFINITION: A written document that defines the desired operational environment. It answers the question: What do we want to accomplish?

PURPOSE: To provide a framework for consistent decision making, and to serve as a rallying point for the whole company.

WHO & HOW: The executives and managers who participated in first-cut education, in one or several meetings, hammer out what the company will look like and what new competitive capabilities it will have after the new approach has been implemented.

TIME FRAME: One to several days.

4. COST/BENEFIT (DRP)

DEFINITION: A written document that spells out the costs of imple-
                   mentation and the benefits of operating at a Class A
                   level.

PURPOSE: To make possible an informed decision about whether
                   to proceed with the implementation; to build a founda-
                   tion for the project; and to ensure there is buy-in and
                   commitment from management to provide the neces-
                   sary resources.

WHO & HOW: Involves the same people and often the same meetings
                   as the vision statement. The top person from each
                   functional area should be accountable for providing
                   the estimate of benefits and the eventual achievement
                   of them.

TIME FRAME: One day to one week.

5. PROJECT ORGANIZATION (DRP)

DEFINITION: Creation of the appropriate management and operational level team(s). Generally, this consists of a steering committee of executives and a project team of key users.

PURPOSE: To assign responsibilities and allocate people resources to the project.

WHO & HOW: Initially, much the same group as above to do the job of identifying candidates. Afterwards, certain executives and managers discuss the opportunity with the candidates to gain their acceptance of the assignment.

TIME FRAME: One day to two weeks.

6. Performance Goals (DRP)

Definition: Agreement of what performance categories are expected to improve and what levels they are expected to reach.

Purpose: To identify improvements that are expected to be achieved and how they will be measured.

Who & How: Essentially the same people who attended first-cut education use the knowledge gained there to set specific targets for attainment (e.g., customer delivery performance, lead time reduction, schedule compliance, cost reduction, productivity increases, inventory reductions, etc.).

Time Frame: One hour to one day.

Please note: In many cases it's possible for most of the activities specified in Steps 3, 4, 5, and 6 to be accomplished by the same people in the same several meetings. This is good, since there is an urgency to get started, and time is of the essence.

DRP: Distribution Resource Planning
Proven Path Detailed Implementation Plan

TASK	RESPONSIBLE	COMMENTS
1. AUDIT/ASSESSMENT I	Top Mgmt. Middle Mgmt.	Assess the company's current situation. In most cases, this is done with the help of an outside consultant with Class A credentials.
2. FIRST-CUT EDUCATION	Top Mgmt. Middle Mgmt.	What is DRP, how does it work, why should a company commit to it? Top management should attend the DRP Top Management Course, key middle managers should attend the DRP Three-Day Course.
3. VISION STATEMENT	Top Mgmt. Middle Mgmt.	A short, concise document defining what we want to accomplish, and when it should be in place.
4. COST/BENEFIT	Top Mgmt. Middle Mgmt.	A clear listing of the costs and benefits, agreed to by the key players.
A. Prepare cost/benefit.	Top Mgmt. Middle Mgmt.	Cost/benefit analysis.
B. Commit to implementation.	Top Mgmt.	Approve the implementation. Communicate the commitment. Deliver clear, consistent messages.
5. PROJECT ORGANIZATION		Create the appropriate management and operational teams.
A. Executive Steering Committee.	Top Mgmt.	Include designation of Executive Torchbearer. Schedule review meetings once a month.
B. Project Team.	Top Mgmt.	Team Leader should be full-time. Other team members from 10 percent to 100 percent depending on their role.
C. Outside counsel.	Top Mgmt.	Outside consultant with Class A experience.
D. Spin-off task groups.	Exec. Steering Committee	Identify initial groups; more may be needed later.
6. PERFORMANCE GOALS	Top Mgmt. Middle Mgmt.	Using the ABCD Checklist, agree on expected performance levels and measurements.

7. Initial Education (DRP)

DEFINITION: An educational effort for all people who are involved in designing and using the new tools.

PURPOSE: To provide a basic understanding of what the company is striving to achieve, why it is important, and how it will enable them to do their jobs more effectively.

WHO & HOW: The groups(s) selected to manage the project (Step 5) must first become more knowledgeable on the approaches. This is usually accomplished through seminars and internal education sessions. These people would then lead the education of the larger group. Business discussions led by managers and supervisors, and assisted by videotapes, have proven to be a practical and effective method of accomplishing this step.

TIME FRAME: Throughout the implementation schedule.

8. THE SALES, LOGISTICS, AND MANUFACTURING PROCESSES (DRP)

DEFINITION: Detailed statement of how the Sales/Marketing, Logistics and Manufacturing functions will perform following implementation, and the detailed project plan necessary to achieve this.

PURPOSE: To ensure that the details of the implementation will be consistent with the vision statement; to verify that the processes that will be affected by the upcoming changes will be prioritized based on those most in need of improvement; and to create the detailed schedule necessary for effective project management.

WHO & HOW: Key people who will be directly involved lay out the detailed project schedule and, where appropriate, obtain concurrence from senior management.

TIME FRAME: One week to two months.

TASK	RESPONSIBLE	COMMENTS
7. INITIAL EDUCATION	Team Leader	Provide the necessary understanding to all people who will be designing and using the new tools.
A. Outside education for people who will be leaders at the in-house series of business meetings, and key managers.	Team Leader	To be effective discussion leaders, these managers need exposure at either the DRP Top Management Course, or the DRP Three-Day Course. The key managers mentioned here are people critical to the design or operation, but who have not been covered under first-cut education and who are not leaders for the business meetings.
B. Outside education for people designated as in-house experts.	Team Leader	Generally, in-house experts are designated in the following areas: Sales & Operations Planning, Master Production Scheduling, Purchasing, Inventory Record Accuracy, JIT/TQC, and Financial Integration. These in-house experts may or may not be part of the project team.
C. Project Team/Discussion Leaders video course.	Team Leader	A series of business meetings where the general principles are translated into the specifics of operation for your company. Acquire the DRP Video Library.
D. Top Management video course.	Executive Torchbearer/Project Leader	A series of business meetings where the top managers apply the concepts to their company.
E. Mixed Management Overview video course.	Discussion Leaders	A series of business meetings covering the overview materials, with a mixed group of managers from each of the different functional areas. The objectives are to understand the concepts, to better understand one another, and to help in team building.
F. Department specific video courses.	Discussion Leaders	Series of business meetings organized by department. The objectives are to determine specifically what changes need to be made to run the business differently in these departments. Typical groups for these meetings include, but are not limited to: Distribution Management, Traffic, Purchasing, Sales and Marketing, Finance, Management Information Systems, Personnel, and Distribution Center Employees.

DRP: Distribution Resource Planning
Proven Path Detailed Implementation Plan

TASK	RESPONSIBLE	COMMENTS
8. SALES, LOGISTICS, AND MANUFACTURING PROCESSES	Top Mgmt. Middle Mgmt.	Develop a detailed statement of how these processes will operate following implementation. The Project Team/Discussion Leaders series of business meetings (Task #7C above) generally provides most of the information needed for this task. Key issues or changes should be approved by top management. In the case of a company with their own manufacturing, this might include MRP II and/or JIT/TQC. If so, see the MRP II and JIT/TQC detailed implementation plans.

9. Planning and Control Processes (DRP)

Definition: Identification of all systems and processes necessary for effective planning and control, from sales & operations planning down through detailed plant, supplier, and distribution schedules.

Purpose: To ensure that the formal planning and control systems either in place or to be implemented are capable of generating and maintaining valid plans and schedules for:

1. Shipment of customer orders
2. Logistics
3. Manufacturing
4. Purchasing
5. Engineering
6. Finance

Who & How: The people throughout the company, in marketing and sales, manufacturing, purchasing, engineering, planning, and elsewhere who will be involved in generating plans and schedules, or in executing them. They do this by using their knowledge of the present operating environment of the company with the knowledge they gained in initial education as to what is required.

Time Frame: One week to three months.

DRP: Distribution Resource Planning
Proven Path Detailed Implementation Plan

TASK	RESPONSIBLE	COMMENTS
9. PLANNING AND CONTROL PROCESSES		Identification of the systems necessary for effective planning. Some of these systems will be implemented using the pilot approach.
A. Sales & Operations Planning.	Top Mgmt.	Can be started right away. Format, policies, unit of measure, and family designations can be developed in the first few meetings and revised as needed thereafter.
B. Demand Management.	Sales Mgr.	Focus on improving the demand side of the business through sales planning, item forecasting, eliminating forecasting wherever possible by interfacing with customer scheduling systems.
C. Master Scheduling (Production or Purchase).	Logistics Mgr.	In a company with manufacturing operations, the term Master Production Scheduling is used. In a distribution operation without manufacturing, the term Purchase Schedule or Master Purchase Schedule is used. Decisions on what items will be master scheduled. Typically started with Distribution Requirements Planning as part of the pilot.
1. Develop a master scheduling policy.	Top Mgmt. Sales & Mktg. Logistics Mgr.	Should address the following: 1. Procedure for changing the master schedule (production or purchase). Who can request a change, how the proposed change is investigated, and who should approve it. 2. Periodic reviews of actual performance vs. the master schedule (production or purchase) with an emphasis on problem resolution.
D. Distribution Requirements Planning.	Logistics Mgr.	Begun as a pilot.

DRP: Distribution Resource Planning
Proven Path Detailed Implementation Plan

TASK	RESPONSIBLE	COMMENTS
E. Transportation Planning.	Logistics Mgr. Traffic	Sometimes implementation is delayed until after master scheduling and Distribution Requirements Planning are fully implemented.
F. Supplier Scheduling & Development.	Purchasing Mgr.	Typically started as a pilot with one or several suppliers.

10. DATA MANAGEMENT (DRP)

DEFINITION: Attaining necessary levels of data accuracy and structure, with timely reporting.

PURPOSE: To make decisions based on current, accurate information.

WHO & HOW: Accountability for data integrity must be assigned.

Data	People
Inventory Record Accuracy	Warehouse and Stockroom Personnel
Bill of Material[3] Accuracy and Structure	Product Engineering, Research and Development, Distribution
Routings (if required)	Manufacturing/Industrial Engineering

TIME FRAME: Up to several months.

---

[3] Often called formulas, recipes, practices, etc. in process flow manufacturing. In a DRP implementation, this step would refer to the distribution bill of material (i.e., which products are stocked at which locations in the distribution network).

DRP: Distribution Resource Planning
Proven Path Detailed Implementation Plan

TASK	RESPONSIBLE	COMMENTS
10. DATA MANAGEMENT		These are the steps required to attain the necessary levels of data accuracy.
A. Inventory Record Accuracy.	Distr. Center Mgrs.	Objective is a minimum 95 percent inventory record accuracy.
1. Measure a sample of items as a starting point.	Distr. Center Mgrs.	Develop an objective assessment of the starting point. Most companies use a sample of 100 items.
2. Provide the tools for limited access and transaction recording.	Distr. Center Mgrs.	Transaction system must be simple and easy to use.
3. Implement control group cycle counting.	Distr. Center Mgrs.	Used to find and fix the root causes of errors.
4. Begin cycle counting all items.	Distr. Center Mgrs.	Done after the root causes of errors have been corrected. Several approaches are commonly used: process control cycle counting, cycle counting by ABC code, random cycle counting.
B. Structure the distribution network.	Logistics Mgr.	Load bills of distribution to represent the distribution network.
C. Item Data.	Logistics Mgr. Purchasing Mgr.	The objective is to have knowledgeable people verify this information.
1. Verify order policies.	Logistics Mgr. Purchasing Mgr.	Decide between fixed-order quantity and lot-for-lot. Dynamic-order quantity calculations are not recommended. Fix the obvious errors in order quantities, use remainder as is.

DRP: Distribution Resource Planning
Proven Path Detailed Implementation Plan

TASK	RESPONSIBLE	COMMENTS
2. Verify in-transit lead times.	Logistics Mgr. Traffic Purchasing Mgr.	Use current lead times, fix the obvious errors. In the case of purchased items, work with suppliers to implement supplier scheduling to get out beyond the lead times.
3. Verify safety stock levels.	Logistics Mgr. Purchasing Mgr.	Applies to independent demand items consistent with master schedule policy. For dependent demand items, restrict to special circumstances only.

11. Process Improvement (DRP)

Definition: Continuous improvement of all processes for sales, operations, logistics, and product design.

Purpose: To ensure survival, growth, and prosperity as a business. This is done by changing those processes that inhibit progress and/or are incompatible with the new vision.

Who & How: Initially, only those people involved with the actual implementation, but eventually everyone in the company, should participate in this step. This is done by creating within the organization a deep commitment to continuing improvement, a creative discontent with the status quo.

Time Frame: Never ending.

DRP: Distribution Resource Planning
Proven Path Detailed Implementation Plan

TASK	RESPONSIBLE	COMMENTS
11. PROCESS IMPROVEMENT		DRP is a planning and control system. JIT/TQC is a change process; changing the business to make it more efficient, more productive, and less costly through the elimination of waste.
		Companies need to do both: Plan and control the business, and change their processes to continuously improve them. For the detailed implementation plan in the area of process improvement, see the JIT/TQC Detailed Implementation Plan.

12. Software Selection (DRP)

Definition: Acquisition of software for planning, control, execu-
               tion, analysis, and monitoring.

Purpose: To provide the information that supports the users in
               doing their jobs more effectively.

Who & How: Software selection should be a joint venture involving
               key users as well as MIS people. This step must be
               accomplished relatively quickly and can be done so
               via the effective use of available information about
               manufacturing and distribution software. (For more
               information, see *The Standard System,* 1989 Oliver
               Wight Limited Publications, Inc.).

Time Frame: Several days to several weeks.

DRP: Distribution Resource Planning
Proven Path Detailed Implementation Plan

TASK	RESPONSIBLE	COMMENTS
12. SOFTWARE	MIS Mgr.	Select and implement the software to support the planning and control systems identified above.
A. Select software.	MIS Mgr. Logistics Mgr.	Select software that meets most of the needs from a user and MIS point of view.
1. Acquire *The Standard System* book.	MIS Mgr. Logistics Mgr.	Available from Oliver Wight Limited Publications, this book provides an explanation of what a typical software package should provide.
2. If needed, schedule software consulting audit.	MIS Mgr. Logistics Mgr.	Helpful in situations where new software is being used or extensive modification and/or interfacing is required.
B. Evaluate systems work and acquire necessary resources.	MIS Mgr.	Includes work needed for modifications, interfacing, and temporary bridges.
C. Implement necessary modules with modifications and interfacing.	MIS Mgr.	Typical modules include: Inventory Transactions, Bills of Material, Master Scheduling (Production or Purchase), Distribution Requirements Planning, Transportation Planning, Purchasing, Financial Integration.
D. Agree on MIS performance standards.	MIS Mgr. Logistics Mgr.	Response times, on-time completion of planning run, reports, etc.

285

13. Pilot and Cutover (DRP)[4]

DEFINITION: Conversion of the current process to the new process.

PURPOSE: To prove that the new tool actually works and to begin to benefit from it.

WHO & HOW: The people directly involved with the implementation begin to operate their part of the business using the new systems and/or processes.

TIME FRAME: Several weeks to several months.

---

[4] Cutover applies only to company-wide implementations. It entails adding the rest of the products/items onto the system following a successful operation of the pilot.

DRP: Distribution Resource Planning
Proven Path Detailed Implementation Plan

TASK	RESPONSIBLE	COMMENTS
13. PILOT AND CUTOVER	Team Leader Project Team Logistics Mgr. Involved Users	Conversion of the current processes to the new processes using a pilot approach.
A. Complete three pilots.	Team Leader Project Team Involved Users	Pilots are: 1. Computer pilot to test the software. 2. Conference room pilot to test procedures and people's understanding. 3. Live pilot to test the new processes and verify they are working. Systems that are typically implemented using the pilot approach are: 1. Master Scheduling (Production or Purchase). 2. Distribution Requirements Planning. 3. Supplier Scheduling and Development.
B. Monitor critical measurements.	Team Leader	Before moving into cutover, verify that the new processes and systems are working.
C. Group remaining products into several groups.	Logistics Mgr.	Three or four groups are typical.
D. Bring each group onto the new systems.	Logistics Mgr. Involved Users	Each group will require intense planner coverage to get them settled down.

287

14. PERFORMANCE MEASUREMENTS (DRP)

DEFINITION: Comparison of actual results to previously established key performance variables.

PURPOSE: To verify that the changes are delivering the expected results, and to provide feedback for implementation corrections.

WHO & HOW: This step should be done by people directly involved in the implementation, perhaps with assistance from other departments, such as MIS, accounting, etc.

TIME FRAME: Duration of the pilot and/or cutover phase.

15. Audit Assessment II (DRP)

DEFINITION: Analysis of the company's situation, problems, and opportunities in light of the newly implemented tool(s).

PURPOSE: To verify the effectiveness of the newly implemented tools, and to define the next steps on the continuing improvement journey.

This is another critically important step. Under no circumstances should it be skipped, since one of its missions is to define the next improvement initiative to follow. Should this step be omitted, the company's drive for operational excellence will stall out, and the company will be left in a competitively vulnerable position.

WHO & HOW: Participants in this step include the executives, a wide range of operating managers, and, in virtually all cases, outside consultants with Class A credentials in MRP II, JIT/TQC, and/or DRP.

The process is one of fact finding, identifying areas of consensus and disagreement, matching the company's current status and strategies with the tools it has available for execution. The end result should be the development of an action plan to move the company onto a path of continuous improvement.

TIME FRAME: One week to one month.

16. ONGOING EDUCATION (DRP)

DEFINITION: A continuing effort to upgrade everyone's awareness and skills.

PURPOSE: To emphasize the importance of people's jobs and to increase their abilities to do them. Ongoing education reinforces initial education as well as being necessary for new employees and employees in new jobs.

WHO & HOW: Department managers and supervisors are responsible for helping their people grow. Aids, such as videotapes, contribute to the effectiveness of the education program.

TIME FRAME: Forever.

DRP: Distribution Resource Planning
Proven Path Detailed Implementation Plan

TASK	RESPONSIBLE	COMMENTS
14. PERFORMANCE MEASUREMENTS	Dept. Heads	Compare actual results to the previously agreed-upon key measurements. Typical performance measurements include: 1. Production Plan (or Open To Buy) performance. 2. Master Schedule (Production or Purchase) performance. 3. Supplier Delivery performance. Other measurements include: 1. Customer Service. 2. Cost.
15. AUDIT/ASSESSMENT II	Top Mgmt. Middle Mgmt.	Re-assess the company's situation. Where are the current opportunities, what needs to be done next. This could be a phase 2 of the implementation, a concentrated effort to improve current levels of performance, etc. In most cases, this is done with the help of an outside consultant with Class A credentials.
16. ONGOING EDUCATION	Dept. Heads	Run a continuing program of outside education and business meetings to improve skill levels and company operating results.
A. Educate key managers new to the business.	Top Mgmt.	New managers in key positions need exposure at either the DRP Top Management Course or the DRP Three-Day Course to continue achieving full operating benefits.
B. Maintain in-house experts.	Dept. Heads	Also important to continue achieving full operating benefits.
C. Continue the series of business meetings.	Dept. Heads	These meetings focus on how to improve the operating results of the business through the use of these tools. It's good to stand back and look at the situation from time to time. Sometimes new people are run through a special series of meetings; more typically, they are included into the ongoing series of business meetings.

Although some steps can be done quickly, while others require considerable time, it is essential to complete each step if the full potential of MRP II, JIT/TQC, and DRP is to be attained. Nevertheless, general managers who confront major problems are often anxious to achieve improvements, and may not insist on a vision statement, a cost/benefit analysis, or a description of the new sales, logistics, and manufacturing processes. These executives need to resist the temptation to minimize the importance of the 16 steps—the success of the company's goals are tied directly to how well each activity is carried out.

Now, keeping the generalized Proven Path in mind, let's look at the Fast-Track Implementation approaches.

Fast-Track
Implementation—
Fail-Safe Mini-DRP

Distribution Resource Planning (DRP) has been in existence since 1975, and is now accepted as the standard method of managing and controlling distribution operations. Many companies recognize that integrating the needs of distribution with the capabilities of manufacturing can best be accomplished using DRP. Since 1984, DRP has also become recognized as a valuable tool for retailers, wholesalers, and distributors.

Despite the impressive results that can be obtained with DRP, only one company in ten has heard of the technique or has actually done something with it. One of the reasons for this is that executives often cannot wait the 12 to 18 months it takes to implement DRP, and they balk at the $250,000 to $500,000 cost associated with a full-scale DRP implementation. Fail-Safe Mini-DRP was created to fill the breach, by helping companies quickly experience the benefits of DRP on a limited scale. Once the company enjoys the dramatic results that inevitably accompany Fail-Safe Mini-DRP, it's much easier to get top management to commit the resources necessary for a full-scale implementation.

Where Fail-Safe Mini-DRP Applies

Situation 1, "Bleeding from the Neck": Top management says, "We can't wait—we're taking on water." Fail-Safe Mini-DRP yields impressive payback in a matter of weeks.

Situation 2, "Jumbo-size Company": DRP is too big—how do we swallow the whole thing? Performing a pilot on a product or product line, followed by a second pilot, enables the company to proceed with small, digestible chunks.

Situation 3, "Middle Up": Top management isn't convinced—does DRP really work? Fail-Safe Mini-DRP provides very quick validation of the program.

Situation 4, "We're Unique": People believe their company requires unique solutions. Fail-Safe Mini-DRP shows them that DRP works for them as well as any other kind of company.

The Components of Fail-Safe Mini-DRP

Fail-Safe Mini-DRP entails using DRP to manage a limited number of high-impact products. It can be implemented in about three months and costs only 5-to 10 percent of an average full- scale implementation. As with the other two Fast-Track Implementation approaches (Quick-Slice MRP and Breakthrough JIT), Fail-Safe Mini-DRP follows the Proven Path implementation route. Several of the steps deserve special emphasis:

Audit/Assessment I

This evaluation is conducted to determine where the company is today and what it must do to successfully implement DRP. This phase eliminates the risk of a false start. It provides all necessary elements needed to arrive at a "go/no go" decision.

Software

The Fail-Safe Mini-DRP project almost always involves low-cost, easy-to-use, micro-based software. This is because, unlike those using MRP II, relatively few companies already have mainframe or minicomputer software for DRP. These high-quality, PC-based software packages exist today, and they're fully capable of supporting a Fail-Safe Mini-DRP implementation. They can be purchased for less than $10,000.

The key issue is not which software package to select; rather a decision must be made quickly and the implementation must move on if Fail-Safe is to succeed. Once Fail-Safe Mini-DRP is operational and the company decides on a full-scale DRP implementation, a minicomputer or mainframe software package may have to be selected. The experience gained during the Fail-Safe implementation will give the company valuable insights into making a better permanent software selection.

THE METHODOLOGY

The methodology for Fail-Safe Mini-DRP has been developed from the Oliver Wight Companies ABCD Checklist, which has four major groupings that are used to measure the effectiveness and performance of a company having a sales, distribution, and manufacturing process. These groupings include:

- Planning and Control
- Data Management
- Process Improvement
- Performance Measurements

PLANNING AND CONTROL

Planning and controlling resources in a logistics organization is concerned with deploying people and equipment, material, space, transportation, inventory investment, etc. A number of planning sequences must be performed depending on whether you're a retailer/wholesaler or a manufacturer:

Sales and Purchase Planning (for Retail/Wholesale): Although only one product or product group may be included in Fail-Safe Mini-DRP, it is mandatory to carry out sales and purchase planning on all product groups. Top management must be responsible for this action, to formalize the high level planning process and link it with other management levels within the organization. The sales and purchase planning process should become operational within 60 days from the start of the Fail-Safe Mini-DRP implementation.

Sales & Operations Planning (for Manufacturers): The sales & operations planning process must be institutionalized across all product lines even though only one product or one product line may be included in the Fail-Safe Mini-DRP implementation.

Demand Management: Companies need to provide sales forecasts for the Fail-Safe Mini-DRP products. These forecasts must then be spread across distribution centers (DCs) that stock the product. This spreading function is usually done by someone other than marketing and sales. The important point is that the sum of the DC forecasts must add up to marketing's forecast. Extra effort is necessary on the part of marketing and sales to improve and monitor forecasts for products in the Fail-Safe Mini-DRP program.

Integrating DRP/MPS: DRP is used to carry out the material planning necessary to support the needs of each DC. For retailers or wholesalers, DRP will communicate to the buyers what they need to buy and when. For manufacturers, DRP will generate the total distribution demand to be input to the master production schedule (MPS).

The information regarding master production scheduling provided earlier in the Quick-Slice MRP section applies to DRP, with one important distinction. DRP provides planning data to the sales & operations planning function in addition to the master scheduling function. DRP takes the sales forecasts and inventory goals by DC and determines how much needs to be produced and when. Therefore, it is critical to recognize DRP's contribution to the sales & operations planning process in manufacturing as well as master scheduling.

For retailers, wholesalers, and distributors, DRP reports what and when products should be purchased. Ultimately, this will lead to formal supplier scheduling arrangements, with the elimination of hard-copy purchase orders, and often utilizing EDI hookups. For Fail-Safe Mini-DRP to work, it is necessary to develop a simple way of communicating DRP's recommended orders (manual or otherwise), as well as DRP's feedback regarding which purchase orders have been created.

Transportation Planning and Scheduling: When appropriate, modes of transport, desired size, frequency of shipments, and distribution lead times need to be determined for the Fail-Safe products. This is necessary to test and verify that transportation planning and scheduling will work properly. In many instances, though, the output will be unusable because most companies ship multiple products at the same time, and products in the Fail-Safe program will only represent a small portion of the total volume that is required to be shipped.

Nevertheless, it is worthwhile to proceed and test the planning module, since valuable insights will result. For example, the results can form the basis for revising the company's transportation strategies and formalizing an important cost area. Thus, when enough products are eventually planned, significant benefits can be realized as the fine tuning proceeds.

DATA MANAGEMENT

The same data management considerations described in the Quick-Slice MRP section above apply to Fail-Safe Mini-DRP. Note that inventory record accuracy of 95 percent plus must be maintained for every DC that stocks the products selected for Fail-Safe Mini-DRP.

PERFORMANCE MEASUREMENTS

If you are a retailer, wholesaler, or distributor, the following performance measurements apply:

• Purchasing/inventory planning performance $+/-2$ percent

• Supplier delivery performance 95-to 100 percent

If you are a manufacturer, the same performance measurements described in the Quick-Slice MRP section will apply to the Fail-Safe Mini-DRP section.

CONCLUSION

Fail-Safe Mini-DRP is the logistics counterpart of Quick-Slice MRP. Therefore, the same concluding comments can be made here as with Quick-Slice MRP: Fail-Safe Mini-DRP is clearly different from the traditional approach but offers true advantages. Already tried and proven, we believe it will become the most common and accepted method of implementing DRP in the near future. It is a major breakthrough.

This concludes our discussion of the three Fast-Track Implementation approaches: Breakthrough JIT, Quick-Slice MRP, and Fail-Safe Mini-DRP. Now let's turn our attention briefly to company-wide implementation.

Fail-Safe Mini-DRP Detailed Implementation Plan

The following pages list the detailed implementation plan for Fail-Safe Mini-DRP. This plan is a modified version of the DRP Detailed Implementation Plan, altered to eliminate tasks that would not be a part of a Mini-DRP implementation. For example, the large education program that would be part of a full implementation has been cut back to an education program for the project team charged with the responsibility for implementing Mini-DRP.

In other cases, the tasks remain the same, but the amount of work is significantly reduced because they happen only for the Mini-DRP items. For example, inventory record accuracy would still have to be attained, but only on the items in Mini-DRP. In fact, the implementation plan for Mini-DRP is not much smaller than the implementation plan for a company-wide DRP implementation. However, the work required to implement Mini-DRP is significantly less and the time required is only a few months.

There are a number of abbreviations used in the RESPONSIBLE

299

column of the detailed implementation plans. The table below shows these abbreviations and their meaning:

Dept.	Department
Distr.	Distribution
Engr.	Engineering (either Design or Manufacturing)
Exec.	Executive
Mgmt.	Management
Mgr.	Manager
MIS	Management Information Systems
P&IC	Production & Inventory Control
Suprvsn.	Supervision

Fail-Safe Mini-DRP
Proven Path Detailed Implementation Plan

TASK	RESPONSIBLE	COMMENTS
1. AUDIT/ASSESSMENT I	Top Mgmt. Middle Mgmt.	Assess the company's current situation. In most cases, this is done with the help of an outside consultant with Class A credentials.
2. FIRST-CUT EDUCATION	Top Mgmt. Middle Mgmt.	What is DRP, how does it work, why should a company commit to it? Top management should attend the DRP Top Management Course, key middle managers should attend the DRP Three-Day Course.
3. VISION STATEMENT	Top Mgmt. Middle Mgmt.	A short, concise document defining what we want to accomplish, and when it should be in place.
4. COST/BENEFIT	Top Mgmt. Middle Mgmt.	A quick listing of the costs and benefits as applied to the Mini-DRP items only.
5. PROJECT ORGANIZATION	Top Mgmt.	Create the appropriate management and operational teams.
A. Executive Steering Committee.	Top Mgmt.	Include designation of Executive Torchbearer. Schedule review meetings once a month.
B. Project Team.	Top Mgmt.	Team Leader should be at least 50 percent on the project. Other team members from 10 percent to 25 percent depending on their role.
C. Outside counsel.	Top Mgmt.	Outside consultant with Class A experience.
6. PERFORMANCE GOALS	Top Mgmt. Middle Mgmt.	Using the ABCD Checklist, agree on expected performance levels and measurements.
7. INITIAL EDUCATION	Team Leader	Provide the necessary understanding to the team members who will be designing and using the new tools.
A. Outside education for team members.	Team Leader	To be effective team members, these people need exposure at either the DRP Top Management Course or the DRP Three-Day Course.
B. Project Team video course.	Team Leader	A series of business meetings where the general principles are translated into the specifics of operation for your company (for the Mini-DRP items only). Acquire the DRP Video Library.

Fail-Safe Mini-DRP

Proven Path Detailed Implementation Plan

TASK	RESPONSIBLE	COMMENTS
8. SALES, LOGISTICS, AND MANUFACTURING PROCESSES	Top Mgmt. Middle Mgmt.	Develop a detailed statement of how these processes will operate following implementation (for the Mini-DRP items only). The Project Team series of business meetings (Task #7B above) generally provides most of the information needed for this task.
9. PLANNING AND CONTROL PROCESSES		Identification of the systems necessary for effective planning (Mini-DRP items only).
A. Sales & Operations Planning.	Top Mgmt.	Start for all products, not just Mini-DRP product(s). Format, policies, unit of measure, and family designations can be developed in the first few meetings and revised as needed thereafter.
B. Demand Management.	Sales Mgr.	Mini-DRP items only.
C. Master Scheduling (Production or Purchase).	Logistics Mgr.	Mini-DRP items only. In a company with manufacturing operations, the term Master Production Scheduling is used. In a distribution operation without manufacturing, the term Purchase Schedule or Master Purchase Schedule is used.
1. Develop a master scheduling policy.	Top Mgmt. Sales & Mktg. Logistics Mgr.	Should address the following: 1. Procedure for changing the master schedule (production or purchase). Who can request a change, how the proposed change is investigated, and who should approve it. 2. Periodic reviews of actual performance vs. the master schedule (production or purchase) with an emphasis on problem resolution.
D. Distribution Requirements Planning.	Logistics Mgr.	Mini-DRP items only.
E. Supplier Scheduling & Development.	Purchasing Mgr.	Slice items only, simple supplier schedules.

302

Fail-Safe Mini-DRP
Proven Path Detailed Implementation Plan

TASK	RESPONSIBLE	COMMENTS
10. DATA MANAGEMENT		These are the steps required to attain the necessary levels of data accuracy (Mini-DRP items only).
A. Inventory Record Accuracy.	Distr. Center Mgrs.	Objective is a minimum 95 percent inventory record accuracy (Mini-DRP items only).
1. Provide the tools for limited access and transaction recording.	Distr. Center Mgrs.	It may be necessary to physically isolate the Mini-DRP items. Transaction system must be simple and easy to use.
2. Implement control-group cycle counting.	Distr. Center Mgrs.	Used to find and fix the root causes of errors.
3. Inventory all Mini-DRP items.	Distr. Center Mgrs.	Done to bring the accuracy of all Mini-DRP items to 95 percent. May have to be done several times to keep the accuracy at least 95 percent if the root causes of the errors have not been corrected.
B. Structure the distribution network.	Logistics Mgr.	Load bills of distribution to represent the distribution network (Mini-DRP items only).
C. Item Data.	Logistics Mgr. Purchasing Mgr.	The objective is to have knowledgeable people verify this information (Mini-DRP items only).
1. Verify order policies.	Logistics Mgr. Purchasing Mgr.	Fix the obvious errors in order quantities, use remainder as is.
2. Verify lead times.	Logistics Mgr. Traffic Purchasing Mgr.	Use current lead times, fix the obvious errors.
3. Verify safety stock levels.	Logistics Mgr. Purchasing Mgr.	Applies to independent-demand items consistent with master schedule policy. For dependent-demand items restrict to special circumstances only.

303

Fail-Safe Mini-DRP
Proven Path Detailed Implementation Plan

TASK	RESPONSIBLE	COMMENTS
11. PROCESS IMPROVEMENT		If process improvements can be done quickly to make it easier to implement Mini-DRP, use the JIT/TQC Detailed Implementation Plan.
12. SOFTWARE	MIS Mgr.	Select and implement the software to support the Mini-DRP. This may be temporary software (like a PC software package) or the current software if it is already up and running.
A. Select software.	MIS Mgr. Logistics Mgr.	A quick evaluation is essential here. In the case of "temporary" software, this can be done with a minimum of evaluation.
1. Acquire *The Standard System* book.	MIS Mgr. Logistics Mgr.	Available from Oliver Wight Limited Publications, this book provides an explanation of what a typical software package should provide.
B. Implement necessary modules.	MIS Mgr.	This should be done with little, if any, interfacing of systems. Typical modules include: Inventory Transactions, Bills of Material, Master Scheduling (Production or Purchase), Distribution Requirements Planning.
13. PILOT AND CUTOVER	Team Members	Typically, there is no pilot in a Mini-DRP implementation. All the Mini-DRP items are brought up on the system at once. However, the following implementation steps for a pilot are still appropriate for the implementation of Mini-DRP.
A. Complete three pilots.	Team Members	Pilots are: 1. Computer pilot to test the software. 2. Conference room pilot to test procedures and people's understanding. 3. Live pilot (or, in this case, Mini-DRP) to test the new processes and verify they are working.

Fail-Safe Mini-DRP
Proven Path Detailed Implementation Plan

TASK	RESPONSIBLE	COMMENTS
14. PERFORMANCE MEASUREMENTS	Team Members	Compare actual results to the previously agreed-upon key measurements. Typical performance measurements include: 1. Production Plan (or Open To Buy) performance. 2. Master Schedule (Production or Purchase) performance. 3. Supplier Delivery performance.
15. AUDIT/ASSESSMENT II	Top Mgmt. Middle Mgmt.	Re-assess the company's situation. Is it now time to implement DRP across all items? What's next?
16. ONGOING EDUCATION		In the case of Mini-DRP, ongoing education typically means initial education for the next phase of implementation.

Inventory Record Accuracy

An inventory record accuracy of 95 percent or better is vital to the success of DRP. Ninety-five percent accuracy means that 95 percent of the items have an actual on-hand balance that is within an agreed-upon counting tolerance of the on-hand balance stored in the system. For example, if the counting tolerance for a group of items is one bottle, 95 percent of items counted should have an actual count that is within one bottle of the count in the inventory record.

This level of accuracy is quite high and, consequently, requires considerable effort to obtain. However, it can be attained; a number of companies have achieved the necessary accuracy by using the following steps:

1. EDUCATE

People make inventory records accurate. People are also the source of inaccurate inventory records. If people understand why inventory records have to be accurate, and how to make them accurate, you have a good start at getting 95 percent accuracy. If people don't understand the need, there is little chance you will ever get the required level of accuracy.

2. PROVIDE THE TOOLS

The way to get inventory record accuracy is to designate a group of people to be held accountable as a group for the level of accuracy. For example, the distribution center manager and his group will be held accountable for the accuracy of the inventory records in their DC. Likewise, the manager of the central supply facility and his people will be held accountable for the accuracy of the inventory records in the central supply facility.

For this to work, the people who will be held accountable must be the only ones who have the opportunity to make inventory transactions. This is called "limited access." Only those people who will be held accountable for the accuracy of the inventory records can have the opportunity to put products away or take productions out of inventory.

In many distribution operations, this is not a problem. As distribution centers typically are isolated, the only people there are the people who will be responsible for inventory record accuracy.

In a number of central supply facilities, however, there are numerous people from the manufacturing facility, the office, etc., and these people are not accountable for the accuracy of the inventory records.

In addition, only the people who will be held accountable for the accuracy of the inventory records should be permitted access to the stockroom. Usually, the stockroom is fenced. The fence or locked stockroom, however, is not the real issue. The key is to only allow access to the people who are accountable for inventory record accuracy.

3. ASSIGN ACCOUNTABILITY

After they have been provided with the tools, the stockroom people can be assigned the accountability for inventory record accuracy. Generally, the job descriptions of the people in the DCs or the central supply facility need to be altered. In the past, these job descriptions involved moving material. Now they should emphasize the importance of inventory record accuracy. The stockroom people must know that first and foremost they are responsible for maintaining accurate inventory records.

4. MEASURE

Cycle counting is the way to measure the level of accuracy in the stockrooms. A program of cycle counting should be established to count all the items in inventory periodically.

5. FIND THE CAUSES

As part of the cycle-counting program, in addition to counting all the items periodically, a small group of items should be counted fairly frequently. The purpose of these frequent counts is to determine the causes of inventory errors.

Typically, this small group contains 100 or so items counted every ten days. There is nothing special about 100 items or ten days. You may choose to have more or less than this number of items, and you may choose to count them more or less frequently. The important thing is to be able to find the causes of the errors. Also, it is a good idea to change the items in this small group from time to time because people learn which items are being recounted frequently.

6. CORRECT THE PROBLEMS

You can do all of the above, but the real key to inventory record accuracy is to aggressively fix the problems that show up through cycle counting. Identifying and solving problems is the way to achieve and maintain accurate inventory records.

Appendix C

Methods for Posting Distribution Demands to the Master Production Schedule

There are basically two ways to post the planned orders at the DCs as distribution demands in the master schedule display. One is to use bills of material to link the items at the DCs to the central supply facility. The second is to have a computer program post the planned orders at the DCs to the master schedule.

Regardless of the method used, a unique identifier is needed for each item in each distribution center. For example, a six-ounce bottle of perfume in the Los Angeles DC would have one number, the same bottle of perfume in the New York DC would have another number, and the same bottle of perfume in the central supply facility would have a third number.

One way to do this is to add a suffix to the item number, to specify the location. For example, the six-ounce bottle of perfume might be item number 45682. Los Angeles is indicated by the suffix -20, New York the suffix -50, and the central supply facility the suffix -00. The item number for the six-ounce bottle of perfume in Los Angeles would then be 45682-20, the perfume in New York would be 45682-50, and the perfume at the central supply facility would be 45682-00.

BILLS OF MATERIAL

If you are using bills of material, each item at each DC will have a bill of material. The bill of material shows the item at the distribution center being made from the item at the central supply facility. It is also possible to have a routing attached to these items, and the routing could show the labor, weight, cube, equipment required, etc.

When bills of material are used, the normal planned and firm planned order logic in most software packages will post the distribution demands to the items in the master schedule. This logic takes planned orders for the parent item in the bill of material and generates gross requirements for the components. Figure C-1 shows how this normal DRP/MRP logic will take planned orders at one level and generate demands at the lower level.

DRP/MRP Display
Distribution Center

	Past Due	Week							
		1	2	3	4	5	6	7	8
Gross Requirements									
Scheduled Receipts									
Projected On Hand									
Planned Orders			200				200		

Master Schedule Display
Central Supply Facility

	Past Due	Week							
		1	2	3	4	5	6	7	8
Distribution Demands			200				200		
Scheduled Receipts									
Projected On Hand									
Master Schedule-Rcpt.									
Master Schedule-Start									

Figure C-1

The planned orders at the different DCs are posted to the master schedule items. As each set of planned orders is posted, the total distribution demands on the master schedule items are increased.

In most cases, using bills of material precludes writing special programs because the normal planned-order posting logic used in MRP software packages posts requirements from the DCs to the master schedule items.

When bills of material are used to link the distribution centers and the central supply facility, all the item numbers are part of one product structure. This structure is contained in a single data base, which means DRP is usually done for all items in all DCs on a single computer, as opposed to each DC using separate computers.

COMPUTER PROGRAM

If a computer program is used to link the items at the DCs to the central supply facility, logic is added to sum the planned orders at the different DCs and post the demands to the master schedule items. Generally, when this approach is used, each distribution center has a separate data base.

After DRP is run for all the DCs, a program reads the planned orders from these data bases, summing all the demands for a particular master schedule item. These demands are then posted to the master schedule item.

When this method is used, it is generally necessary to write the program. Most software packages do not yet include this type of logic for distribution companies. Fortunately, this program is a simple one.

This method makes the most sense when each distribution center has its own computer because a separate data base exists for each DC. Each DC can run DRP and transmit the planned orders to the central supply facility, where they will be posted to the master schedule items.

Methods for Handling Changes in Supplying Distribution Centers

Basically, there are two methods to indicate changes in the way distribution centers are supplied. They are:

1. Changes based on dates.
2. Changes tied to specific orders.

These methods are the same ones used with MRP to handle changes to bills of material. Not unique to distribution, they are general purpose techniques used to handle changing relationships in a scheduling network.

In the past, distribution planning systems tended to assume that the distribution network is static and unchanging. These systems represented the way the product was distributed, and it was assumed that this would continue to represent the network for an indefinite period of time. But as DRP was implemented to plan a distribution network for a year or more into the future, some problems were bound to develop. A distribution network is not static. Companies eliminate or add DCs, they change from DCs to RDCs feeding the satellite DCs, etc., and the planning system must be able to cope with a changing distribution network.

CHANGES BASED ON DATES

One solution is to tie the changes in the distribution network to a date. This method uses effectivity dates, and is more commonly known as "engineering change." Dates stored in the system are used to determine how a DC will be supplied. These dates might indicate, for example, that the Montreal DC may be supplied from the central supply facility up to June 30. From July 1 until August 31, it will be supplied from the stockpile. From September 1 on, it will again be supplied from the central supply facility.

There are, however, some problems with effectivity dates. This method is a date-driven change system. In practice, some distribution network changes are driven by a date, but others are not. An example of a date-driven change is one when the plant is scheduled to shut down March 1. This type of change is best handled using effectivity dates. An example of a change not driven by a date is when the inventory in a stockpile is to be used up before switching back to the central supply facility. This type of change is best handled using changes that are tied to an order.

CHANGES TIED TO SPECIFIC ORDERS

A second way to handle changes to the distribution network is to allow a deviation from normal distribution channels, with this deviation tied to one or several specific orders. A deviation tied to an order means the deviation is bound to a specific order, and does not apply to any others. Because the deviation is tied to the order and not determined by date, the deviation moves as well if the order is rescheduled. In the situation above where the inventory in the stockpile should be used up first before going back to the central supply facility, this eliminates the need for the planners to continually update effectivity dates when sales are different from forecast or as inventory adjustments occur.

THE MECHANICS OF THESE TWO METHODS

Appendix C explained two methods for posting the distribution demands to the master schedule: using bills of material and using a computer program. Both of these methods can be used to show changes in the way DCs are supplied.

Using Bills of Material

If bills of material are used, bill-of-material effectivity dates are used to handle changes in the distribution network that are based on a date. Bill-of-material effectivity dates are generally available in most bill-of-material systems. The dates are stored as part of the descriptive information for a parent-component relationship. With DRP, each planned order date is compared to the effectivity dates. If the component (supplying facility) is active on the date of the planned order, distribution requirements are generated and posted. If the component is not active, distribution requirements are not posted. In the case where a component is not active there is generally another component that is active. To illustrate this, a bill of material is shown in figure D-1 with effectivity dates to handle the depletion of a stockpile inventory.

Bill of Material
2½ Lead Pencils
Montreal Distribution Center

COMPONENT	EFFECTIVITY DATES	
(SUPPLY FACILITY)	START	STOP
Central Supply	———	6/30/XX
Stockpile	7/1/XX	8/31/XX
Central Supply	9/1/XX	———

Figure D-1

If bills of material are used, it is sometimes possible to tie deviations to an order. Some software packages provide this capability and others do not. If possible, deviations tied to an order are normally provided by allowing the planner to maintain the distribution requirements for firm planned orders. The planner is able to add distribution requirements, delete distribution requirements, or change the distribution requirements for an order.

Using this method, the planner selects the orders that will be supplied differently from the normal method and makes them firm planned orders. In the above example, the planner makes all the orders between 7/1 and 8/31 firm planned orders. Then he or she deletes the distribution requirements to be supplied from the central supply facility and adds distribution requirements to be supplied from the stockpile.

Using a Computer Program

If a computer program is used to post the distribution demands, date-driven changes to the distribution network are handled using a table. This table is stored in the computer and contains the item, supplying facility, and the start and stop dates. It closely resembles a bill of material with effectivity dates. An example appears in figure D-2.

Supplying Locations
2½ Lead Pencils
Montreal Distribution Center

	EFFECTIVITY DATES	
SUPPLY FACILITY	START	STOP
Central Supply	————	6/30/XX
Stockpile	7/1/XX	8/31/XX
Central Supply	9/1/XX	————

Figure D-2

This table works in the same way as bill-of-material effectivity dates. With DRP, each planned order date is compared to the effectivity dates. If the supplying facility is active on the date of the planned order, distribution requirements are generated and posted. If the supplying facility is not active, distribution requirements are not posted.

If a computer program is used, it is also possible to have deviations that are tied to an order. This can also be done using a table. The difference is that the table lists the specific orders that deviate from the normal supply facility. The table in figure D-3 is an example of this concept.

Supplying Locations
2½ Lead Pencils
Montreal Distribution Center

NORMAL
SUPPLY FACILITY

Central Supply

DEVIATIONS: SUPPLY FACILITY	ORDER NUMBER
Stockpile	23980
Stockpile	45927

Figure D-3

CONCLUSION

It is important to realize that either of the two methods--bills of material or a computer program--will work. The choice should be based on the amount of work needed to provide these capabilities within the system. If you use a software package that provides effectivity dates and deviations tied to an order, and figure all the processing on a single computer with a single data base, it is simpler to use bills of material. However, if the software does not have these features, and you calculate DRP on separate computers at each DC, a computer program is probably less work.

Methods for Planning DC Shipping Schedules

Two methods can be used to adjust the planned orders in a DRP system based on the planned DC shipping schedules. Both methods, which require a computer, are applicable in the following situations:

1. *Weekly bucketed system*: One or more distribution centers receive shipments less frequently than every week.

2. *Bucketless or plan-by-date system*: There is a fixed shipping schedule by day.

METHOD 1: MODIFICATION TO THE BASIC DRP LOOP

Using this method, the DRP logic is expanded to include the DC shipping schedules. The DRP logic (as explained in chapter 3) will create a planned order when the items are needed at the distribution center, but does not take the DC shipping schedules into consideration.

The modification is to include a section of logic after the planned orders are created but before they are stored, and before the distribution demands are posted to the master schedule items. This section of logic compares the planned-order start date, or shipment date, to the fixed shipping schedule for that distribution center. If the planned order is not due to ship on one of the fixed shipping dates, the date of the planned order can be changed to the next earlier shipping date by using a table that stores the shipping schedule for each DC.

This method has an advantage when bills of material are used to link the items at the DCs to the items at the central supply facility because the planned orders are created and immediately posted as distribution demands on the master schedule items. By adjusting the planned order dates before they are posted to the master schedule items, it is not necessary to readjust both the planned orders and the distribution demands.

The disadvantage of this method is that most software packages for MRP do not contain this logic for adjusting the planned orders by the DC shipping schedules, and the modification typically has to be made to a fairly central, and sometimes complex, section of logic. However, the modification merely involves inserting a section of logic, and does not disturb or modify the existing logic in the system.

METHOD 2: SEPARATE COMPUTER PROGRAM TO ADJUST THE PLANNED ORDERS

Using this method, the DRP logic is unchanged. The planned orders are created based on the need dates and stored in the data base. Then a special computer program reads the planned orders and adjusts the planned order dates based on the shipping schedule. Any planned order that is not due to be shipped on one of the shipping dates is changed to the next earlier shipping date.

The advantage of this method is that it does not require modification of the order planning logic in the commercially available MRP software packages. Instead, a separate computer program is written to adjust the planned order dates.

This method has an advantage when DCs have their own computers or separate data bases. The program can be run after the planned orders are created for the DCs, but before they are posted as distribution demands on the master schedule items.

Index